CHRONICLES OF FAITH

CHRONICLES OF FAITH

The Autobiography of Frederick D. Patterson

Edited by
Martia Graham Goodson

With a Foreword by
Harry V. Richardson

The University of Alabama Press
Tuscaloosa and London

Library of Congress Cataloging-in-Publication Data

Patterson, Frederick D. (Frederick Douglass), 1901–1988.
 Chronicles of faith : the autobiography of Frederick D. Patterson
/ edited by Martia Graham Goodson : with a foreword by Harry
V. Richardson.
  p.   cm.
 Bibliography: p.
 Includes index.
 ISBN 0-8173-0459-2
 1. Patterson, Frederick D. (Frederick Douglass), 1901–1988.
2. Tuskegee Institute—Presidents—Biography. 3. United Negro
College Fund—History. I. Goodson, Martia Graham. II. Title.
LC2851 1935. T817P38 1991
378.1'11—dc20   89-4894
[B]   CIP

British Library Cataloguing-in-Publication Data available

Dedication

To my wife, Catherine,
a helpmate and counselor over a period of fifty years.
As a devoted mother, she provided our son with love and care
during the many absences required of me
by Tuskegee Institute (now Tuskegee University)
and the Phelps Stokes Fund.

and

To my sister, Wilhelmina B. Patterson,
who as the oldest of six children, when we lost our parents
before my second birthday, became my surrogate mother.
At whatever the cost, Wilhelmina provided for my education
and kept before me goals of achievement.
For this my gratitude is without end.

Contents

Foreword

This book is the story of a man and his indomitable faith in himself, in the causes he espoused, and in the essential goodness of human nature. According to this man, if a social need exists and ways of meeting it are shown, people of goodwill will respond. Because in every instance his faith was vindicated, the present book is a chronicle of faith triumphant.

Frederick Douglass Patterson had the ability to see social needs clearly and realistically, as calls for action, not simply as subjects for emotional oratory. Having identified a social need, he was not content to rest until something corrective had been done.

But corrective work is hard. It requires endless persistence in making plans, in forming organizations, in finding competent personnel, in fund raising, in maintaining morale both in givers and receivers, and in seeing that everything is done faithfully and efficiently. Patterson had the capacity for all of these tremendous labors and has extended them even into his later years, not for profit, but for human betterment and national welfare.

His founding and development of the United Negro College Fund, which I regard as his magnum opus, illustrate the point, but he had other achievements, too, especially his introduction of military aviation at Tuskegee, an innovation which gave black people access to this field for the first time. Later, in wartime when the government took over this effort, black young men, like their fathers before them, came forward to offer their lives in defense of America, not only on land and sea, but in the sky as well. No less impressive an accomplishment was the establishment of the

School of Veterinary Medicine at Tuskegee. The university now graduates more black veterinarians than all of the other eighteen American veterinary schools combined.

Then, too, in the pages of this book the reader will see American democracy at its best, as hands reach out, sometimes in sacrificial ways, to help a person striving to address a social need. Finally, this book may suggest ways of helping our world in these troubled, anxious days. For all of these reasons it will be read with profit and inspiration.

Harry V. Richardson

Preface

Chronicles of Faith emerges from a series of recorded interviews I conducted with Frederick Patterson in 1980 and again in 1986–87. The original interviews formed part of an oral history of the United Negro College Fund collected by the Oral History Research Office at Columbia University. The later series was conducted when Dr. Patterson decided to record his reminiscences more completely on paper.

Patterson was born before the twentieth century was two years old. *Chronicles of Faith* is therefore not only his life story but a story of the twentieth century as well and embodies the perspective of a participant in important national and international events of the period. It is, primarily, a history of institutions: Tuskegee Institute, the United Negro College Fund, the Phelps Stokes Fund, and the Robert R. Moton Memorial Institute.

A reading of *Chronicles of Faith* not only reveals the perspicacity which Patterson employed in the interest of African and African-American youth throughout his life but also illuminates the characters of other people active in the first half of this century. Patterson helps us remember some names that may be fading from historical memory.

This retrospective view of Patterson's life carries the reader to a variety of places: places as far apart economically as the White House (in the city of Patterson's birth) and the wooden shacks of sharecroppers and tenants on plantations in rural Alabama (at the time when Patterson was a college president); places as far apart geographically as Prairie View, Texas, and Kakata, Liberia; and places generally unheard of, such as Chehaw, Alabama, and Capahosic, Virginia. Patterson's offices in New York, in university laboratories, and in institutions of technical education in colonial East and West Africa are stops on the journey recalled here.

The significance of this collection of oral reminiscences lies in the spectrum of activities in African-American and African life with which Patterson has been associated. His story fleshes out a picture of the social, economic, and educational scene and therefore provides the political backdrop for African-Americans in the American South from the turn of the century to the present. He does the same thing, though to a lesser extent, for Africans in the final days of the British Empire. *Chronicles* provides evidence of historically consistent support—both financial and spiritual—in the African-American community for education and especially for its traditional institutions of higher education. Patterson's creation, the United Negro College Fund, was the first ongoing cooperative fund-raising organization for higher education in America.

Patterson's life serves as a reminder that the institutions with which he was affiliated reflect, in their present form, many years of thought, study, discussion, and struggle. Their maintenance and advancement require more of the same, with an extra measure of vigilance. Within Patterson's memoirs, we find no contradicition of Du Bois's assertion that the problem of the twentieth century is the problem of the color line. But clearly, Patterson's recognition of the absurdity of that line did not deter him from using it as a whip to promote opportunities both for African and African-American people and for the American nation. His work challenges us to do no less.

Acknowledgments

My thanks to many friends and associates who have encouraged me to write this book. They felt that I should describe my part in events at Tuskegee University, the Phelps Stokes Fund, the United Negro College Fund, and the Robert A. Moton Memorial Institute as a personal experience.

I feel that the events detailed herein should be recorded. They are historic and should be recognized in the context of the progress made by this country and by its black citizenry. In this effort, I wish to thank the many persons who are related to each event, to the extent that memory permits.

I must first thank Dr. Matthew Jenkins and his wife, Roberta, both graduates of Tuskegee, he from the School of Veterinary Medicine. They generously agreed to underwrite publication of this book. I also thank Dr. Nathaniel Colley, another Tuskegee alumnus, who graciously contributed to the cost of production, and Dr. Martia Goodson, for her diligent, persistent, and satisfying editorial efforts. Dr. Hobart Jarratt read the manuscript and offered helpful constructive comments.

Several project areas discussed in this book deserve more extensive and scholarly research than was possible here. In all instances, the issues in question have not been limited by race or region. They are problems of human well-being, of housing, health, nutrition, education, and human understanding. Surely each will continue to receive study and will see improvement (at least I hope so) as people everywhere seek better lives.

Finally, I thank Christopher Edley, president of the United Negro College Fund. Ever since my semiretirement in 1979, Edley, with board approval, has allowed me full use of an office in the UNCF/Urban League building. Through his influence and with the approval of UNCF's member college presidents, I was offered a stipend for life. I did not accept it apart from support in a form that would give me the use of my office. My thanks also to the UNCF administrative officers and staff members, whose warmth, friendliness, and cooperation are greatly appreciated.

Frederick D. Patterson

Work on this autobiography with Dr. Patterson was a pleasure and a learning experience that would not have been possible without help and encouragement. My thanks to Jamie Graham, Danny Williams, Paula Williams, and Glen Johnson for archival and research help and to Catherine Patterson, Z and Malik Goodson, Martin Graham, Janice Judge, and Marilyn Russell for encouragement, understanding, and inspiration. I am also grateful to Eleanor Charris, Vivian Andrist, and especially Carolann Greenup for help with typing and transcription and to Hobart Jarratt and John Henrik Clarke and Sister Alma Nomsa John for opinions, advice, and help graciously offered. I have been guided in this endeavor by the spirit of my ancestors, who brought together two alumni of two colleges soon to be UNCF members to make me.

Martia G. Goodson

CHRONICLES OF FAITH

1 Early Years

I remember chiefly what my sisters and brothers told me. Apart from one brief instant when I remember seeing my father, I knew neither of my parents. I have no memory of having seen my mother at all. My father was William Ross Patterson, and my mother was Mamie Brooks Patterson. They both died of tuberculosis, my mother when I was eleven months old and my father when I was a year and eleven months old.

I recall my father from a visit with him when he was ill at Freedmen's Hospital in Washington, D.C., where he died. I had brought him some candy, and instead of eating it, he fed it to me. I have never forgotten being fed candy by my father. In my mind, it explains the sweet tooth that I've had all my life.

My mother and my father both graduated from Prairie View State Normal and Industrial Institute, a state school in Prairie View, Texas. Father had been principal of a high school in Calvert, Texas, and actively identified with the Republican party there before moving to Washington. He did not fare well in Calvert because of race relations. For a person of his ability and ambition, the political climate was too restrictive. In search of a better environment both for himself and my mother and for their five children, all born in Calvert, my parents moved to Washington in 1898 or 1899. My sister Bessie was the oldest child. Then followed James and John and next my sister Lucille. After her came Lorenzo, who was five or six years old when I was born.

My father had formed the impression—probably through his political connections—that, if he went to Washington, he could get a job of some substance with the U.S. government. When he arrived, I am told he found that he could work only as a messenger. He was not satisfied with that job. Perhaps he could have worked for the post office if he had wanted to, but he must have felt that he could and should do better. At any rate, he decided to go to law school at Howard University, even though he had a wife and five children to support.

By the time he finished his law courses at Howard, I had been born, on October 10, 1901, in an area known as the Buena Vista Heights section of Anacostia. My father named me for Frederick Douglass, near whose home we lived. At about this time my mother died. Father passed the exam for the bar, but he, too, died before he was able to practice.

He had, however, drawn up a will:

Know all person to whom these lines may come greeting that this is the last will and testament of Wm R. Patterson written [in] his own hand. On the demise of the said Wm R. Patterson, it is his wish that Mr. Solomon G. Brown of Ellvi[r?] Avenue shall take my daughter Willie May (Bessie) and her piano as his own child and his own instrument to use in his own way till she arrives at majority.

Second it is my desire that Dr. and Mrs. Hunter should take Lucille and her violin and the family library to have as their own child and their own instrument and library till Lucille shall become of age then the instrument and library shall become Lucille's property.

Third it is my request that Mrs. Webster of Staton Avenue should take James Gillespie and with [him] one of the bedroom suits in the house. I desire Mr. Charles H. Armstrong and wife shall take John Ross and with him the sideboard, glassware, silver or whatever in the way of dishes there may be in the house. I wish that Mr. [&] Mrs. Ivy Brown shall with the understanding of my executor use every possible mean[s] to secure government [assistance] in maintaining him. It is my desire that Aunt Julia Dorsey shall keep Frederick Dougglass [*sic*] and shall have one of the bedroom suits in the house and all the chairs and other articles of furniture. I desire that James shall have his mother's picture, and prefer that Bessie should take mine. I desire Lucille shall have her mother's watch and I desire that John shall have his mother's wedding ring. I desire that Lorenzo shall have my plain gold ring but that Bessie shall hold it in trust for him till he is old enough to use it. James may have my silver watch.

Undertaker W. E. Mason of Nichol[?]s Ave. is requested to prepare my body for burial on my demise at a cost not to exceed sixty dollars. Said sixty dollars to be paid by any executor from the Equitable Insurance Fund of $98. From the balance of said Equitable Insurance of $98, my executor is required to [pay] said W. E. Mason $31 balance due of funeral expenses of my wife.

Frederick D. Patterson with his brothers and sisters, ca. 1904. Front row: James, Frederick, Lorenzo, and John. Back row: Wilhelmina Bessie and Lucille.

Of the $250 I set apart fifty dollars to reimburse my executor for any outlay he may have been compelled to make. I want Bessie and Lucille, James, John, and Lorenzo each to be given $10. I want Frederick Dougglass to have fifty dollars. I wish that the remaining $100 shall be given to Miss Harriet A. Gibbs of 14 N St. N.W. to be used by her in furthering the interest of Bessie's and Lucille's musical training.

Several individual families had apparently made the trek to Washington with my father at the turn of the century. Some were related to us, and some were just close friends. "Aunt" Julia Dorsey was a friend. As very often happened with black families, "Aunt" didn't necessarily mean the sister of one's mother or father. So I really cannot say how she got to be my aunt, but after my parents had died, I remember, I lived with her in the house where I had been born. I called Aunt Julia my "Civil War" aunt because she was born during slavery, though she was about eleven years old when the Civil War ended. I was a toddler living with Aunt Julia, learning to venture out, going down with my playmates to what we called The Caves, which were the remains of the fort near the family home. At other times, we fashioned trains out of sardine cans and made other toys that helped us pass the hours before we were old enough for school. Later, Aunt Julia and I moved to a fairly large house off Morris Road. We lived in this house when my school days began.

After our parents died, their children couldn't stay together. My sister, Bessie, who became my guardian after a few years, was living in the city of Washington itself and had to work to support herself while she went to school. She lived with a fairly prominent family, the Ivy Browns. After graduating from high school, Bessie was able to attend the Washington Conservatory of Music, where she studied under Mrs. Marshall and received a diploma. When she finished school, she wanted to work as a music teacher and earn money by giving concerts.

My brother John was placed with the Armstrongs, who lived in Buena Vista Heights, a few doors away from where I was born. James was with Mrs. Webster. It's not clear to me who was to care for Lorenzo. In time all three of my brothers were sent to St. Paul's, a vocational school, in Lawrenceville, Virginia, where they were registered in the mechanical department. Little money was available, but even St. Paul's had some sort of student work program, and they each had jobs of some type. The oldest of the boys, James, became proficient in carpentry and construction and followed this trade throughout his life. The next brother, John, lived with different families at different times and was noted for running away from home. Somebody always found him and brought him back. He stayed for a while, and then he would be gone again. He was a rambling sort of child who, having no parents, adjusted to life using whatever resources he felt he had. Lorenzo, the sickly one, returned to Washington and worked for James in the construction business.

Lucille Emma Patterson, my second sister, married at an early age. She was only nineteen when she married Henry Dale, of the John Henry Dale family. The Dales were also a large family. They had migrated to Washington from Mississippi. All of the Dale brothers went into the U.S. Postal Service, which offered just about the only decent job that literate blacks could have in Washington at that time.

During the time I lived with Aunt Julia, I started attending the Birney Elementary School. I went for one or two years. It was several blocks from my house. Each day, someone would take me—in my long plaits and the little sailor dress that I hated—to school.

In due course Bessie finished at the Conservatory and contemplated her next move. Being the oldest of the children, she was aware that my parents had relatives in Texas: Uncle Walter and Aunt Josephine, also Aunt Sara Woods and Aunt Emma Bailey. Bessie thought the best place to get a job was where she knew people who would help her. Since most of her contacts were in Texas, she decided to return there, and she took me with her. Bessie had always visited me, so it seemed natural to begin living with her and to move to Texas. It meant saying goodbye to Aunt Julia, but I never forgot her and remained grateful for her love and care during the years when I needed it most. Now I was off on a new adventure with Bessie, whom I dearly loved.

For the trip, my braids were cut, short pants replaced my dresses, and I became a boy. I was about seven years old and Bess was nineteen or twenty when we boarded the train for the trip from Washington to Gainesville, Texas, traveling through the Colorado canyon and the Rocky Mountains and scenic areas further west. These sites were breathtaking to me as we traveled to the state our parents had left just ten years earlier.

After several days of traveling we arrived in Gainesville, where we stayed a year or less. I was in the third grade, and Bessie taught. Then she and I were separated while Bessie worked at teaching jobs where I couldn't be with her. So for the next few years I lived with several families who kept me.

First, I lived in San Antonio while Bessie got a job in Oklahoma. She left me with Uncle Walter Patterson, my mother's half brother, who was also named Patterson. He was a retired barber, an older man in his fifties, living, as a I recall, in a modest house with porches around it. He had two grown sons, Eddie and Cephus. Cephus was like my brother John; he loved to roam around. I don't know how he died, but I'm inclined to think that his death was probably a violent one. Eddie became a police officer and remained on the police force for many years. He had a family, but he was not married. His common-law wife wanted marriage, but apparently he kept putting it off, even though he raised two daughters, Josephine and Mary.

Uncle Walter and his wife were separated during the year or two that I stayed with him. Bessie and I knew his wife, Aunt Josephine, and spent some time with her too. She was not a blood relative, but she felt close to both Bessie and me and later on even willed us some property in Victoria, Texas.

I was not in direct contact with my brothers and Lucille during this time. I knew more or less where they were and what they were doing, but I did not see them until I made a summer trip back to Washington to visit the family. I spent some time with Lucille and Lorenzo. The oldest boy, James, was a contractor and had given jobs to both the other brothers.

When I returned to Texas from this visit back East, I found that Bessie was working in Austin. She brought me to live with her again at the home of our aunt, my father's half sister Sarah Woods, who was about Uncle Walter's age. Aunt Sarah was married to a carpenter. They had no other children living with them. Bessie taught, and I was enrolled in the elementary school of Sam Houston College.

I began studying at the fourth or fifth grade level at Sam Houston. I finished the eighth grade many whippings later. My sister had overall say-so about what was going to happen to me. When she put me in school at Sam Houston, she paid the tuition, about eight dollars a month. I don't imagine she made over twenty or twenty-five dollars a month.

While I was living with the Woods family, I worried my sister until she bought me a bicycle. I got quite good at riding until I ran into something that got in my way. I broke my leg. I didn't go to the hospital but was treated instead at home. My leg was splintered and I stayed out of school for six weeks. During my spare time during those years, I enjoyed spending hours under the house playing with my favorite pet, an old black cat.

At one point, Bessie left me in Austin in order to take another job in Oklahoma, and she put me in the school's dormitory. Without her there, she thought, I needed supervision, and the Woods were too elderly to keep up with me. At about this time my brother John joined me in Austin. He had been working for James but became restless and decided to return to Texas and work. I was with him when we learned that Lorenzo had died in Washington at the age of twenty-one. Lorenzo was really the sibling that I liked most, I guess because he didn't seem to be very strong. He died from tuberculosis, the same illness that had claimed my mother and father.

Sam Houston was a boarding school. Although it was called a college, it had primary and high school departments. I was in the primary department and wore short pants. James Brawley, who later became president of Clark College in Atlanta, was an upper-class schoolmate of mine in the college department at Sam Houston, where I attended the seventh and eighth grades.

My dormitory housed two or three students to a room. A string of showers and toilets adjoined our rooms. We assembled for meals in the dining room in a separate building. Mr. Brown supervised our dormitory, and Mr. Marshall, the dean of men, had charge of all the students in the school.

I didn't object to school, but I didn't do much with it. At the time I didn't take my studies seriously. I played tennis a lot and loved baseball. Some subjects I handled fairly well, but mathematics and scientific subjects did not interest me. I was the typical boy, and without parents to encourage me, I was certainly not diligent. I took life as I found it. I was frequently in trouble. Bad language and absence from class were infractions at our school. I got whipped by most of the school administrators. Dean Marshall once whipped me in front of my girlfriend, Stella Brewer. (She didn't know she was my girlfriend, but I was her secret admirer.) Stella later had a great career as a teacher at Clark after Brawley became head of the college.

Sam Houston was a church-supported school, and the budget was quite tight. As a result, the meals were not good. There was lots of grits and gravy and cornbread. You got hamburgers or frankfurters once a week. That was about all. The only time a really good meal came along was at Thanksgiving. Then they gave you all you could eat. But grits and gravy were standard fare.

Sam Houston was located in the countryside where I had once played hookey and had gone hunting with a couple of white boys. On that occasion I had one of my most memorable adventures. The white boys were hunting rabbits and squirrels, but they wound up threatening to shoot me. I think that we had lost some of the game they had killed, and we had to go back and find it. They said that if they didn't find it, they were going to shoot me. Although they probably didn't mean it, they might have meant it. I managed to get back to school and was determined never to repeat that experience. Despite my regular attendance from that point on, however, my eighth grade classmates voted me least likely to succeed.

Bessie, on the other hand, had a tremendous amount of drive, not only for herself, but also for me. Although I didn't take my studies as seriously as I should have, she gave me the impression that she expected me to stay in school and graduate from college. She thought I should go to law school and study international law. Frankly, I didn't know anything about national law, to say nothing of international law. In fact, the legal profession did not appeal to me.

During summer vacations, I went to stay with relatives, like Aunt Josephine in Victoria or Aunt Emma in Davilla. Aunt Emma was my father's full sister, the mother of twelve, some of whom were grown by the time I began visiting. I used to spend the summer with them, picking cotton and living in the primitive, country way, using kerosene lamps and lanterns. We'd have to go twelve miles to church in a wagon, sitting in a chair or something similar, pulled by a team.

I was always around a lot of children during the years when I was growing up. Aunt Emma's children took care of me, and I tagged along with them when they went into the town of Davilla. During the summers there I made enough money picking cotton to buy my clothes for the next school year. I enjoyed going into town with the ten or twelve dollars I'd earned to get some clothes. I think I bought clothes before my aunt and her family wanted me to buy them, but I had already spent the money. I got some suits and other things. I've always been independent. Whatever I had I controlled whenever I could. I remember, though, one time when I was with some of the older of Aunt Emma's sons. We were in the little town of Davilla. We passed a little white boy who was selling soda water, and he offered to sell me some. I don't know whether I didn't have the money to buy it or didn't want to. At any rate, when I *didn't* buy it, he spat in my face. I was going to go after him, but my relatives held me back. They said, "Don't do that, that's dangerous." Fighting back was dangerous. "If you start fighting with him, somebody might kill you." They didn't say the words, but they let me know that I wasn't free to fight as I wanted to because the boy was white and I was black. My fighting, they had me understand, could have jeopardized not only my safety but that of my cousins, Aunt Emma herself, and her children who were not living at home.

On some school holidays I didn't leave the campus at Sam Houston, but I never remember feeling lonely. There were always other children around and always things to do. I never had parents, so I didn't feel myself separated from them. All I felt was the separation from my sister. When I finished the eighth grade, however, Bessie and I were reunited. She got a job teaching music and directing the school choir at our parents' alma mater, Prairie View Normal and Industrial Institute.

When Bessie moved to Prairie View, she sent for me, and I lived on the campus with her. That four years was the longest period of time we ever had together. When I joined her there, I was about ten or eleven years old and overweight, a problem that has plagued me all of my life. By the time I was fourteen, I weighed 214 pounds and measured five foot seven or eight inches.

Prairie View was a boarding school located out in the country about forty-five miles from Houston and about five miles away from the nearest town, Hempstead. It was called a "normal school," one which trained teachers. The school offered a two-year training program and granted a teaching certificate. "Normal school" students had already finished the eighth grade or had gone beyond it.

Prairie View Normal and Industrial Institute was a land-grant institution operated by the state of Texas. Land-grant colleges came into existence in the 1860s. They were designed to train students in agricultural and technical fields, in contrast to the liberal arts and the so-called learned professions. As the land-grant programs developed, however, their requirements of intelligence, application, and content eventually approached, and in some cases exceeded, the demands made by the liberal arts colleges and universities. Land-grant institutions were created by the U.S. government to make the kinds of education that led to basic productivity—in agriculture, home economics, and veterinary medicine—become practically equivalent in standing to the programs at the universities, where liberal arts and the professions were emphasized.

Liberal arts universities were largely state supported to begin with. The land-grant institutions, on the other hand, were subsidized by the U.S. Department of Agriculture. Blacks were excluded from these institutions when they were created, but by the 1890s the first black land-grant institutions, such as Mississippi Alcorn, had come into being.

Prairie View was a coeducational school. Most of the students came from Texas, particularly from Houston and Beaumont. In addition to training teachers, Prairie View taught the trades. The school had a power plant and generated its own electricity.

During my early years at Prairie View, I did as much work as I had to to stay in school, but I did not really take the work seriously. I was assigned to work in the shoe shop, where I promptly showed a lack of interest.

I stopped spending summers picking cotton in Davilla with Aunt Emma after Bessie and I moved in together. Instead, I spent part of the summertime with Aunt Josephine, Uncle Walter's former wife. She lived in Victoria, and when I went there I always enjoyed myself, although work was always involved. Once I was on a visit when I was about twelve years old. I had not hitched the horse to the wagon properly; a chase ensued, and before it was all over, the horse had kicked me in the face, causing me to lose several of my front teeth. Although my injuries were serious, I was taken not to a doctor but to a faith healer. Aunt Josephine was a Seventh Day Adventist and didn't believe in doctors; she believed in praying. Although I was prayed over and prayed for, I wasn't satisfied. I can't recall how I managed to get hold of some hydrogen peroxide, but I did, and I treated myself. When I returned to Prairie View, I had the broken teeth replaced with bridgework. I never had strong teeth, but most of my dental work did not begin until years later. Even before the accident, my teeth were not sound and were irregular on the edges. I ate a lot of candy and probably didn't brush my teeth as I should have. As a result, and after suffering many toothaches, I lost a good many teeth.

Some summer breaks from school I spent in Dallas. When I was about sixteen, I took a job with a family that required a driver. I didn't know how to drive. In fact, I hadn't even ridden in cars very much until that time. But I believed that you learn by doing, and I learned to drive by driving. It was something I wanted to do anyway, and the requirements of the job gave me the opportunity. The first car I tried to drive was the Hudson owned by a Jewish family that hired me to drive and do quite a number of other things.

At Prairie View, I saw tennis being played and I began playing. It replaced baseball, which had been dear to my heart until that time. I borrowed someone's racket to get started on the grass courts on the campus. Tennis was not an elitist sport as I saw it played; anybody played tennis.

Life for me at Prairie View was business as usual until I came in contact with two veterinarians, both of whom, because of my love for animals, impressed me favorably. The first was named Carson, and the second, Evans. Bessie knew Evans, because they worked together, and she knew him to be an outstanding person. She also knew Carson, an older person who had been there before Evans arrived at the school. My fascination with these two men was encouraging to her: she was glad to find something that held my interest. From the moment when she took over my care, Bessie was constantly reminding me, regularly urging me to do well and to become something.

I became interested in school when I was assigned to the Agriculture Department and came in contact with these two veterinarians who were teaching and practicing with the large number of swine, cattle, and horses, sheep, and dogs that belonged to the school as well as with animals in the nearby community. At about the time of the close of World War I a very young man, Dr. Edward B. Evans, had come to Prairie View from Iowa State College, where he had had a brilliant record as a student. He had made an average of ninety-two or ninety-four during his four years at Iowa in Veterinary Medicine and really should have been the top person in his class. That honor, however, went to someone else, H. H. Dukes, a brilliant man who became professor of veterinary physiology at Cornell University. Evans and I became friendly, and I was impressed by him.

As a veterinarian, Evans knew exactly what he was doing. He was young and enthusiastic, with a pleasant disposition. I had the good fortune of riding with him as he went out to treat the animals at the school and in his private practice. To me, he was ideal in his personal life, his ability, and his commitment to the field of veterinary medicine. By that time, I was beginning to show some interest in scientific subjects and particularly in the practical aspects of working with a veterinarian. My dedication to veterinary medicine had been awakened. I did my work assignment with Evans during my junior and senior years in high school and decided then that I wanted to attend the same college he had attended and to major in veterinary medicine as he had done.

In order to enroll in Iowa State College, I had to earn some money. I had already learned that college fees for Iowa residents were lower than for students from out of state, so it was decided that I should establish residency in Iowa before I reached the town of Ames, where Iowa State was located. Soon after graduation from high school at Prairie View, I took a train to Des Moines, Iowa, where I spent the summer working. I lived with a man named Fields, to whom I had been directed by someone in Texas who knew him. Right away I found a job at the Hotel Fort Des Moines as an elevator boy and bellhop. When the summer ended, I traveled to the Iowa State College campus and felt no shame in replying "Des Moines" when the college registrar asked me where I was from. She looked at me and smiled, knowing that I wasn't a legal resident, but she allowed me to register as a resident anyway. The price of registration was seventeen dollars and fifty cents at that time, and I'm not sure I had that sum. My sister had to send me the balance of the registration, although I must have had a little money from working during the summer. The college registration fee for nonresidents of Iowa would have been fifty dollars—more than I could ever have managed to pay at the time.

I'm not sure that Iowa State had dormitories then, though I remember the fraternity and sorority houses. Of course I wasn't eligible: I wasn't white and had very little money anyway. There were only a few other black students at Iowa State. Most of them were discharged army personnel and had some veterans' benefits that they used to take vocational programs, mostly below the college level.

I joined a group of six or seven other black students, and we rented the upstairs floor over a ten-cent store in the town of Ames, a mile or so from the campus. We had a kitchen, a front room, and a very large room in the rear for sleeping. We just lined up beds in that large room and lived as though were in an army barracks. We christened our quarters the "Interstate Club." The rent was about sixteen dollars a month, which, when divided among several of us, was two or three dollars each. Somehow we managed, but most of us had to find jobs to pay our share of the rent and buy food.

Although the campus was an open one, I had little social life. There was really no time for it. What little time we had, apart from that devoted to the pursuit of our studies and perhaps an occasional weekend to socialize, we spent working to meet our school expenses.

I, in particular, had to have a job because I had absolutely no source of support except for whatever help Bessie could give me. I found work in a sorority house. But despite my need to work, the demands in the sorority house were so hard—waiting on tables, cleaning, doing any and everything the members wanted done—that I couldn't study after work because I was too tired. So I quit. Next I was employed at the local hotel, where I did a variety of jobs, mostly waiting on tables. Over the course of the four years I spent at Iowa State, I changed, altered, and adjusted work to fit the circumstances of my situation.

My earlier experiences with Dr. Evans didn't help when I got to my course work at Iowa State. I had assumed that the little bit that I had learned under Evans was not anything like what I'd have to learn to get a degree as doctor of veterinary medicine. And I was right. A high school diploma was considered adequate for starting college, but I wasn't even well prepared with that. In some subjects, particularly English, I simply hadn't been taught very well. I was good in memory subjects such as geography and the sciences.

Fortunately, at Iowa State, particularly in the veterinary subjects, most classes consisted of lectures. There wasn't the abundance of textbooks that you find in colleges now. Instead, the professor told you what he thought you ought to know about his subject matter, and the student listened and took notes. Usually we were examined on what was said in the lectures; so I learned to listen very well and to take good notes. In that way I was able to pass most of my courses. Initially I worked and went to class and then studied as best I could, but I flunked some of my courses. I found that I couldn't stay in school unless I did better, and so I applied myself more diligently to my studies, notwithstanding the hours I had to spend working.

When I was employed at the hotel, I went to school and then worked the dinner meal. But the waiters didn't have their dinner until the guests had eaten and the dining room had closed. At that hour, unfortunately, I tended to overeat and fell asleep as soon as I got home. For this reason I didn't do well in school initially. But in time I learned to adjust. I had a variety of jobs. Once I took a job as a cook in a restaurant, though I didn't know how to cook. Another time, I was a janitor and had to get up at four o'clock in the morning. I learned after several experiences that the best time for me to study was early in the morning, because although I could open a book at night, it wasn't long before I was asleep. But by studying in the morning, I managed.

Iowa weather was different from Texas weather; the temperature sometimes went down to eighteen degrees below zero, and lots of snow stayed on the ground for a month or so. Almost always I walked to the campus from our apartment in town, although a streetcar ran from town to the campus; to save money, I found it better to walk back and forth to school. At one point, and for a brief while, I had an old Overland car that ran on and off.

Classes in veterinary medicine, except for the basic subjects like English, math, or chemistry, were taught in a cluster of buildings that belonged to the veterinary college. In my freshman year, anatomy was the one course directly related to veterinary medicine. I went to the anatomy class, and as soon as I was assigned a seat, I reached over and took a model of a horse's head from another desk. The professor said, "Oh, you're going to run things to begin with?" Embarrassed, I promptly replaced it. The remark didn't faze me, though. I was pretty hard to insult in those days.

After gross anatomy of the whole body, we studied microscopic anatomy, examining each organ under the microscope to learn the structure of the organ in minute detail. We went next to physiology, the way in which the normal organ functions, and then moved on to pathology, what happens to organs when they are diseased. Another very important course was pharmacology, the study of drugs and doses, using materia medica, books on drugs. The same books are used for humans, but the dosages are different. Some species of animals are more sensitive to particular drugs than others. The simple medicines such as Epsom salts and castor oils were store bought. Most other medicine was compounded, or put together in certain combinations which we had to learn. We had to master the administration of drugs in a syringe intravenously or subcutaneously, under the skin. Another part of our medical training involved learning how to restrain animals. Restraining a horse or a cow, for example, is quite an operation in itself. The animals had to be tied down and secured by the right method. If you didn't follow the right method, you'd get kicked!

We got to handle the dead animals in the first year. But the live animals we didn't practice on until Junior Clinics. Most of the surgery we did during our senior year.

I didn't do badly in anatomy, after I had settled down to it the first semester. I had two years of it and at least two years of physiology, one of my best subjects. In fact I did fairly well once I decided to study more in order to stay in school.

When I went to see the counselor to whom I had been assigned by the school, he said, "Well, how are you getting along?" I said, "I seem to be doing all right, but I just don't have any time." He leaned back in his chair and laughed. "You're not supposed to have any time. You're supposed to spend it all working on your subjects." So with that orientation, I didn't have to see him much. I knew what to expect.

Bessie and I corresponded frequently. She knew how I was doing in school, and she knew that I had to work to pay my way through; if she could help, she did. I worked hard during the summers and put as much away as I could. When school was over for the year, I held two jobs, working in the hotel and for a tailor. I drove between meals at the hotel. When I was put on the night shift at the hotel, running the elevator, I could spend more hours driving for the tailor, so I was usually able to manage two jobs during the summer. My school tuition wasn't that much, but if I still needed money, Bessie would let me have it. In fact, we maintained that relationship throughout our lives. If I needed money and she had it, she sent it to me. If she needed money and I had it, I sent it to her.

When I went to Iowa, Bess knew that she didn't have to urge me to do well. She knew that if my mind was made up to become a veterinarian, I would work at it. If I had problems, I would discuss them with her, but as far as school was concerned, I was motivated. I wanted to do well both for her sake and for my own.

J. R. Otis, a classmate of mine at Iowa State, was a Mississippi boy who had come to Iowa from Three Oaks, Michigan, where he had gone to high school. I don't know how he got to Three Oaks, but he lived with a white family and had learned a great deal about dairying. At Iowa, he wanted to study animal husbandry and work with livestock. He joined the group at the Interstate Club, and I got to know him well. In the summer after my freshman year I had tried to start a little business of my own as a means of helping to cover my expenses. I put all I had saved into buying an Overland car and set myself up to do rug cleaning and clothes cleaning. I had worked for the Ames Pantorium, a dry cleaners, and I figured I knew enough about the business to give it a try. But the venture proved to be totally unwise. The other students I had counted on to help finance the business were without money. This left the entire responsibility to me, and the fledgling business went bust.

Then Otis came along and, having a little money of his own, he too wanted to earn more. He had worked for his keep in Michigan and wanted to earn his way at Iowa. So he picked up on this idea of doing clothes—cleaning and pressing—as a good means of self-help. He rented space, opened a shop, and bought a secondhand truck. I was to do the delivery and work at the shop between deliveries. The two of us operated the business for only a short time because the work was more than we could manage while we were in school.

In the veterinary program, I did not feel odd being a part of the group of students working in the veterinary clinic although I was the only black person there. The absence of animosity encouraged me to see veterinary medicine as a field in which I could practice without being hampered by the racial stereotypes and obstacles that would confront me as a medical doctor, for example. I found the teachers of Iowa State helpful whenever I approached them. Educationally, it was a fine experience.

The vet school had a program called the ambulatory clinic, where students were assigned to observe a doctor as he drove around, answering calls. Animals were either treated on the spot or, if necessary, brought back to the hospital. Several times three other boys and I were assigned to Dr. Walsh, an ambulatory clinician, as the doctor was called. We all raced to get a seat in the car that was not behind the driver. In those open cars, Walsh's tobacco juice didn't always go where he wanted it to go.

Once as a student I had to care for a show animal, a boxing kangaroo being treated at the school after something happened to its eye. Doctors had removed the eye, and I was charged with caring for the animal while it recuperated from surgery. The kangaroo and I had a good time shadow-boxing with each other during the two weeks he was with us before he returned to the show. I didn't hit him in his eye, and he didn't hit me in mine.

There were a few black people in the town of Ames, working at whatever jobs they were able to get, as cooks, janitors, custodians, and the like. We black students early established a relationship with these people, and they were very kind to us: they were glad we were there, and they opened their homes to us. So we had a pleasant though limited social life with them.

We encountered some prejudice and some effort to segregate black students at the theaters and restaurants in the town, and it was hard to get a haircut, so we cut each other's hair. The dollar always creeps into the way you're treated. If entrepreneurs think that treating you differently from others helps them to get the most money for whatever it is they are selling, then that's what they will do. On the other hand, if they fear losing money by treating you differently, they will conform and refrain from discrimination.

For the most part, the town was pleasant. By and large, Iowans were impartial, indifferent, and not overly friendly, as compared with many

Patterson, a student of veterinary medicine at Iowa State College, with kangaroo patient, Ames, Iowa, 1921.

southerners. I remember one white southerner who was in school with me and who used to hang around me. He once said, "I don't care for this place up here. You can stand on a corner and choke to death and nobody'd ask you what's the matter!" But I found that wherever I needed to deal with the townspeople, race was not a factor of any great significance. If anything, Iowans tended to lean over backward to help me as a poverty-stricken student in need.

I never returned to Texas while I was in college. I spent my summers from 1920 to 1922 working in Ames. I had an opportunity to see my boyhood idol, Dr. Evans, however, when he came back to his alma mater to visit. He wanted to know how I was getting along. Evans tried to advise me and keep up with me to some extent. He never offered to pay any of my expenses, however, and I never asked him for financial help. I was working, and if I needed money, my sister would usually forward it.

Since I was on a military subsidy as a member of the Student Army Corps in my junior and senior years, I was obliged to spend the summer of my junior year at Carlisle Barracks in Pennsylvania. It proved to be a memorable experience.

For all able-bodied male students at Iowa State, a two-year course in military science and tactics in the Student Army Corps was required. If one wanted to go beyond the basic training, he could stay for an additional two years and receive the subsidy. After four years in the Student Army Corps, the graduate received not only the college degree but also a second lieutenancy in the reserves. I decided to take the full course. Our training included drilling, obeying commands, marching, shouldering a rifle, and going through the manual of arms. The whole thing was military. All of our training was conducted by the army, and military officers were stationed on the campus. Colonel Bowles, the man in charge, had a remarkable memory. It was said that he could remember the names of four thousand students; he was just that good. I appeared before him only once or twice, and he always called me by name. It might not have been too difficult to do so because there were no other black students at Iowa who were in the Student Army Corps. The majority of the blacks were, as I've said, veterans. Everything was integrated at Iowa except the fraternities and sororities. And there was no segregation in the Student Army Corps until we were sent to a Pennsylvania camp during the summer. The Carlisle Barracks are close to Harrisburg and were a government school for the Carlisle Indians at one time. Today they are the site of the Army War College. When we went, the Indian school had been broken up. It was a military training installation and the scene of a very unfortunate experience for me.

Although the U.S. military itself was segregated, I had not expected to have any experiences in Carlisle Barracks that I had not experienced in school. But the authorities had already segregated a black student from Kansas by placing him at a separate table in the Carlisle Barracks dining room! When I arrived, I was expected to be similarly placed. I protested, but the other student had already been assigned a table by himself in the dining room. If he hadn't already accepted it, I wouldn't have accepted it. Rather than create a lot of confusion, and because I didn't want to make him look bad, I acquiesced, and the two of us were served together. He and I were the only two blacks in fifteen hundred students at the camp who were treated this way.

Our table was as close to the whites as the whites were to each other, and so the separation was purely symbolic. After all, we marched together, slept in the same barracks, showered together, and did everything else together. But it was considered unacceptable for us to eat together. More food was always put on our table than we could eat. When we had finished, the white boys would say, "Let me have some of those potatoes" or whatever, which just shows how absolutely stupid the whole thing was.

I knew it was also stupid for me to have allowed myself to tolerate that segregated arrangement. It changed the whole complexion of the attitude of the other Iowa State students at the camp toward me. They treated me very differently after we returned to the campus, because I had become a pariah. Until that time, we wrestled, kidded around, and enjoyed a warm relationship. There were no differences based on race. But after Carlisle Barracks, the other students didn't want to be as friendly as they had been before; I learned a lesson with regard to race that I never forgot: how people feel about you reflects the way you permit yourself to be treated. If you permit yourself to be treated differently, you are condemned to an unequal relationship.

Personally, I didn't let the change bother me too much. I didn't like it, but there wasn't anything I could say or do. I wasn't in school for their friendship anyway. I was there to be educated, and if I was doing well in my classes—as by that time I was—I was satisfied.

Some of the same students who showed their prejudice would come to me for help with their schoolwork when they needed it. By their actions they showed me that they were willing to make whatever change was necessary to get what they wanted. This experience was a lesson in itself.

By the time I graduated from college, I had lost the boyish fat I had when I entered. Bessie came to see me graduate in 1923, and she came back again when I got my master's degree in 1927, after I had spent two years teaching at Virginia State College. I had to look for a job after commencement in 1923. I had two leads. First, I had taken the examination for meat inspector with the Bureau of Animal Industry and was awaiting the results. Also, prior to graduation, I had been promised a job at North Carolina Agricultural and Technical College, known as A&T, in Greensboro. Just before graduation, the director of A&T's Agriculture Department wrote to me that the appropriation hadn't come through and therefore I couldn't be employed. I hadn't yet heard about my bureau exam results, and so I was finally "Dr. Patterson, veterinarian" but without a practice or even a job.

My brother John had moved to Columbus, Ohio, by this time and so when I left Ames, I went to work with him during part of the summer of 1923. When I first arrived, John was painting a house. The first thing he did was give me a paintbrush. Before I realized what had happened, he had disappeared and left me to paint. Since I was in Ohio, I decided it was prudent to take the state board exam in veterinary medicine. When I passed it, I was licensed to practice in Ohio, but lacking money to start a veterinary practice, I was still out of luck.

I found a job in an engraving company. While I was working there I heard that Dr. J. M. Gandy, the president of Virginia State College, had come to town to see about his son, Theodore, who was a medical student at Ohio State University. I got an appointment with Gandy and rushed over to see him. I wanted to tell him that I was a graduate in veterinary medicine from Iowa State College and was looking for a job. To my pleasant surprise, he offered me one. When we spoke about salary, I don't remember whether he offered me twelve hundred dollars a year or whether I asked him for that much, but I took the job for a hundred dollars a month and thought I was well off. Later, when I began the job, I found out that the salary was much less than I needed, and I think it was less than I would have received had I initially asked for more.

Nonetheless, Virginia State College in Petersburg, Virginia, gave me my first teaching job, one to which I reported in the fall of 1923. Sometime during that fall, I received a telegram from the Bureau of Animal Industry saying that I had passed the exam for meat inspector, that my federal appointment had been made, and that I was to report to Chicago for my first assignment for the bureau. As a meat inspector, I would receive a salary of $1,760 a year. This offer came after I had already agreed to work at Virginia State for twelve hundred! In considering what to do, I remembered that, during my senior year, my dean at Iowa had stated unequivocally that he did not regard meat inspection as more than a temporary occupation for a vet graduate of Iowa State College, the implication being that more was expected of an Iowa State graduate because of the excellent training we had received. I had more or less decided that I would not take the government job, but I decided to show the telegram to President Gandy, just so that he would know I had had another job offer. He encouraged me not to take the federal job but to stay on with some salary increase the next year. In fact, I was influenced by more than Gandy's encouragement and my Iowa dean's advice. I was really moved by my increasing knowledge of my father's life and circumstances.

By the time I reached Virginia State, I had had an opportunity to talk with some of my brothers and sisters about our parents and to learn more about them, particularly my father. Both of my parents, it seemed, had had the highest education possible for people of color at the time they attended school in Texas. Their oldest child, Bessie, had undoubtedly been influenced in her choice of music as a career by my mother, originally a San Antonian who was trained as a music teacher at Prairie View. After meeting my father and marrying, she taught with him at the school for blacks in Calvert, Texas. I am told that she played the piano well and gave piano lessons to her own children and to white and black children of the neighborhood. I was also able to find out that my maternal grandparents were Salisbury Brooks, a carpenter and builder, and his wife, Mahalia Wallace Brooks.

According to Bessie, our father had been born on a farm in Bell County, Texas, the son of Emily and Harry Patterson. My paternal grandmother was the daughter of a Choctaw Indian woman and a man of mixed Irish and Negro descent. My father was one of eight children raised by this couple, who between them had the skills of farmer, midwife, basketmaker, and coffin maker. My father managed to get to Prairie View. There he met my mother, graduated, married, and left for Calvert, where he was instrumental in organizing the first "colored high schools" in the state. The absence of schools for black people in Texas made finding suitable teachers difficult, so our father conducted training sessions in Austin, Waco, Houston, Galveston, and other places in Texas for black teachers who needed state certificates to become teachers. Not satisfied with this work, he became the editor of the *Calvert Republican,* a community newspaper, and was active in politics and state affairs, "always lining up with good government." He named his eldest son for James Gillespie Blaine, just as he would later name me for another American statesman he admired.

Father took the civil service examination in Texas and was declared qualified as clerk during the administration of President McKinley. Feeling, no doubt, that his chances for opportunity and advancement would be better in Washington, D.C., than in Texas, my father moved with his wife and five children to the nation's capital, where he was assigned to the War Department, with messenger's pay! It seems that father did everything he could to overcome the racial prejudice that obstructed his career plans, but his efforts provided futile. Even volunteer overtime during the Spanish American War without compensation did not help. Finally, he must have decided that he needed to try another tactic. He entered Howard University Law School and graduated with honors. Although he died before he could practice—and I don't know how great a lawyer my father might have become—I came to respect both the choices he had made with regard to his career and his efforts to overcome obstacles to his advancement, despite the fact that he had a family to support.

As I thought about the offer of the job as the meat inspector, it was apparent to me that it was rather deadend work, even though the salary was higher than that which I received teaching at Virginia State. I think that my growing knowledge of my father's experience led me to pass up the federal job and keep teaching. I also hoped to practice veterinary medicine. That seemed to be the more promising career for which I was really prepared.

I had been hired to teach several subjects at Virginia State. I taught chemistry and bacteriology to students in the nursing program and animal husbandry, physiology, anatomy, nutrition, and pathology to the agriculture students. My job was not to do any serious veterinary training but instead to impress upon students the importance of caring for animals. In addition, I taught geography and astronomy—of which I knew absolutely nothing—in the summer school. Although I liked Virginia State, this was a very embarrassing period for me because some of the many different subjects were unfamiliar to me. But I could keep the job and receive compensation through the summer only by teaching the courses I had been assigned, so I did the best I could.

In Petersburg I was able to resume my tennis playing. I even competed in some of the tournaments there. I remember playing and winning against Lester Granger, a man who later became head of the Urban League. Much to my annoyance, his girlfriend kept taking my towel and wiping his face with it!

In addition to enabling me to play tennis regularly, my time at Virginia State gave me my first chance to have a social life with black women in any significant way. (There had been only one female black student at Iowa State, and she was already going with another student.) At Virginia State, there were faculty and staff with whom I could socialize.

The job at Virginia State also enabled me to practice the veterinary skills I had learned in college. I recall repairing the legs of a horse that was walking on the front of his feet instead of his hooves. The trouble was that, from pounding pavements, the horse's tendons had shortened and the animal's feet were bent under. I had never seen the corrective surgery performed, but I knew what was supposed to happen and where you had to put the knife in order not to strike some sensitive parts of the leg. This operation is performed on a table if you have one, but I didn't. Instead I used the ground with a sheet underneath. After the surgery, when the tendons had been separated, they had to be kept apart, and so I had to put on a metal brace which pulled the leg back to its proper position. This allowed the horse to walk. Finally, I had to put horseshoes on the hooves. I considered the operation a success. Later, I saw that the horse had healed and was pulling a wagon!

In the days when I began practicing, there was no reciprocity between states in the licensing of veterinarians. Although I had taken and passed the state board exam in Ohio, I had to take the Virginia exam to practice there. I passed the Virginia state board and, for the second time, did so well on the examination that I was congratulated on my performance. I believe that my success on the two exams was due to the extensive training that I had had at Iowa State. Our veterinary medical education went beyond the bare necessities, and for that reason, and some others, such as the quality of the faculty and facilities, Iowa State was known as one of the top schools of veterinary medicine.

Despite the school's reputation and my training there, my education suffered from an omission that became apparent when I began practicing in Virginia and performed abdominal surgery on a cat. Throughout the years of my acquaintance with veterinary medicine, no one had told me not to use catgut as suture when operating on a cat but to use silk suture instead. I learned on my own. When I went in the next morning to check on the cat, I found the cat's remains all over the cage and floor: the cat's own enzymes had acted on the catgut suture and had dissolved it. Consequently I had a dead cat and a floor to clean. It was a difficult situation to face and to have to explain to the cat's owner, but I did it somehow. I don't remember what I said, but it was less than the whole truth.

My schoolmate J. R. Otis graduated from Iowa State and joined me on the faculty in Virginia. Once, when we were broke, we came into possession of a mule that had recently died. Otis and I had the idea that a mule's hide, which we assumed would be good for leather, ought to be worth something. We worked on skinning the mule for nearly two full days, ending up with a hide that brought us only two or three dollars! We had evidently been mistaken about the value of a mule's hide.

One of the dairy farms where I used to practice in Virginia was owned by a woman named Wherry, who used to offer me homemade wine when I visited to treat her cattle. At Virginia State, drinking was frowned upon and little drinking went on. I wouldn't say there was no drinking at all, but the faculty was supposed to set the right example for the students. What you did when visiting friends in the community was a different matter, but we weren't supposed to have liquor or to drink in any place where the students could have contact with you. I knew of the prohibition and adhered to it. Mrs. Wherry offered me some of her wine, however, and I accepted. I didn't particularly like it, since it was not sweet, so she would put a spoonful of sugar in it for me. Once I had returned to campus and was seated at the faculty dining table, everything that was said and done seemed very funny. I came to realize that I had had too much of Mrs. Wherry's wine and was tipsy.

The school did not frown upon dancing at faculty-organized events, and the faculty took advantage of that fact. There was always dancing; we used to do the Charleston all over Petersburg, along with the waltz, the one-step, and the two-step.

In my third year at Virginia State, I received a fellowship from the General Education Board of the Rockefeller Foundation to do graduate work in veterinary medicine at Iowa State. So in the fall of 1926 I took a leave from my teaching and returned to Ames. Thanks to the fellowship I did not have to work while I was in school. I had encouraged Norman Dale, the son of my sister Lucille, to begin studying at Iowa State and to pursue veterinary medicine. We lived together and I looked after him. I washed his clothes and mine and often cooked for the two of us. The course work at Iowa was not as interesting to Norman as it had been to me. When I left at the end of the year with my master's degree, Norman left, too. He returned to Washington, where he followed his father's people into the Postal Service. He had found his career and he remained a postal worker until retirement.

While I was earning my master's, I learned from Bessie that she had accepted a job offer at Hampton Institute, the school both of my future predecessors at Tuskegee had attended in Hampton, Virginia. She was to teach music and work with the distinguished composer R. Nathaniel Dett. I was happy that I was able to help her financially as she made the transition from Texas back to the East. Meanwhile, James, my oldest brother, had also married into the Dale family, just as Lucille had done, and was living in Washington, working as a contractor.

When I returned to Petersburg in the fall of 1927, the seeds were being sown that would lead to my departure. At that time, there were very few black veterinarians, and those associated in any way with teaching institutions were particularly few. As a result, I suppose, Charles Gibson, a friend

Frederick D. Patterson attending master's degree ceremony, Iowa State College, 1927.

at Tuskegee Industrial and Normal Institute in Alabama, learned that I was doing graduate work in veterinary medicine. Gibson's father was comptroller at Tuskegee Institute, and the younger Gibson was a member of the school's faculty in agriculture and animal husbandry.

Soon after I had returned to Virginia State, I received an invitation to join the faculty of Tuskegee, which had such a fine reputation that when I received the opportunity to go there I didn't think it was necessary for me to visit the school before accepting: I had high enough regard for Tuskegee to believe that, for me, this was an improvement over the position I was holding in Virginia. I decided, however, not to accept before the fall of 1928, when the new school year began. When I went to President Gandy, I told him of the Tuskegee offer and indicated that I would like to retain my position at Virginia State until August of that year. Gandy was displeased, especially since I had received the fellowship and had more to offer Virginia State as a faculty member than before. I too was concerned that it might be considered improper for me to leave so soon after returning from my fellowship leave.

I discussed my situation with Jackson Davis, a local field agent of the General Education Board, who had made the fellowship award. Davis assured me that the board was just as interested in improving the quality of higher education for blacks in Alabama as it was in Virginia. He assured me that I would not be dishonoring an obligation to Virginia State or the GEB and encouraged me to accept the new offer. President Gandy, however, was not of a similar mind: he tried again to persuade me not to take the position at Tuskegee. Then, when he found out that I was going to take it anyway, he fired me! Consequently, instead of teaching from June through August, I spent the time with my sister Lucille and her family at their home in Washington, going to movies and playing tennis. I had nothing else to keep me busy but my thoughts of the new school for September.

At Tuskegee I don't remember having had a contract for more than one year at a time, although when I went there, knowing that Dr. Bias had been there many years and that veterinary medicine was part of the institution's ongoing program, I naturally assumed that if my work went well, I would be there for a fairly long time. I had heard of Tuskegee for many, many years because of the outstanding reputations of Booker T. Washington, the founder of Tuskegee, and of Dr. George Washington Carver, the plant scientist who was brought to Tuskegee by Washington. I knew some things about Tuskegee before I went. Furthermore, as it developed, Russell Atkins, the director of the School of Agriculture, knew something of my work through my friend Gibson. Dr. Bias, for years the veterinarian at Tuskegee Institute, was about to retire, and I was invited to replace him.

What an honor, I felt, to be invited to Tuskegee! Carver had already won renown as a researcher in chemistry and in plant sciences. The story goes that, in his appearance before a committee of the U.S. Congress, he was scheduled to take just a few minutes to talk about the peanut. But the committee was so interested in what he had to say that it kept him for hours, talking about the potential of the peanut and the sweet potato in the South, which was then wedded almost completely to the cotton economy. The South was not diversifying as it should in order to meet the nutritional needs of the people or to provide alternate sources of income.

At Tuskegee, veterinary science was already an established program covering the essentials of animal care. My teaching responsibilities were similar to those that I had had at Virginia State: animal science, including a little bit of anatomy and physiology, first aid, and inoculation. Agriculture students needed to know the routine illnesses the average farmer would encounter—particularly one who did not have enough money or enough valuable livestock to justify his spending a lot of money for professional services. Tuskegee's agriculture students were headed for jobs in which, among other things, they would need to teach farmers what they themselves could do to keep animals healthy and to treat sick animals.

And I was to be their veterinary science teacher as well as being a bacteriology instructor to students in the nursing program. It was the fall of 1928 and I was headed for Alabama and the site of the research laboratory of the esteemed Dr. George Washington Carver, who was also, as I knew so well, a graduate of Iowa State.

Like me, Dr. Carver was a graduate of Iowa State College. Feeling a kinship with him, I immediately sought him out. My impression of him, of course, by the time I reached Tuskegee, had already assumed large dimensions. He had been on the faculty at Iowa, and I knew a great deal about his work there. Carver's efforts reflected the philosophy of Iowa State, which was, as I have previously noted, a land-grant institution dedicated to making lives better in practical fields such as agriculture, home economics, and engineering. I knew of Carver's reputation and knew that I could learn from him. An incident that occurred early in my days at Tuskegee brought us even closer together: a number of the Institute's swine herd were dying, and as the newly appointed veterinarian, I was consulted about the problem.

First, I wanted to see whether the affected animals were eating something from the dining room that might have been causing the trouble. I found that they were not and were living largely in a pasture. After examining other possibilities, the thought occurred that maybe they were dying from eating poisonous plants. At that time, the soil of Alabama around

Tuskegee was not very fertile. As a result, animals would eat almost any-thing they could get and often developed symptoms of poisoning. I men-tioned my concern to Dr. Carver, and he expressed a willingness to make a number of early morning field trips with me to see if we could recognize anything in the pasture which might be causing the damage to the swine. As we began, I was impressed with Dr. Carver's marvelous knowledge of plant life. All of the plants we saw he knew both by their scientific names and by their common ones. We came to the plant *Phytolacca decantra,* known as poke salad, whose leaves people boiled and ate just as they would greens of any kind.

Carver said, "We ought to look at the roots and the stems of this plant because it's filled with oxalic acid." We took some of the plants to his labo-ratory, where he cut thin slices, put them under the microscope, and let me see that they were, in fact, packed with oxalic acid crystals. "All right," I said. "I'll take some of those pigs that are not affected and feed them poke salad, and I'll keep the other unaffected pigs as controls." I was able to produce exactly the same lesions found in the dead animals that were eating in the pasture. By destroying all the poke salad plants, we were able to correct the condition. This experience gave me a close relationship with Dr. Carver, and we remained friends throughout the remainder of his life.

My responsibility, in addition to teaching, included inoculation of the swine. The nearby Veteran's Hospital was established by the federal gov-ernment on land donated by Tuskegee Institute during the administration of Dr. Robert Russa Moton, who succeeded Booker Washington at Tuskegee. This hospital serviced more than two thousand black veterans. Housing and feeding such a large number of people resulted in a good bit of garbage. In order to use the garbage, the government kept a fairly large swine herd. Dr. Bias had been responsible for inoculating these animals against hog cholera and administering medical treatment for internal para-sites. After I arrived, Mr. Bray, who was in charge of the swine herd, gave me the job.

When hogs are inoculated, the usual sanitation precautions against soiled or infected needles—boiling and sterilizing all the equipment—are taken, but the operation itself is fairly common. A smock or some kind of covering is used to protect the veterinarian's clothing. Hogs needing to be inoculated were usually in a pen. Someone caught them and threw them on their backs. On the underside, where there was no hair, the skin was disinfected before they were inoculated.

Tuskegee Institute was a mailing address as well as an educational in-stitution. It had a separate post office from that of the town, with its predominantly white clientele. Also there was Greenwood, an established black community which was related to Tuskegee Institute. Many faculty families and other people lived there. Even when I arrived in 1928, Greenwood had a large number of homes and small businesses. It has grown tremendously through the years.

Much of the housing occupied by Tuskegee teachers was rented from the Institute. Some faculty members were able to buy land and build their own homes, but the school provided most of the housing for the teachers when I went there. There was housing for the unmarried male faculty, most of whom lived on the campus, where the most convenient and the least costly form of housing was located. I lived on campus in a frame building which had a number of single rooms and shared bathing facilities. We ate our meals in the faculty dining room, which was located in Tompkins Hall. Faculty members also lived in student dormitories. For example, Dr. Carver lived in Rockefeller Hall for a long time before he was transferred during his later years to Dorothy Hall, which had become the campus guest house. At Dorothy Hall, Henry Ford installed an elevator to help make Dr. Carver more comfortable.

I arrived at Tuskegee cold, as they say. I didn't know very many people, but that didn't last long. We didn't teach all day: class was held during certain periods, and so there were times when the school day was more or less over. A good many of the faculty indulged in card playing, but I was never much of a card player. There were other social activities, such as dances, too. There has always been a sort of picture show at Tuskegee for faculty and students, and there was a movie theater in the town; some recreation was possible. Then, too, of course, Montgomery, Alabama, was only forty miles west and Columbus, Georgia, was only forty miles east.

Tennis remained an important part of my life, and I always had time to play. I was among those who introduced tennis to Tuskegee in a serious way. Along with softball, it was relatively popular with the adults; baseball and football were more popular with the students in school. When I went to Tuskegee, people were playing a little bit of pitty-pat tennis. Later on, we became organized and played tournaments. My regular partner was E. W. Ramsay, a baking instructor. We were doubles champions in 1930, thanks largely to Ramsay. I was a fair player, but I was considered to be pretty good. I played every day with people who were more or less at my level. In the tournaments, people came from all over to play. Although not very many people were playing, tennis was gaining in popularity. Doctors and nurses from the Veterans Hospital played. On the edge of Columbus, Georgia, Fort Benning had a good athletic program and plenty of personnel among the elite group of military there, including the noncommissioned officers. Tennis players at Tuskegee early developed a relationship with those at Fort Benning, and we played games in both places. College students from different parts of the country participated in our annual August tennis tournaments at Tuskegee.

Just as at Virginia State, we were expected to observe some rules as Tuskegee faculty members. For instance, drinking and even smoking were somewhat restricted at the time I arrived. Drinking was totally prohibited for students and discouraged for teachers, but school policy didn't mean that people didn't drink. Smoking was grounds for expelling or at least suspending a student.

The head of Tuskegee Industrial and Normal Institute was called the principal. Dr. Moton, who had come from Hampton Institute to succeed Booker Washington in 1915, was principal when I arrived at Tuskegee. Later his title was changed to president. Although I was hired during Moton's tenure, he did not hire me. A social occasion gave me my first chance to meet him. One of the functions which was held shortly after I got to Tuskegee in 1928 was a farewell luncheon for R. R. Taylor, the vice-principal. Taylor, an engineer from M.I.T., was going to Africa—to Kakata, Liberia—to help establish the Booker T. Washington Institute, a school made possible by a gift from Olivia Phelps Stokes. At this luncheon I met a good many of the top people at Tuskegee: Monroe Work, head of the Department of Records and Research; Mr. Roberts, head of the Academic Department; Russell Atkins, director of the School of Agriculture; the head of the trade school, known as the Department of Mechanical Industries; and, of course, R. R. Taylor, for whom the reception was held. Taylor was very distinguished for his work in the engineering field. He had designed most of the buildings on Tuskegee's campus and had supervised their construction by students and faculty.

Of course Dr. Carver was there, as were many of the women who had top responsibilities: Mrs. Jennie Dee Moton, wife of the principal; Mrs. Carrie Ramsey, one of the older Tuskegee people; and Mrs. Terrell, who was from a distinguished family in Washington, D.C., and was in charge of the Institute's elementary school. The dean of women, Mrs. Edna S. Landers, was also a person of high standing.

In a sense, Tuskegee Institute could be called a regional institution. Although the majority of students came from Alabama, Louisiana, Texas, and Oklahoma, a number of other states provided substantial numbers of students because of the great reputation that Tuskegee had achieved under Booker T. Washington. For many elementary and secondary schools, Tuskegee was the preferred source of teachers, especially in home economics, agriculture, and the trades.

A job applicant from Tuskegee was practically guaranteed employment in Alabama and any of the surrounding states. The training at Tuskegee was practical as well as theoretical; it was considered the training that a developing South needed: people well trained in technical and applied fields. When I arrived in 1928, the school offered training from the first grade through two years of normal school work. College-level work in the field of education had recently been added.

Tuskegee taught almost twenty-five different trades, including plumbing, carpentry, masonry, shoe repair, and just about any artisan skills needed in society. These were fields in which black people had worked in great numbers during slavery. After Emancipation, Tuskegee was a welcome source of tradespeople. Some few of the graduates of the trade school became teachers themselves; most of them, however, went on to practical vocations. Even in those days, alumni not only had businesses of their own but were also employed by local governments. I can remember some Tuskegee graduates in the mechanical trades working in the power plant of the city of Pittsburgh. The school offered rather cosmopolitan, diversified opportunities, depending on the level of training the students pursued.

Originally, Tuskegee did not attempt college training in the liberal arts. In fact, when the college division was begun, Tuskegee received much unfavorable criticism. Some observers felt that we should remain a trade school. But education in the trades was beginning to be available in the southern states, and it was necessary for Tuskegee to advance in order to train teachers to meet the increasing demands of schools in the surrounding states.

Tuskegee Institute's Department of Mechanical Industries had a larger number of students enrolled than any other department because the trades were so diversified. Even so, there was an ample number of students in the Department of Agriculture, to which I was assigned, but the number decreased over the years. While there may have been some agriculture students who intended to farm or to go into business for themselves, the vast majority of students had one of two jobs in mind. And the importance of those two jobs—as teachers or government field agents—reflected a redefinition of the South that was taking place at that time. The process of redefining the South went on continuously while I was in Alabama. When I entered the state, two major issues confronted blacks in the South in general and especially in Macon County, in which Tuskegee was located. First, cotton was diminishing in importance in the South because places such as Egypt, Ethiopia, and the Sudan were providing alternative sources of this staple. As a result, the southern cotton culture was not as predominant as it had been during the era of the big cotton plantations.

This decline in cotton culture and a reevaluation of the potential of the South—what its climate, its soil, and its people were capable of—brought a shift toward livestock, foodcrops, and forestry. Second, the shift meant a decline in the resources of those who grew cotton. In the South, large numbers of tenants lived on farms and worked either for the landlord or as sharecroppers entitled to a portion of the crop. The system created disadvantages for the sharecroppers, to put it mildly. Many stories circulated then about landlords who had central stores out of which the sharecropper was advanced not only seed and fertilizer but also bacon and certain other foodstuffs.

The tenant farmers were largely illiterate, and most of them certainly did not know how to keep good records. Too often, at the end of a particular season, the sharecropper went to the landlord to see what he had made and found that he had earned a little less than his indebtedness. This system guaranteed the landlord the labor for making the crop and guaranteed that the sharecropper would never get ahead financially. As I have said, there are many, many stories of this type of exploitation. The government attacked the problems of poverty and ignorance through various educational efforts. For example, most of the schools in the South at that time were rural and had 4-H Clubs sponsored by the U.S. Department of Agriculture (USDA). These clubs began at the grade level and went up through the eighth grade. After the eighth grade, students could become New Farmers of America or New Homemakers of America and could work in clubs at activities that taught them some of the things they would need to know in agriculture and homemaking. Boys, for example, studied the care of livestock, truck vegetable farming, and forestry. Girls, on the other hand, studied homemaking, health, and hygiene. Since all education in the South was segregated, both black and white teachers were needed for the students. Vocational teachers of agriculture or home economics could readily find employment throughout the South, and Tuskegee Institute offered the training they needed to do so.

Many of the Tuskegee Department of Agriculture students aspired to and attained other jobs that were also designated by gender: these were jobs as county agricultural agents (male) and home agents (female). Agricultural agents, or "ag men," as they came to be known, were trained to call on farm people—the men and their wives—and determine whether they were following the best known practices at that time. Home agents did similar work with the farm women and children. Like the male agents, these women had local offices and circulated in the counties where their offices were located. Occupations such as county and home agents were considered the better professional jobs at the time I went to Tuskegee.

Agents were hired by the county, but part of their salary was paid by the U.S. Department of Agriculture. One of the biggest educational resources in Macon County was Tuskegee Institute, and many of the local county and home agents were based on the school's campus.

Of course, the entire system operated on a segregated basis. There were black home agents and white home agents; there were white agricultural agents and black agricultural agents. Usually, the blacks were under the overall supervision of the whites, although the whites were not necessarily more competent. On the contrary, very often some of the black agents, because of their specialized knowledge in some field, served both white and black farm families. But their primary work was more or less arbitrarily divided along racial lines.

The agents based on Tuskegee's campus covered anything from better livestock to tree planting, to harvesting crops and preservation of crops, to nutrition and sanitation. One black county agent named O'Neil became well known for his ham and egg show, which all members of the community could attend.

Tuskegee's famous Moveable School began as a wagon drawn by two horses or mules and equipped with the things the farmer ought to have. Conducting this "school" were a county agent, a school nurse, and a nutritionist. These people were able to bring the farm families together in a given location and set up a one-, two-, or three-day series of lessons. When the Moveable School had done its job in one place, it moved on to other farms or locations. Usually the meeting would be held on a farm where people could learn something that everybody needed to know—tree planting, for example, or the proper care of animals. Where there were a large number of children, the agent would discuss the best approach to health problems.

As with people everywhere, there were good farmers and poor farmers. The more progressive ones welcomed the Moveable School, and every effort was made to notify all local farmers that instruction and demonstration would be given and that participants would be able to learn from specialists. Of course, there were different kinds of farmers, including some who were not dissatisfied with their old-fashioned methods. I can remember one story of a county agent who was trying to persuade a farmer to come to a meeting. The man had missed a number of such demonstrations, and so the agent went to call on him. The farmer said, "Professor, I'm not doing all I know how to do *now.* So, no need for me to go to that meeting because I'm not going to do any differently." Such farmers were not in the majority. I think even Dr. Carver, in the early days, accompanied the Moveable School on many occasions. I can recall a special tribute that was paid to him for having provided plans for the construction and equipping of the original Moveable School. Later, the school was motorized, and several different vehicles were used before it was phased out.

I was not part of the Moveable School, but I was frequently asked to come and give a demonstration on the inoculation of animals or to lecture about animal health and nutrition: how to avoid problems, how to have better grades of livestock, and how to care for these animals so that they would be productive. I enjoyed doing this work; it gave me a chance to leave the campus and to meet and help people who were facing very real life problems.

Thomas Campbell was a USDA field agent who worked in the lower South. His counterpart in the upper South was H. D. Pierce, who worked out of Hampton Institute. Between them they divided the fifteen southern states and visited the county agents, held meetings, and talked about what the USDA could do. In short, Campbell and Pierce saw that the agents became aware of all the benefits that the various government programs could offer. Campbell was located at Tuskegee for many, many years and he died while still working for the government. Campbell was a Tuskegee graduate from Georgia. I don't know the circumstances of his original appointment, but when I went to Alabama, he was already a person of stature and enjoyed wide recognition for his work. He made a trip to Africa with Jackson Davis of the General Education Board and, upon his return, wrote the book *The Moveable School Goes to the Negro Farmer.*

Robert Russa Moton, who was Tuskegee's second administrative head, inherited with the presidency of Tuskegee a degree of national influence. The head of Tuskegee was generally recognized as the leading spokesman for black people in the United States. He had the ear of presidents of the United States. He sat on presidential commissions and attended national conferences and meetings as an advocate for his people; he was the head of the Negro Business League and president of a bank. The fine reputation that the school enjoyed, I learned, was shared by its top administrator.

Of course, there were less prestigious experiences in Dr. Moton's life. Bob Moton, Dr. Moton's son, told me an amusing story about an experience that the Motons had had while traveling through the South. The summers, he said, were a special time for the Moton family: Bob and his sister, Catherine, or Kitty, as we call her, and their brother and sisters. There was no summer school at Tuskegee, and when their father's work was wrapped up for the term, they would pack into the family car—five kids, mother, father, and the pet dog, a Russian wolfhound—and head for Dr. Moton's home in Virginia. There they'd spend the summer visiting family and fishing. There were also times when Dr. Moton would entertain guests who were friends of Tuskegee Institute. And of course, the summers included a visit to Moton's alma mater, Hampton Institute. When the summer was over, the Motons once again packed into their car and headed back to Alabama.

The Negro Business League had given Dr. Moton the car, a big Cadillac, which was quite full with the family, the luggage, and the dog. On one of these return trips to Tuskegee, as the Motons were passing through a town, they pulled up to a stop and found themselves alongside three young white boys sitting on a rock or a stump. There they were staring at each other, five black children and three white. The Motons did not speak, but the other children did.

Said the first, "Look at that car!"
Said the second, "Look at that dog!"
Said the third, "And niggers, too!!"

W. E. B. Du Bois and Dr. Moton were good friends. Du Bois gave an address at Tuskegee during my early years there. He was a quiet speaker, but his language could cut right through to the heart of anything he wanted to condemn. He wasn't eloquent, but he was absolutely articulate, if that distinction can be made. He droned on; he spoke quietly and most of his speech was dry and historic as he led up to his point. He laid the groundwork for what he was going to conclude with things that the average listener didn't know, nor did the average listener necessarily understand just where Du Bois was going in much of what he was saying. By the time he finished laying the groundwork, some were almost asleep. Then he woke everybody up by making cutting judgments about the status quo. He was brilliant and he knew history in an amazing way.

Usually, when Du Bois spoke to a white audience, they hissed him, especially when he condemned the capitalist system as exploitative. On this occasion at Tuskegee, however, he was on the platform with Jessie Daniel Ames, a white woman who had been heading the antilynching organization. She spoke first. She was a southerner and wanted to take things in the gradual way.

Du Bois ended his long, dry speech with a biting indictment of segregation and discrimination. He said that black children were encouraged to be Uncle Toms, but he didn't use the words "Uncle Tom." Black children, he said, are indoctrinated so that they will be docile, accepting. He continued, "I may not be able to do anything about some of the discriminations that we are suffering, but I resent them with every fiber of my being." The audience, including myself, applauded him. Du Bois took his seat. Everybody was now waiting. The chapel was dead silent, waiting for Dr. Moton to close the meeting. People asked themselves, "What's he going to say about what Dr. Du Bois said? What's he going to say about what Jessie Daniel Ames said?" Dr. Moton got up, stood at the front of the platform, and hesitated for a few moments. Then he said, "That was a great game we had yesterday!" Everyone in the chapel roared.

I continued to gain experience as a veterinarian both in my work at the school and in the private practice that I conducted. I remained somewhat unsuccessful in treating cats. My dry cleaner, Mr. Nofles, arranged for me to operate on a cat that belonged to his wife. I have never gotten over the embarrassment I felt when, after I had administered ether or chloroform and operated, the cat never woke up. I think the reason was the ether, but, of course, I didn't tell the Nofleses that.

On the other hand, there were instances when my practice was more rewarding. I treated a mule with a tumor on his tail. To eliminate the tumor, I shortened the tail. The mule was healthier than before the operation because the poison from the tumor was no longer in his system. When I saw him later running around, doing work, I felt proud of my success as a surgeon.

In other surgery, I opened up cows and removed rubber heels and everything else from their stomaches. A cow has four stomachs and anything she grabs usually goes to the first stomach, which is simply for collecting. The food moves on and is regurgitated. If what cows eat goes all the way through, there's no problem; but if it doesn't, it can cause trouble.

The General Education Board (GEB) of the Rockefeller Foundation had field people stationed in the South who were trying to improve the quality of teaching in the black colleges. There was Jackson Davis in Virginia, Leo M. Favrot of Louisiana, and the McQuistan brothers of Tennessee. These agents visited black colleges—schools such as Fisk, Dillard, Hampton, Virginia State, North Carolina A&T, Morehouse, and Tuskegee—and made recommendations to the GEB concerning grants to these schools and their faculties. Many of the giants in the field of higher education for blacks at this time were recipients of the grants, several of which took the form of fellowships for graduate work which would strengthen the faculty of the colleges. I had received a GEB fellowship to complete my master's degree while I was at Virginia State. Now I had a chance to work on the doctorate of philosophy in bacteriology through another GEB fellowship. I chose

Cornell University. My professors at Iowa State, with whom I was still in contact and correspondence, had advised me that, after doing both the basic veterinary degree and the master's degree at Iowa State, I should move to a different institution rather than remaining there. Knowing of Cornell's distinction in my field, I wanted to take advantage of the different experience I could get there.

In 1931, I therefore left Alabama for Ithaca, New York, in pursuit of a doctorate. I was familiar with Cornell as an excellent academic institution. It was also the school where black students had started my fraternity, Alpha Phi Alpha, which spread throughout the country. I became an Alpha in the year that I graduated from Iowa State, in a chapter that was organized just at that time. (College fraternities were new for blacks, and Alpha was the first and oldest of them. When I was at Iowa, a fraternity man from California came to Ames to set us up.)

I had no difficulties with my studies at Cornell, though I did encounter minor problems in English and math—some things I should have mastered in high school and college. But as I have already indicated, I had not worked as hard as I should have in school in Texas and Iowa. During the year and a half that I spent at Cornell, however, I was elected to the honor society, Phi Kappa Phi. My doctoral program involved research and course work, and so I had problems to solve or to attempt to solve in the field of animal disease, particularly diseases of chickens. At the same time, I had a series of courses such as entomology, bacteriology, and pathology and all the related sciences in veterinary medicine. My Ph.D. thesis dealt with the viability of a particular species of parasite that was causing extensive destruction in the poultry field all over the United States. I was able to determine that these parasites could live in the soil for a certain number of years. My project required me to put parasites in soil that had been sterilized and then, after a period of time, to see whether the parasites were still alive. This experiment was carried out under controlled conditions so that the results were measurable in terms of the longevity of the parasites. I had to design much of the equipment I used, including a sterilizer and a micropipette for isolating single cells.

I had intended to stay away from Tuskegee for two years, but by December of my second year at Cornell, I had satisfied the requirements for the doctorate, and I returned to Tuskegee, where I was the first person on the faculty to have earned the degree, Dr. Moton and Dr. Carver both being recipients of honorary doctorates. I was earning two hundred dollars per month at Tuskegee when I left for Cornell, and I was paid two hundred dollars when I came back. I was disappointed that my superior did not increase my salary, though I had not been promised an increase and

Tuskegee had financial problems at the time. So despite my disappointment I did not think of leaving. Besides, there were no other opportunities equivalent to the one that Tuskegee offered me.

Roosevelt came into office in about 1932. I was at Cornell University when he and Herbert Hoover were vying for the nomination. Roosevelt had been in office for two or three years when he began to identify the South as the nation's number one problem. After a time he switched and called it the nation's number one opportunity. He emphasized the importance of the individual and the importance of helping each person to reach his or her potential. In other words, thanks to Roosevelt, education emerged as one way in which the nation would improve the status of the South and of the country as a whole. When the rest of the United States was objecting to Roosevelt's emphasis on the South as the nation's number one opportunity, his reply was to describe what the lack of opportunity had meant to the South. To the non-South he said, "You're gonna have to marry some of these people, so you might as well educate 'em! With the birth rate in the South"—the South was the only section of the country that was repopulating itself—"these are going to be the only people available for you to marry." That was Roosevelt's clever way of saying that a number of southern women would marry New Yorkers and other people who were not southerners. And to some extent, I guess, men of the South would marry northern women.

By that time Roosevelt had become handicapped. He was also a very wealthy man. Often wealthy people don't care what happens to those who are not wealthy. But his handicap seemed to make him aware that physical handicaps are no worse than the handicaps that deny people the opportunities to be what they ought to be. Roosevelt saw that the non-South was depleting its resources. The major industries were beginning to wane. But the South had unexploited territory—the climate, people, and just about everything else needed to build a nation. And the South was being neglected. Roosevelt was wise to regard the South as an area of opportunity.

About a year after I returned to Tuskegee from Cornell, and under very tragic circumstances, I became director of the Department of Agriculture. A paranoid killer at large in the community shot three people, the last of whom was Mr. Atkins, the director of the School of Agriculture and the man who had originally hired me. As the person with the most advanced training, I was asked to assume the directorship.

I was not well prepared as an agriculturist. Although veterinary medicine was a related field—I was knowledgeable in the handling of livestock and animals of all sorts—when it came to the growth and care of plants, I knew much less than was called for. I tried to carry on my work teaching and to maintain an animal practice while I served as director. I realized that this juggling of so many jobs was not fair to the director's position because my practice limited the time I had available to prepare for classes. Sooner or later we had to find replacements on our faculty, and we did. As a believer in the idea that Tuskegee must continuously move forward, I was careful, as director for those two years, to hire people who were better prepared than the ones they were succeeding. During this time, my Iowa classmate J. R. Otis, joined the faculty and was in charge of livestock. He remained a number of years before he also went to Cornell to earn his Ph.D. in soil science. Otis had an excellent mind. He came back to Tuskegee from Cornell and was later appointed president of Alcorn Agricultural and Mechanical College in Mississippi. His roots in Mississippi (he had spent his boyhood there) probably helped him get the job. After a while—I don't know whether because of politics or for some other reason—Otis left that job and returned to Tuskegee. He remained there until his death.

Dr. Moton retired in 1935, but he had indicated his willingness to retire about a year beforehand. The Tuskegee trustees spent the ensuing twelve months deciding on his successor. I had no idea that I was being considered. Despite the fact that Dr. Moton had sent me on several trips to represent Tuskegee Institute, I did not think that I was regarded as a candidate for the presidency.

Dr. Moton, as I knew him until that time, was not an unfriendly person, but he was a person of great stature. If you didn't know him, you never felt quite comfortable just going in to discuss anything you had in mind. I wanted him to know me, and I wanted particularly to draw his attention to various matters relating to the Department of Agriculture on which I thought his point of view and endorsement would be helpful.

I was so overawed by Dr. Moton, however, that I was almost tongue-tied in his presence. Although he was extremely kind and considerate, I think my reaction was natural. I've gone to see presidents of the United States, and usually I have felt the same thing; the petitioner compares his own stature with that of the person he is trying to convince and finds himself wanting. Certainly one wishes to do well in the conversation. I can remember even making lists of remarks that I could make when the moment came.

When I thought of candidates for the position of third president of Tuskegee, my name never appeared on the list. Both Booker T. Washington and Dr. Moton seemed to me to have been persons of great distinction and

Robert Russa Moton and Frederick Douglass Patterson, 1935.

national stature. As far as I could see, Tuskegee would have to go outside for Dr. Moton's successor.

Of course, a great many people were mentioned as possible candidates. One Tuskegee graduate who was working in South Carolina and had merited a lot of recognition was being considered. The administrators of the Julius Rosenwald Fund, longtime friends of Tuskegee, were very anxious for Charles S. Johnson, who was a professor of sociology and later president of Fisk University, to succeed Dr. Moton. But neither Dr. Moton nor Dr. William Jay Schieffelin, who was chairman of the Tuskegee Board of Trustees, wanted Johnson in the post. Moton had his candidate, and Schieffelin worried that the Rosenwald Fund might exercise control of Tuskegee. Johnson was a brilliant sociologist, but he was not considered. Apart from opposition to his candidacy from the president and chairman of the board, Johnson lacked technical training; he was trained in the social sciences. I have no doubt, however, that would have done a good job as president of Tuskegee if he had been chosen.

I was interviewed in Dorothy Hall. I was thirty-three years old. I told the selection committee that I was thirty-four. I was actually in my thirty-fourth year, but I wanted to sound as old as possible. I didn't think they were looking for youth. I was asked what I thought the future of Tuskegee should be under a new administration. I don't exactly recall what I said, but I firmly believed that Tuskegee was very close in commitment, program, and opportunity to Iowa State. Iowa, as I have said, was a land-grant institution. Tuskegee had been modeled on the land-grant institution, although technically it was not one. I knew that agriculture, engineering, and home economics were the areas in which Tuskegee offered advanced training. In describing the future role that I envisioned for Tuskegee, I was mindful of the lack of availability of similar opportunities in the South. My remarks were, I believe, important in helping the committee decide to appoint me.

After I knew that I was being considered, I became anxious about it. It was a frightening experience! When the decision was made and my appointment was announced to the Tuskegee Institute community, some people who saw me said that I looked shrunken and withdrawn, as if I had the weight of the whole world on my shoulders.

The determining factor in my selection as president of Tuskegee was Dr. Moton. He was a powerful influence there, and the desire of the trustees and faculty to please him—because of his remarkable record of achievement—meant that they were going to lean over backward (unless I proved to be completely undesirable) to give me the opportunity. I have often said that Dr. Moton helped me to get the job, but he didn't help me to keep it. I had to do that on my own.

Once I became president, I was on a totally different footing with Dr. Moton, and I felt comfortable with him, probably because he put me at my ease. I was not presumptuous in any way and I was still awed by him. The more I knew of him—his simple, friendly, kindly manner as well as the scope of his knowledge—the more comfortable I felt in his presence. I had already started calling on his daughter, Catherine, at the president's home. And I had visited the home Dr. Moton had built for his impending retirement on the York River at Capahosic in Gloucester County, Virginia.

Catherine had been in school at Oberlin College. She was born at Hampton and her father had planned to send her to Hampton Institute until a family friend intervened. Catherine is a musician, a pianist and harpist. President John Hope of Atlanta University was impressed with her talent. He prevailed upon Dr. Moton to send her to Oberlin, where she could receive the best training in her field. When she finished Oberlin, she went to Texas to teach music at Bishop College.

I used to attend Tuskegee basketball games. At one game, I saw her sitting alone, went up to her, and, with her permission, sat with her. I wanted to meet her; she was an attractive girl. We started talking, and conversation was easy. At this time a school of music was being started at Tuskegee. There had been a department of music, but with the beginning of a school, Tuskegee would issue degrees in music. Kitty resigned from Bishop and returned home to help start the school of music. That's when our relationship became serious. She wasn't the only girl I was interested in. Before going to Cornell I had been seeing a young woman from Wisconsin who taught home economics at Tuskegee. Once I started seeing Kitty, however, and when she returned to Tuskegee, everyone else faded out of the picture.

My inauguration was scheduled for October 28, 1935, but I took over the responsibilities of president in the spring of 1935. In June, Kitty and I married at Capahosic and took off on what we thought was going to be a honeymoon. We drove to Washington and visited Lucille and her family there. Lucille's son, Almore, had dropped out of school. I was concerned and when I went looking for him around Washington, I spotted him outside the grocery store at King Avenue and Talbert Street where he was working. I said to him, "Why don't you come on and go to Tuskegee and get an education?" And Almore said, "Why not?" He felt that he wasn't getting anywhere, so we agreed to start off together at Tuskegee when my honeymoon was finished. In 1939, I'm happy to say, Almore was one of the first of "my" students to graduate from Tuskegee.

Honeymooning, Kitty and I drove on to Chicago. No sooner had we arrived than I received a message from the chairman of Tuskegee's Board of Trustees, "Come at once to New York to discuss the problem of the budget." I had yet to be inaugurated and the honeymoon was already over.

2 Tuskegee Years, I

When I became president, Tuskegee Institute was suffering from a large deficit of about fifty thousand dollars a year. Dr. Moton, of course, had retired, and so the responsibility for the budget devolved upon me as president-elect. As president I did not have a contract. I served at the pleasure of the Board of Trustees. Anytime the trustees were not pleased with what I was doing, they would let me know. If they didn't see the changes they wanted, they could let me go. This fact weighed on my mind as I headed east to meet them. When I reached New York in answer to their summons, I made my way to the offices of Goldman Sachs, where they were meeting. For my part, I hardly knew what a budget was, much less how to eliminate deficits. Winthrop Aldrich, a member of the Rockefeller family who was chairman of Chase Manhattan's board and a member of Tuskegee's board, walked into the room with a sheaf of papers in his arms, dropped them on the table, and said, "If you don't cut this budget a hundred and fifty thousand dollars, I'm going to get off the Tuskegee Institute Board." With that, he turned around and walked out. The other trustees either agreed with Aldrich or felt that they should express no disagreement because he was a powerful man. His membership on the board was a great asset to Tuskegee Institute. I formed the impression that Winthrop Aldrich laid down the law.

Dr. Schieffelin, the board chairman, was presiding. He said only, "Well, that's a pretty rough statement to face this young man with." Nevertheless, I took it as a command.

I consulted with Dr. Moton and, with his guidance, immediately began calling on a few of the longtime friends of Tuskegee Institute. My wife and I were joined by the Tuskegee Quartet, and we traveled to several cities and towns in New England, trying to raise money. The quartet sang. I described the history of Tuskegee, spoke of the need for continued support, and appealed for funds.

The time was the 1930s. Mr. Roosevelt was just coming into office. A good many people were angry with him because he was instituting new measures to tax the rich. Many people who represented affluent America believed that Roosevelt was sympathetic to minority people or to poor people. For example, I was on the train going from New York to Washington when an announcement of Roosevelt's death came over the loudspeaker. A man who was sitting near me in the parlor car said, "I'm glad of it. It should have happened a long time ago!" This man represented the wealth of the North, the business interests. He was reacting to the new taxes. Since the North, comparatively speaking, had the wealth, Roosevelt's tax measures were drawing on the North's unused resources in order to help the South. I suspect my neighbor on the train was thinking, "Roosevelt's a rich man who ought to be protecting our wealth, but he sees his mission as taking our wealth away from us." Such people responded predictably to our fund-raising appeal: "You elected him; suppose you go to him for money rather than come to us." Actually, most black people were not allowed to vote at that time and had therefore not helped elect Roosevelt. Nonetheless, such was the attitude toward Roosevelt that we frequently encountered, whether it was voiced or written or implied.

Besides going to individuals, I made initial fund-raising efforts that included calling on the foundations that had helped Tuskegee in the past, such as the General Education Board. I soon got word back that the GEB would no longer underwrite the fifty thousand dollar deficit. While it had helped indebted colleges in the past, it preferred to support the forward movement of the school; deficits were an indication of bad management, and the GEB was not interested in funding while a school sought to eliminate them.

The rebuff from the General Education Board was a turning point. College presidents, particularly presidents of small black colleges, frequently used the deficit as an argument for raising money and with some good supporting reasons. One of the basic rationales was that the students that we were trying to serve were so poor that they could not afford the tuition that would have been needed to enable their schools to circumvent deficits. But when that argument failed to win support from sources such as the General Education Board, we began to realize that, although the students were poor, they probably were not paying as much as they could. At Tuskegee, tuition was only fifty dollars per year. Tuskegee—where a part of the tuition could be satisfied by work—had since Washington's day had the reputation of being a school that would give a chance to anyone who seemed worthy, no matter how financially needy. Now we had to do something new.

When I returned to Alabama from my truncated honeymoon, I began to work closely with the business officer, William H. Carter, who had been there a great many years and who was considered quite proficient in his management of Tuskegee business affairs. I also began to look forward to my inauguration. It took place as scheduled in October and was one of the high points of my life.

The ceremony was memorable. The formal inauguration took place at eleven in the morning in the famous Tuskegee chapel with the "singing windows," the stained glass art that depicted the travail of the slaves as reflected in their religious music. The students marched in at about ten thirty, and as the chapel filled, the programs were handed out. My sister Bessie and my brother James both attended, as did Lucille's son, Almore. Dr. Mary McLeod Bethune, the moving spirit and founder of Bethune-Cookman Institute, was the main speaker. I remember her saying, "Put your hand in God's hand, Fred Patterson, and keep your feet on the ground!"

As the new president of Tuskegee, and on the basis of my experience at Iowa State and my general knowledge, I had a vision of the direction in which Tuskegee should be heading. I felt that the school had to advance the level of its educational program. Under Dr. Moton, it had moved from high school work to the beginnings of a baccalaureate program. Now, I felt, the time was right to develop that program and move on to graduate education. But first there was the overriding concern with the deficit.

Carter and I began to examine the budget, especially assessing the personnel who had been there a long time. Some staff positions seemed not to contribute to meeting the demands of the times. The question was: could we reduce our budget by eliminating some of those people? In fact, we could and we did. In the end, a number of people, including Carter himself, left Tuskegee Institute.

I was under orders to reduce the budget. I told the chairman of the board, Mr. Schieffelin, of any cuts I thought should be made. After I had made my recommendations, and with his approval, we were able to notify the people that we were no longer able to retain them. Dr. Schieffelin himself notified some people, such as Mr. Carter and the head of the Home Economics Department, both of whom were longtime employees. It was

my job to make it well understood that Tuskegee Institute was facing difficult times. In order to preserve financial integrity, we had to make some
unpleasant adjustments. It would have been difficult for me as a young,
inexperienced person to meet with older people who regarded their authority as both substantial and not subject to change. I wouldn't have had
the strength to call on them and tell them they were fired, but the chairman of the board did.

Mr. Carter was the last person to be asked to leave. Earlier he had
helped me eliminate many questionable positions on the staff and faculty.
He didn't know at the time, I think, that we would have to reassess his
situation. For this reason it seemed wise to let the chairman of the board
speak to him. I'm sure I was criticized more than I knew for letting people
go. Everybody discussed the cuts. After all, my action was unprecedented,
unheard of. Tuskegee had been considered a comparatively wealthy institution; it had between seven and ten million dollars of endowment. Our
costs were increasing at a much faster rate than our income. Under the
circumstances, the action to be taken was clear.

I also had to contend with the fact that a number of people had been
retired by Tuskegee. Although the pensions we paid were not large, they
were a charge against the income from our endowment, and they were
costs which the persons then retired had not participated in funding. In
practice every retiree received one hundred dollars a month or more—
but not much more, I would say, for this was the 1930s. An important part
of our endowment income was thus going to pay pensions, for which the
operating budget showed no comparable benefit. Employees had been
promised these pensions, and we had to try to live up to the promise, but
we had to face the severe financial problems involved. We soon contracted
with the Teachers Insurance and Annuity Association (TIAA) so that teachers could contribute to their own retirement. This wonderful benefit came
just when we needed it most.

Another important problem that compromised our financial condition
was that Tuskegee funded the school which gave our education students
their practice teaching, a practice school for the kindergarten, elementary
grades, and high school. Tuskegee thought at one time that it had sufficient
funds to operate this school, but upon closer inspection, this proved not to
be true. Dr. Moton had initiated work at the college level in 1925 because
of the demand for teacher training in technical fields. In reviewing the
services we were providing, I had to consider what the state of Alabama
and Macon County should have been doing in this regard and were not
doing. Eventually the state did assume the costs of the high school, but the
shift occurred gradually. Changes couldn't be made overnight. With hard

selling, persistent effort, and assistance from some of the trustees from Alabama, we were nevertheless able to reduce our costs. We readjusted first by dismissing extra staff and offering whatever pension plan they were entitled to; second by using TIAA to reduce and manage our pension costs; and third by eliminating programs below the college level. I think my action gave the trustees' confidence in my early administration.

As president, I typically started the day with a four-mile walk at six o'clock in the morning. I walked by myself and encountered only a few people on their way to work. Afterward I returned to my home, the president's house, which was a three-story residence with a large porch located on the campus. There was no fence around it, so that when people passed they were close to the house, and usually they'd speak. The house had a nice living room, dining room, and kitchen on the first floor, with a winding stairwell close to the front door. The family had rooms on the second floor, and there were rooms in the basement and on the third floor for the students who stayed with us and helped by waiting on tables and cleaning up.

When I returned from my walk each day, I showered and had breakfast. I reached the office at about eight or eight-thirty. The first item on my office schedule was correspondence. On certain days at certain hours I saw people, and appointments had to be scheduled. Also in the president's office, we had a vice-president, W. T. B. Williams, a Harvard graduate, whom I named to the position. In addition we had a secretary to the board, Mr. Holsey, as well as two or three secretaries who took dictation.

When I went home for lunch, as I did every day, I tried to relax for ten, fifteen, or twenty minutes after eating. Then I returned to the office to work until four or five. While I was young enough to play tennis, I went to the tennis court after leaving the office. As my presidential responsibilities became heavy, however, I played tennis less and less.

There was almost always some group or person visiting the campus. People who came to the campus, if they were the least bit important, wanted to see the president. They felt offended if they couldn't see him. So I had to set time aside for them. Sometimes I took them home to lunch. In fact, many times when we had guests on campus they were invited to share meals with us. We always had a pretty good cook to prepare meals and to do the housework.

During the entire eighteen years of my tenure as president of Tuskegee Institute, my wife presided over the president's home. As Dr. Moton's daughter, she had of course lived in the president's home with her parents, and as my wife, she played an indispensable role as Tuskegee's official

Dr. and Mrs. Frederick D. Patterson, ca. 1935.

hostess. There was an almost continuous stream of visitors to Tuskegee's campus. On various occasions she greeted such persons as Eleanor Roosevelt, Mrs. Bethune, Pearl Buck, W. E. B. Du Bois, Duke Ellington, Andrés Segovia, Paul Robeson, and many other notable people. Often after concerts given by such artists as Roland Hayes, Phillipa Schuyler, or Etta Moten Barnett, we hosted a reception to which faculty, community, and students were invited. My wife's competence in these affairs was a great relief to me.

I chaired some meetings, but mostly the meetings were held in departments and were chaired by faculty members. I didn't see people at home in the evenings unless there was some urgent need to do so. Instead, in the evenings I spent a lot of time reading. My wife spent a lot of time playing and practicing. Usually, if there were no concerts or evening cultural events, and if no people were coming in, I listened to radio news. Most of our guest artists' performances and guest speeches took place in the evenings and on weekends.

As president, although I attended all of the official functions, I did relatively little socializing. My work kept me busy. I was even at some distance from those who had been my friends. I wasn't really buddy-buddy with anyone, but those with whom I had been friendly before I became president pulled away from me. I suppose they didn't want to be accused of being a footstool or an inside person.

I had to tread carefully. Some people had called both Booker Washington and Dr. Moton Uncle Toms. To some extent, I found that I too needed to bow to the exigencies of race relations. When I saw things that made me angry, I didn't react as strongly as I felt. I didn't want to tarnish the image of Tuskegee Institute, and so I couldn't be a spitfire. If being a spitfire was what I had wanted to do, I would have left Tuskegee rather than blemish the record of an institution to which many people had contributed and which was important to its students. I didn't feel that I truly could be a spitfire; perhaps some people did call me an Uncle Tom.

Still, I never felt that I was one. In Alabama in the 1930s and 1940s, however, it was considered unusual for blacks and whites to eat together. Our board consisted of both blacks and whites, from the North and the South. All trustees met together to conduct our business. Usually at the time of our board's meeting, they met with me and the business manager for about two hours. The rest of the time we put on special programs for them to see. But other aspects of their visit to the Tuskegee campus— beyond the conduct of business—were separate. For example, our northern trustees stayed at our campus guest house, Dorothy Hall. Most of the southern trustees were from Montgomery, and so they didn't stay overnight on the campus. The black trustees, however, stayed in student dormitories when I became president. Likewise, at mealtimes, black and white trustees were separated. The whites were served in the Dorothy Hall dining room, and the blacks ate in the faculty dining room.

I decided to put an end to the separation. First I advised the chairman of my intention to have all the trustees dine together. I said, "Mr. Schieffelin, I feel that you ought to know that I intend to invite *all* of the trustees to dine together, black and white, at Dorothy Hall." He said, to my surprise and pleasure, "Well, it's about time." Next I had to inform the southerners.

I went to Mr. E. B. Norton, the secretary of education in Alabama, and told him the same thing. He said, "Wait just a moment, please. I'll be right back." Shortly afterward, he returned, presumably after consulting with the other southerners and checking the floor plan of the dining room, which is not very large, comparatively speaking, maybe twenty feet by twenty feet. Norton said, "Well, all right. Seat us at an all-white table but not an all-southern table."

For dining at these meetings, we used tables that seated ten, and we usually needed two of these. I conceded to Norton's wishes. All of the southern white trustees and some of the northern white trustees ate at one table. And the rest of us ate at the other. The following year, however, we had one large table big enough for everyone.

I can remember a good many of the people with whom I worked in my early years as president. They included the head of the Academic Department, Mr. Ezra Roberts, and his wife, who was trained in physical education. Ralph Davis, in the Sociology Department, stayed until his retirement. Another one of the senior male people at Tuskegee at that time was Monroe Work, who had developed the *Negro Year Book.* It had gained substantial recognition for its documentation of changes in the lives of blacks. Work's statistics on lynching were published annually and were widely quoted. Robert R. Taylor had returned from Africa. Many of the elderly members of the faculty in agriculture remained during my early tenure, persons like Mr. Perdue, the incomparable Dr. Carver, and Mr. Matthew Woods, who had charge of the horse barn and handled the judging of livestock. Also, there were a good many senior people in the trade school, such as Mr. West, who had charge of shoemaking; A. P. Mack, in charge of the plumbing division, and his lieutenant, Mr. Webb. Henry Lee Moon, who died recently in New York, worked in President Moton's office and served in my administration. Later he became editor of *Crisis,* the magazine of the National Association for the Advancement of Colored People (NAACP).

As I have said, I did not do a great deal of socializing and I did not develop any strong allegiances in my early years. I was aware of many people and of their work. I respected them, and they seemed to respect me. It seemed to me that Tuskegee Institute, with its reputation for working with the hands and for trying to accommodate the primary needs of people, could do no better or worse than to take its own community—a low-income community—and make it a laboratory to demonstrate what could be done elsewhere.

One feature of the Tuskegee Institute educational program was the All-Institute Conference, which developed into a fairly professional reunion of the faculty at the beginning of each school year. The conference had a theme and, in the latter years, we usually had an outstanding speaker—a professor or a college president, an expert in one particular area who would serve as a consultant or resource person. To some extent, these meetings served as professional gripe sessions; one purpose of the conference was to talk about things that were wrong and about what should be done to right them.

Since the days of Booker Washington, much of the school administration had been delegated to the staff because both Dr. Moton and Dr. Washington spent so much time away, either raising money or expanding the influence of Tuskegee. The various department heads were relied upon to run the institution.

As I've said, there was a time when Tuskegee did not have a summer school, and so the beginning of the fall term was an important time of the year. The faculty members were fresh; they had ideas; they were rested; and they were looking forward to the months ahead. The whole purpose of the first faculty meeting was to set the tone for the year's work. When this schoolwide faculty meeting took place—it later developed into the All-Institute Conference—everybody participated, and the department heads reported on their areas. I discovered that Booker Washington had used this meeting to learn what had been going on. In the process of reporting, faculty sometimes criticized each other, and Dr. Washington learned a lot that they did not intend him to know.

The annual Farmers' Conferences were another outstanding feature of the Tuskegee program. They tied in both with the vocational agricultural program and with the agricultural agents' program. Tuskegee Institute personnel went out to work with rural people, and once a year rural people assembled on campus for a meeting characterized by two features. One was a demonstration by Tuskegee of what students in agriculture could do. The other was an opportunity for Tuskegee to learn from the farmers themselves what they had done to raise livestock or farm produce of better quality for the market; how they were able to develop breeds of chickens that were primarily for meat production or for egg production; and how they could diversify their effort by at least raising much of the food they needed. Our programs in agriculture and home economics encouraged people not only to raise crops but also to prepare food properly, to look after the health of their families, and to be sure that their well water was potable. The focus was on how to make rural life on a comparatively modest income as wholesome as possible.

Tuskegee was of course located right in the heart of the cotton belt. Prior to Tuskegee's influence, people were growing cotton right up to the door and depended for their cash income entirely on the money from the crop's sale at the end of the year. But cotton crops fail just as other crops do. The sharecroppers were living on somebody else's land, and the landlord was more interested in the cash crops of cotton than he was in the health of the tenants. As I said earlier, these landlords, especially if they had a big plantation, had a company store. The people who were raising the cotton would go to the store to get what they called a "furnish"—cottonseed, food, and just about everything else they needed. At the end of the year, when they had sold the cotton crop, they would go to see where they stood. They inevitably found themselves in the red. Even the small one-room and two-room shacks in which they lived belonged to the plantation owner. These people owned nothing. Their value to the owner consisted only in their labor for the production of the cotton crop.

Tuskegee wanted these farm families to realize that they were suffering from malnutrition and were sinking deeper in debt. They weren't even buying clothing, for example, that they could have afforded if they had raised eggs or meat for sale. The whole idea was diversification. Tom Campbell's book *The Moveable School Goes to the Negro Farmer* sets forth very well the doctrine that Tuskegee Institute preached to rural people.

Landowners opposed what we were about, particularly since Tuskegee taught tenants how to keep books, so that they would know when they were losing money and would know that they were being cheated out of their livelihood. If we went on a plantation and tried to offer instruction to tenants without the approval of the landowner, we were considered to be interfering with his private business. As a result, of course, the teachers had to be diplomatic, even in helping people to learn what their problems were. We tried to show landowners that such instruction resulted in the better management of their land. Of course, it turned out that many times it was not in their best interest as they saw it. For the sharecropper, migration was one of the answers to the problem.

The town of Tuskegee was surrounded by plenty of poor sharecroppers or small tenants who could not afford the little adequate housing available in the area. But Tuskegee Institute developed a program that enabled the people themselves to build improved homes by providing a new building material as well as the necessary inspiration and guidance in carpentry, masonry, and plumbing.

Many people lived in old wooden one- and two-room houses with the kitchen on one side, the sleeping quarters on the other, and a covered porch in between. We called the open space a "dog run." The amazing thing was that if such a house caught fire, several people were likely to burn to death. For the life of me, I could not understand why on earth, when fires struck, the people remained in the house. Why couldn't they just knock a hole in the wall and get out? I learned that most of the fires started at night, and the wood was so flammable that families found themselves locked in by fire before they could realize what was happening. A concrete block house, I realized, would eliminate the problem.

I'm a great copycat. If I see something that's pretty good and that I can adopt or transform into something useful, I use it. The person who gave me the germinal idea of the Tuskegee concrete block was a Tuskegee graduate, a young fellow by the name of Walter Nickens. He was one of those people who is good at a number of different things. One day as I passed by his home, I noticed that he was constructing a small building using a block which he had made. It was different from the commercial concrete block, which was poured with holes in it. Nickens was creating the air spaces for insulation by putting his unique solid blocks together in a unique way. I was very much impressed, by the assembly and most of all by the fact that he used materials which were, for the most part, lying on the ground right around him. He was using sand and gravel. The cement he bought.

Macon County was noted for its poor soil. Sand, or sandy loam, as they called it, was everywhere. Every ditchbank had almost pure sand and gravel in it; to make concrete blocks all you had to buy was the cement. Nickens built wooden molds for casting the blocks that produced the finished product.

I had no construction experience, but I decided that an institution such as Tuskegee ought to be concerned about the way people lived. Moreover, I saw the concrete block's practical application to the distressing housing situation.

Because it was a trade school, Tuskegee had people who knew carpentry, electrical wiring, plumbing, and masonry. I said, "Let's take some fellow who is pretty good and train him in all of these different things and let him go out and get poorly housed people to build their own homes." In other words, we would supply the technical skill; and by making the blocks and helping to construct the building, we would show them that they themselves could build a house for a fraction of what it would cost otherwise. Instead of "cheap houses," we used the term "low-cash-cost houses." Although the skill was largely donated and supervised by Tuskegee Institute, and although nature had placed the required raw materials, except for the cement, right at hand, the houses required just as much workmanship and skill as would any house of similar size and construction, regardless of the cash cost.

The School of Mechanical Industries began experimenting with the idea. Simplified wooden forms were developed that were adaptable for pouring fifty blocks or thousands of blocks. Next, the "tie-end" block, or half block, was developed. The technique for laying the Tuskegee concrete block differs from that used for other masonry materials in that two blocks are laid parallel with an air space in between. Sometimes, for decorative purposes, the blocks were tied in with brick rather than with the half block.

I decided that the first house to be constructed ought to go on my little forty-acre farm. I always wanted to do things that had to do with either agriculture or business, and I didn't have the time. But I had the farm and wanted to see how the experimental techniques we had devised would actually work out, and so a house was built. Today it's still standing and occupied.

We pronounced the experiment a success and proceeded to take the idea to the people whose plight was our concern. We built fifteen homes in Macon County in cooperation with people who would own the houses and live in them. We found in the agricultural engineering section the ideal person to lead the program. We said to George Williams, "We want you to learn how to lay brick. We want you to learn how to lay pipe, and we want you to learn how to string wire for electricity." He had innovative ideas, resourcefulness, and the willingness to help fulfill an important need. We used the simplest of all methods, the simplest of all procedures, and our plan worked.

The only things that could be destroyed in the newly built homes were the window frames and doors and a very few other wooden components. As a matter of fact, after fifty years, all of the houses are still there, despite the inadequate maintenance they have received.

Shortly after we began the program, we decided to construct some houses on the Tuskegee campus. Our home economics students needed a home in which they could practice the skills which they were learning. A practice house would allow the students to live in for a short period of time and to carry out all of the functions of living in a home—cooking, cleaning, planning, maintaining, and so forth. Two practice houses were built of Tuskegee concrete block near Dorothy Hall. Then we reasoned that if the block was good for practice homes, it could be used for homes for faculty.

A large part of the faculty was transient at that time. There was no tenure system for teachers, and there was always a certain amount of movement in and out. For those who had not decided whether they wanted to make a permanent residence in Tuskegee, we built twenty homes. Actually, instead of using brick to tie the two rows of blocks together, we often simply broke the block in half and used the halves as cross-ties. Each block was supposed to be the equivalent of seven bricks. The U.S. government became interested in our housing project and made a small grant of ten thousand dollars. We were then able to issue publications about the Tuskegee concrete block. One booklet *Low Cash Cost Housing* used the catchphrases "Native Sand" and "Family Labor" on the cover.

When the federal government entertained visitors from countries where low-income housing was a significant problem, delegations were sent to Tuskegee. Our system of construction was early recognized as one of the useful approaches to low-cash-cost housing. When Congress passed the Housing Act of 1949, it made provisions for rural housing. The secretary of agriculture, Charles Branham, designated the Farmers Home Administration to administer the farm housing program. Officials from the FHA in Washington, D.C, Montgomery, Alabama, and Macon County studied the experimental work of Tuskegee Institute in rural housing. In December 1949, the FHA of Alabama approved the Tuskegee concrete block as a material for constructing farm homes and farm buildings financed by the FHA. Secretary Branham visited the campus and saw the block being laid.

George Williams went to South America with the block and to Africa as well. The block became fairly widely used. But I think it was never widely exploited as it should have been. On the campus of the Institute, however, we were able to find several uses of the block beyond building residences. Laboratory tests showed that the block had the structural strength required for the walls of large buildings. A few years later, we used the block in heavy construction of two new wings of the home economics building and in the new School of Veterinary Medicine which was being established. By using the Tuskegee concrete block, we reduced the construction cost of these buildings 50 percent.

We attempted another experiment but without great success. We worked on the malnutrition problem that we found among families in Macon County. People were not getting enough to eat, and their health was being seriously affected. In many instances children were not getting the proper food or corrective treatment for the attendant ailments. Hookworm and other diseases associated with malnutrition were very common.

The idea occurred to me that perhaps goat milk—such a high-quality food that it was used to feed invalids—might alleviate malnutrition. Goat milk is naturally homogenized. Its fat globules are smaller than those in cow's milk and are widely distributed. Also, goat milk tastes good. My son, who is now six feet four inches tall, drank goat milk as a child and loved it. I don't particularly care for milk, but even I discovered that goat milk is really quite good.

Again, I used my little farm to experiment. I developed a small goat herd of four or five goats there. I believe they were called Toggenbergs. We moved them to the campus after a wealthy visitor from Westchester County in New York wanted to know what he could do to help the school. I told him my idea about goat milk, and he gave Tuskegee Institute enough money to build a small barn on the campus and to buy additional goats. We tried to promote the idea in the rural community, but goat farming just did not catch on as I had hoped it would. Eventually, I learned why. We bought excellent feed for families to give to their goats, but the families ate the feed, and later on, they ate the goats. We ended the goat project at that time. I'm told that Tuskegee has tried to do it again, and I'm not sure what the story is now.

There are always people who do not like change, and they include some graduates of Tuskegee Institute. They wanted the institution's name to remain what it had been when they were educated there. The school was Tuskegee Normal and Industrial Institute in 1925 when Dr. Moton introduced college-level training by adding teacher training courses at the bachelor degree level in education, agriculture, and several of the trade programs, such as construction. When the various states were looking for black teachers, they looked to the Tuskegee-trained person. It seemed to us that, as a college, we should shorten the name to Tuskegee Institute.

It was no longer a "normal" school. Normal really meant two years leading to a teaching certificate, whereas Tuskegee Institute, as a four-year college, gave a B.S. degree. We had made realistic progress in the educational program of Tuskegee Institute, and the name should reflect this headway, I thought.

Some alumni criticized Tuskegee for changing its name. They thought we were straying from the technical and agricultural aspects of education. That was not the case. Our aim was not only to prepare people in applied fields but also to educate them so that they could qualify as bona fide teachers. Later, under the school's fifth president, Benjamin F. Payton, the institution became Tuskegee University in line with the upgrading of curriculum, faculty, and programs.

Tuskegee, like Hampton, prided itself on educating youth from disadvantaged families by giving them work that would help pay for their education. This had been a Tuskegee tradition when I came to the Institute. During my early years as head of the School of Agriculture, I was charged with administering part of the work program. One of the criticisms from the faculty and staff was that the students did not work long enough to become proficient in what they were doing; therefore, the system was uneconomical for the college. Student inefficiency was blamed for the deficits which the college was running. On the other hand, when the students failed to do as well in the classroom as they should, the reason was said to be that they were working for their board and room and lacked sufficient time to study.

Jobs were assigned by the registrar, who tried to send as many of the boys to work on the school farm as possible. At this time, we were growing much of the food we served in the cafeteria. We depended on the school's large farm to keep our costs low. A story used to circulate around the campus that when the registrar would ask new enrollees, "Boys, would you like to work on the farm?" the boys would say, "No, sir, we didn't come here to learn *about* the farm; we came *from* the farm." The registrar would say, "Well, would you like to be involved in agriculture?" The answer then was, "Oh, yes, that's all right." The word "agriculture" sounded big enough. And they found themselves right on the wagon, with a bucket of George—"George" was the name they gave to their cornbread and syrup—headed for the farm. Of course, not all students did farm work. Under the student work plan, the students did just about everything that needed to be done. But the system was inefficient in its operation.

An improved system emerged from a fiscal crisis at the John A. Andrew Hospital, the Institute's medical facility. When I went out to Stanford University to study for a few months, we had a big deficit in the hospital operation. The people in Macon County were poor and couldn't pay for their medical treatment, yet we tried to serve the community. When I returned after six months, I found that we had a deficit of $150,000. The trustees called a second meeting with me on the Institute's budget: they wanted to meet once every month until the deficit had been eliminated. Feeling that my administration had been challenged, I advised against monthly meetings and declared that I would decrease the deficit. When I looked into the charges at the hospital, I found that we had about eighteen people working as nurse's aides, earning about eighteen hundred dollars a year plus retirement benefits. In studying the expenditures, I made inquiries of the business manager and ultimately discovered that, although the aides were not even high school graduates, they were receiving salaries only slightly below those paid to people with M.A. and M.S. degrees in various disciplines.

I decided to eliminate all of the aides. People on cash salaries cost money, and we were spending money that we did not have. I said to the business manager, "I'll tell you what we're going to do. We're going out and advertise: Any young woman"—I think we restricted it to young women—"who has a high school B average or better but for financial reasons can't get into college can come to Tuskegee. We will give her a chance to work all day and go to school at night." The young women would do a full day's work and a half day's academic program at night for two years. They would then have achieved the freshman year. We agreed to pay them twelve hundred dollars in services rendered rather than in cash. Their earnings would be a book entry on which they could draw with a part-time job during the next three years, when they were going to school full time.

All the prospective student needed to enter this work-study program was fifty dollars. Tuskegee Institute would see that they finished their entire degree program without spending further money. This became known as the Five Year Plan. The students had to have a B or better, and so they had screened themselves before coming to Tuskegee. All they needed was the opportunity, and the Five Year Plan guaranteed that they would have one.

As a result of this strategy, which was sound for the student and for the Institute as well, we replaced a deficit of $150,000 with a surplus of $300,000. We did not restrict the plan to nursing; instead we generalized it. By so doing, Tuskegee made it possible for the students in carpentry, masonry, and plumbing, by working a full day under their instructors, to become proficient until they were actually worth the wages they were being paid. Then, when they went on a part-time job for three years, they were skilled rather than being inexperienced novices. The success of the Five Year Plan, over and above its financial value, was the educational security that it provided to the students.

Nathaniel Colley, an attorney in Sacramento, California, gave Tuskegee fifty thousand dollars more than once. He recently gave the NAACP a hundred thousand dollars for its new building. Colley is a very wealthy man. He graduated from Tuskegee as one of our outstanding Five Year Plan students, went into the army's Chemical Corps, and subsequently took a law degree at Yale University. Colley's wife was also a Five Year Plan student. There are many stories of students who developed well under the Five Year Plan and took from Tuskegee Institute important skills they learned while working as well as knowledge from their classroom instruction. I was sorry to see the Five Year Plan eventually discarded. In my opinion, Tuskegee would have avoided much of its later indebtedness had it continued the Five Year Plan.

In 1940 the Tuskegee students went on strike. The strike had not been anticipated; it happened rather suddenly. As I look back on it, I assume that it stemmed in part from my efforts to give the students some experience in self-government. They decided to make their feelings known and, in my opinion, took things to an extreme.

The strike took place in 1940 and lasted, as I recall, three or four days. I learned a great deal from it, especially how beneficial it was for us to bring the students even closer to the operation of the school than they had been in the past.

The students struck for better food in the cafeteria and for more social privileges. Students never get enough social privileges or enough food, no matter how good it is. I can't even remember with much certainty what the students wanted in the way of social privileges. We didn't have as much dormitory visiting as there now is. Dormitory visiting wouldn't have been tolerated for an instant. But the students wanted more dances or more movies or something else. They refused to go to classes, and they stopped eating in the cafeteria.

I had created the cafeteria five years earlier. When I became president, meals for Tuskegee students were served in the dining room in Tompkins Hall at long tables with several students seated on either side. Food placed at one end of the table often did not reach the other end. If there wasn't enough food to pass along, only the students who served themselves first were able to eat. There was reaching, grabbing, a lot of noise, and an absence of manners at mealtimes in Tompkins. The faculty ate with proper decorum in a separate dining room with table service. I think at one time teachers had sat at the tables with the students, but when I headed the administration, only students ate in the dining hall. The students were consequently free to do as they pleased, and what they chose to do often wasn't very good.

As I did frequently during my career, I adopted a solution with which I was already familiar. I had been in cafeteria lines at Iowa, and I had been in cafeteria lines at Cornell. It had seemed to me an orderly process, and I thought it would be better. I instituted the conversion to the cafeteria system at Tuskegee and had the dining room renovated before the 1935–36 school year began.

Soon after my arrival on Tuskegee's campus, twelve years before the student strike, Dr. Moton had hired Harry Richardson to replace Dr. Whitaker as chaplain. Richardson and I had been friendly all along, but we became especially friendly as a result of the student strike. Everybody else put some distance between themselves and me, but Harry didn't, and I have always appreciated his loyalty to me, especially at that time. The students had chained one of the important buildings. Harry went over with me to try to open it and to calm the students who wanted to fight; some wanted to fight to go in, and others wanted to fight to keep them out. Harry and I sorted everything out, and the strike resumed without other major incidents on the campus.

Shortly after the strike began, I heard from the trustees. They wanted to know what had happened and why. Some of them wanted to take a vote of confidence in me. But President Edmund Ezra Day of Cornell University, who was on the board, said, "You don't need to take a vote of confidence in him: the place is not burning down. The vote of confidence is an apology. Let things go on as they are, and simply let the President know that we are fully in support of him in whatever he wants to do." So I was on my own.

It wouldn't have been as bad as it was, but the students started interfering with the delivery trucks that came to the campus, and the drivers reported the interference. Then the law became involved. I had to prevail on the state troopers not to arrest the students who were blocking the entrance but to give us a chance to work things out, which they did. We had wonderful cooperation from the troopers, but they had the biggest guns I'd ever seen in my life. I said, "Don't touch these students." They responded, "We wouldn't do that, Dr. Patterson." I said, "I think we can get this situation under control."

The students got in trouble only when they wouldn't stop striking. We said to the students, "We will talk with you; we'll discuss anything at all. But after we tell you the best that we can do, we expect you to be back in classes. And if you're not back in school, you have to leave the campus." By this time, hunger had taken over and a considerable number of students had already returned to meals in the cafeteria.

When we met, the students expressed their grievances and we listened. About the cafeteria, they complained of the food—the quality, the quantity, and the service. I said, "We're not trying to make money off the food. We're simply trying to help you get the best food we can give you for the price you can afford to pay. But you don't have to put up with what we serve you. You can take it over. We'll turn over to you that dollar a day"—and I think that's what the amount was that we put into food for each student. "Now you buy the food. You can go to the Business Office. You can go to any of our people who are involved and ask them to help you. But the food service will be your responsibility, now *you* have to do it. But remember, you've got to put aside a certain amount for cooks, for insurance, for replacement of equipment. That dollar has to be broken down to cover these things as well as food. Only a portion of it goes for raw food."

The students loved the idea; they thought it was wonderful. They kept it for two weeks! Then they came back and said, "Dr. Patterson, we haven't got time for all this work. We didn't know there was all this involved!" So we resumed management of the cafeteria, but they had learned the hard way, by trying to do it themselves. And the experience was something worthwhile.

It's very easy for the average college administration to become dictatorial, to say "You must do as I say." I think that's wrong. During the student strike, we of the faculty had to learn to hear what the students had to say. Some of the faculty criticized me when I turned over the food service to the students. I didn't think the students would keep managing the food service, but if they had, I would have been willing for them to do so. They couldn't, yet they learned from trying.

When the students complained about social privileges, we decided to include students in the college's committee structure. We said, "Let them come closer to what goes on here." I felt that we were reasonably creative when we said, "We're not just going to tell you what we can't afford. We're going to give you the responsibility and let you find out for yourselves." We helped the students to see all the things we did to run the institution. We said, "Let them have something to say about the way the dining hall is run. Let them be a part of the process of deciding who is going to be invited as guests for the Entertainment Course, our social calendar on campus. Let's give the students a forum so that when they want to talk about anything else, they don't have to create an emotional furor before they're listened to." To the student council, which already had one faculty person, we added several faculty members. But we left the student majority. The students could have controlled the vote on any issue that came up, but they never did. There was never a time when all the students were on one side and all the faculty on the other.

We put students on every college committee except the Faculty Governing Board. Today, they're even on that. When the students became more involved in the running of the school, they learned and we learned. After the student strike, my wife invited junior and senior girls to come to our house and visit with her. And whenever we entertained campus guests at the president's home, we always had student hostesses.

Some of the students refused to stop striking and were dismissed for not returning to class. When they reached their homes, their parents immediately ordered them, "You get on back up there and go to school as you're supposed to." In later years, it amused me to recall the students who were sent home. I enjoyed telling alumni like Daniel "Chappie" James, who later became a general in the U.S. Air Force, "Just about every one of you that we dismissed seems to have done well since you graduated from Tuskegee. It was you smart guys that I should have kept on the campus and dismissed the dullards!"

For a year or two after the strike, the students treated my administration very coolly. After we changed the way we dealt with young people, brought them in as participants in decision making, and gave them a chance to see the results, I couldn't have had warmer support from the students. When the strike was over, however, I remember shedding tears. This was one of three occasions when I did so.

While I was president, P. H. Polk became the official photographer for Tuskegee Institute. Polk was establishing a good reputation, and in due time, he was recognized nationally. Polk was a tremendously conscientious, diligent, energetic, and competent photographer. He was ubiquitous: no important gathering on the campus escaped him. He was, of course, wonderfully skilled in his work, much of which was portraiture. Unquestionably, Polk made an important contribution to the historiography of this period through his photographs of Tuskegee Institute. Some of his work is included in this volume.

The many gatherings that Polk recorded included the meetings of the Board of Trustees. Other than one or two local whites and one or two blacks, Tuskegee's board consisted largely of northern business people. They were mostly wealthy people who had been interested in the education of blacks for many years. They gave fairly generously at that time or helped contact people of wealth who were generous contributors. The trustees were people of national standing, mostly in the financial field, or people of wealth which had been acquired from relatives in the financial field.

Their job as trustees of the Institute was clearly defined. The board is the body which controls the Institute. It holds the properties. The physical plant is under the supervision of the trustees, who are naturally concerned with how the plant is used for educational purposes. They were also concerned about the resources which the institution had or needed to acquire, and to this end, they constantly received financial reports from the president about the institution's welfare. The trustees also appoint an auditor, who reports independently.

Apparently several of the trustees had become interested in Tuskegee because of Booker T. Washington and contacts with the Hampton Institute. General Armstrong, who was the founder and first principal of Hampton Institute, brought the interest of the whole Boston contingent to the two schools. Sometimes membership on the Tuskegee or Hampton board became a tradition within a family. When one family member died or resigned, another family member would take his or her place. The trustees were great supporters of Washington and Moton. They did not participate in any organized form of fund raising, but they gave to the school. Dr. Moton had been successful in the Hampton-Tuskegee fund-raising campaign in the 1920s, and I guess a good many of the trustees had been involved at that time. But during the years that I functioned under the board—until the United Negro College Fund (UNCF) was developed—Tuskegee trustees did not involve themselves in routine fund raising. Still, fund raising was definitely what was needed.

Procession, Founder's Day, 1946. Front: Dr. William J. Schieffelin, chairman of the Board of Trustees; Basil O'Connor, trustee; Vice-President Henry A. Wallace; Frederick Patterson. Rear: Claude Barnett, trustee; Harry V. Richardson, Tuskegee faculty; A. A. Alexander, trustee; D. W. Andrews, trustee.

During the last few years of his administration, Dr. Moton hadn't been well. When I became president, I ran into an interesting problem: the auditor, who was white, was trying to dictate the way the institution was to be run. When he had decided that some things needed changing, he had gone to faculty and other staff to institute changes, completely bypassing me in the process. When I became aware of what he was doing—something I'm confident he would not have done if he had been in a white school with a white president—I insisted that if he found anything wrong, he was to let me know. He was *not* to dictate to anyone on my faculty any changes which neither I nor the board had approved.

At the beginning of my presidency, Dr. Schieffelin, of the Schieffelin Drug Company of New York, was chairman of the board. He served as a trustee of Hampton or Tuskegee or both for forty years. Later, Basil O'Connor took over the chairmanship. Henry S. Bowers of Goldman Sachs, also of New York, and Edgar Stern of New Orleans, Julius Rosenwald's son-in-law, were also members. As I was made president, Stern resigned because of a disagreement with the chairman of the board. His brother-in-law, William Rosenwald, succeeded him and served for forty years or more. Another of our members, Mr. Mason, attended our meetings accompanied by his wife, who was the granddaughter of the Civil War governor of Massachusetts, John A. Andrew, after whom the Institute hospital had been named. Winthrop Aldrich, the brother-in-law of John D. Rockefeller, Jr., and chairman of the board of Chase Manhattan Bank, was a member of our board. It was he who had told me on my honeymoon that if I didn't cut the budget by $150,000, he wasn't going to stay on the board.

Claude Barnett was also a member of the Tuskegee board. An impressive figure who stood about six feet six inches tall, Barnett was president and chief operator of the Associated Negro Press in Chicago. He was a Tuskegee graduate and prided himself on having been Booker T. Washington's office boy as a student, he was to become one of the most loyal and effective trustees we had. He was such an efficient newsman that people used to say that Barnett gave his business card to all the GIs in Europe during the second World War just so that they could send stories back to him. Most black newspapers were affiliated with the Associated Negro Press. Each week they received a mimeographed document of current happenings with which they could enrich their publications. Barnett also made a point of being on many important boards, particularly those that were related to blacks.

My friendship with Claude Barnett began while I was still director of the School of Agriculture. I remember discussing with him a project I wanted the board to approve: I wanted Tuskegee to purchase eighteen hundred acres of land known as the Russell plantation, which was located some distance from the campus. It was rich land in contrast to the soil in the immediate vicinity of Tuskegee. I felt that we could establish housing on the acreage and provide some practice work in agriculture for the students. Although I wasn't there when the matter came before the board, I'm sure that Barnett helped us secure the board's agreement to purchase the plantation. It turned out to provide a fairly rich source of timber. We paid roughly seventeen hundred dollars for the acreage, and we were able to sell about fifty thousand dollars' worth of timber in different cuttings off that land. Although I had not anticipated income from forestry—I had originally been interested in its use for our teaching program—I was nonetheless pleased that we had it.

Barnett supported my administration when I, as a young president, was being vigorously criticized by alumni and others for various steps I was taking in running Tuskegee. I frequently visited him and his wife in Chicago, stayed at their home, and shared my concerns with them. Etta Moten Barnett was a distinguished artist in her own right in the fields of music and drama. She and Claude were also deeply interested in education, both in the United States and in Africa.

As I've already noted, the financial situation at the time that I assumed the presidency was not good. We needed more money, and it was my job to figure out where we could get it. Washington and Moton had been such effective fund raisers that the trustees had more or less delegated the job to them. The board members contributed to the school, but their contributions alone were not sufficient to improve our plant, our course offerings, and our faculty.

I did not have a background in fund raising, nor did I have the acquaintances, other than the people to whom Dr. Moton had sent me—friends or acquaintances of his. I really had to strike out on my own to develop resources.

First, I went to the state of Alabama, which had been using Tuskegee Institute's resources and had been giving very little. Then, when I looked beyond the state, the idea of a united appeal for the private black colleges occurred to me. It originated in the following way. Basil O'Connor was the head of the National Foundation for Infantile Paralysis. The March of Dimes was a national fund-raising campaign of the foundation. It was a campaign in which people all over the nation were asked to contribute dimes to fight the curse of polio. That campaign was off to a good start and was recognized and supported nationally. O'Connor later became head of the American National Red Cross, and through his leadership, I was made a member of the Board of Governors.

In both of those national organizations, the direction was moving from the control and contributions of a few to a larger giving constituency. The idea occurred that this was the direction of national philanthropy, with the masses brought in to contribute. Only by going beyond any immediate constituency such as alumni and trustees could a campaign have a national appeal. Could black colleges, perhaps through a united effort, make a case for the needs of black youth now being severely restricted and handicapped by lack of resources?

The answer to the question lay within an organization that I founded, the United Negro College Fund. Many people know of my connection with UNCF, but only a few are aware that the inspiration for that idea grew directly out of my experience in creating programs and addressing the financial needs of Tuskegee Institute. In fact, I am just as proud of many of the programs I was able to introduce at Tuskegee as I am of my work with UNCF and subsequently with the Phelps Stokes Fund (PSF). I remained

Frederick D. Patterson and Basil O'Connor, president, National Foundation for Infantile Paralysis, and Tuskegee trustee, ca. 1946.

president of Tuskegee for eighteen years. During that time, the innovations I've described earlier became part of the educational landscape of Tuskegee and of Macon County. In addition, four programs were created that I recall with particular pride: commercial food service, veterinary medicine, aviation, and engineering.

These programs reflected the results of Tuskegee's effort to give our graduates new employment opportunities by training them in fields that were up and coming. Each program arose from slightly different circumstances; each had unique features; and several had their genesis in efforts in the South to maintain segregation as long as possible.

The U.S. Supreme Court decision of 1954 banning school segregation was inevitable. It was a good decision and one that I welcomed. Prior to that time, however, segregation in schools was the de facto law of the land. For black students, therefore, any program of study that was not offered at a black school was unavailable to blacks in the South. Most black youngsters seeking a college education did not have an opportunity to leave the South and attend integrated schools such as Iowa State and Cornell, as I had done. But when students came to Tuskegee, I felt, they should have the best that could be offered. Tuskegee's programs were superior to those at many black colleges but were sharply deficient when compared with those at the best of the white schools. We needed more.

The focus of my efforts during my eighteen years as president was on creating programs that operated and finding the necessary money. I am proud of the results of my efforts. Little by little, as these programs were established, the ideas that went into the United Negro College Fund began to take shape. But before I discuss UNCF, I will describe the Tuskegee experiences that convinced me that collective fund raising was an idea whose time had come.

3 Tuskegee Years, II

Commercial Dietetics, 1935

A member of our faculty, G. L. Washington, was approached on a train by a man in the Alabama restaurant/hotel business who said that the nationwide need for good, intelligent cooks was inexhaustible and that Tuskegee might consider this field in planning new programs. When G.L. told me of this conversation, I recalled my stay at Cornell University, where, in the hotel management school, the practice facility was Willard Straight Hall, a hotel in which Cornell alumni and many other visitors to Cornell and Ithaca stayed. The thought immediately occurred to me that if the Cornell hotel school model could be modified to emphasize commercial food service rather than guest housing, Tuskegee should adopt it. Very few colleges or institutions over the country as a whole considered food preparation and service a discipline that could be learned in academic terms as well as practical ones. The uniqueness of the commercial dietetics program we instituted was the fact that none of the so-called educational institutions serving black youth were doing anything in this area.

The preparation and service of food is one of the biggest businesses in this country today. Yet the top people in the food industry have never had as much experience as many black people in the preparation and serving of food. The industry was far smaller in 1935 when we started the commercial dietetics program, but even then I could see that we had received an excellent suggestion.

In slavery and afterward, the majority of professional cooks in the country were black. Black cooks in white homes and businesses, as well as in commercial establishments such as bakeries and catering services, had already become a part of American culture at the time we studied the idea. Cream of Wheat cereal featured a picture of a black man on its packages, the Uncle Ben on the rice box was black, and so was Aunt Jemima on the pancake package. Obviously blacks were identified with good cooking. I asked myself why, having always cooked, we couldn't cook better. People were making millions from activities that blacks had always done. At Tuskegee, we strove to prevent people from exploiting us; instead, we exploited our own talents and elevated them to the level of sound business.

In all fields, we taught Tuskegee students not to downgrade work they had to do but to upgrade it to something worth doing for which there was real compensation. In considering a commercial food program, we refused to allow the domestic work of slavery to discolor the practicality and good business value of food preparation and service as a career.

The American economy reflected the growth of the common occupation. This truth was Booker T. Washington's philosophy, and it is inscribed on the Washington monument at Tuskegee Institute: "We shall prosper as we learn to glorify and dignify labor and to put brains and skill into the common occupations of life." Commercial dietetics was strictly within the Tuskegee tradition.

It was also a logical extension of home economics. Our graduates in home economics would have opportunities as homemakers, or as teachers in vocational high school home economics programs, or as home agents with the Department of Agriculture. These opportunities were not unlimited, and we thought that salaries for those in commercial foods who were successful would be equal to or better than those for teaching home economics or for teaching in general.

We had apparently found an area of wide opportunities. Since the need was great, we went to the leaders in the hotel and restaurant organizations to persuade them to invest money in our program. Although they enthusiastically endorsed our program, we were disappointed that they did not underwrite it properly.

Commercial dietetics involved cooking and serving food, budgeting food, and learning to consider the cost of food in establishing the price paid for it by the customer. As in any other business, this work encompassed public relations, personnel, business and accounting practices, and management—all the things that would create a growing and thriving enterprise. The Institute had a large do-it-yourself program that could help us. We prepared all the food served for students and faculty in the cafeteria and guest house dining room. We planted, grew, and harvested. In animal husbandry, we had the expertise to raise, slaughter, and cure meats. We had a dairy, and we had home economics teachers already on staff. In fact, home economics people who came to understand the commercial value of food preparation and service often became much more interested in the new program than they were in routine home economics instruction.

The person we employed to take charge of commercial dietetics was Robert Spicely, whom I had known when he was a student at Virginia State. As an undergraduate, Spicely had insisted on taking home economics, and everyone had laughed at him. Home economics had seemed to be a program for young women only. But there was nothing feminine about him. When we set up the commercial dietetics program, we thought he was the best person to head it, and he joined us from Chicago, where he was working.

Spicely brought his young wife with him to Alabama. They were, in every sense, worthwhile members of the Tuskegee Institute organization. He turned out to be a teacher of very high caliber—a little bit profane but nonetheless highly dedicated. He knew how to roll up his sleeves and get the job done. Spicely and G. L. Washington did the necessary organizing to launch the program, including establishing an annual food show for the students in this program. The situation resembled a medical clinic in which students meet, observe, and learn from experienced practitioners. The show featured a guest chef. We'd look over the country as a whole to find especially talented chefs. Annually we invited a few to attend the show and do some teaching. The guest chefs were an inspiration to the students. They demonstrated artistry in the preparing, serving, and marketing of food services. Our guest chefs also shared their view of the field as a future vocation.

One of the people who surveyed our program was Lucius Boomer, the manager of the Waldorf Astoria Hotel in New York. Boomer attended the Tuskegee food shows and joined in the discussion of an appropriate name for the program. Since dietetics had to do with the serving and preparation of food, and since this was not home economics but work on a commercial basis, we put the two words together, and thus it became the Department of Commercial Dietetics.

As the program grew, we developed internships. Tuskegee Institute had

beginning stages, flying was open almost solely to whites. There were only twenty-five black pilots in the whole of the United States when flying instruction began at Tuskegee.

I was personally aware of a few of them. I first saw a black person fly a plane in Iowa when I was a graduate student. A black student there owned an airplane and could fly, but he was the great exception. Flying was expensive. Most blacks, for various reasons including lack of money, did not aspire to fly.

I had also known of a Tuskegee graduate who had done some flying and had been a part of the military aviation program in Ethiopia. There was a black woman flyer—an aviator named Bessie Coleman–who had excited people in general, not only because she was a woman who flew, but also because she was black.

I can remember my own first passenger flight. During meetings with foundations in New York City in 1938, I learned that Henry Ford would be visiting Dr. Carver at Tuskegee Institute on the next day. I wanted to be there, and so I took my first plane trip. It was quite exciting initially, but meteorology was not what it is today. The flight was grounded in Richmond because of bad weather, and I had to spend the night there. I missed Mr. Ford's visit and had to finish the balance of the trip from Richmond to Tuskegee by train.

In the 1930s "Chief" Charles Anderson, together with a member of the Wright family of Philadelphia, flew to Tuskegee en route to South America. Wright was interested in importing coffee to be sold by black merchants in the United States. Anderson, his pilot, stopped in Tuskegee and landed the plane in an area near the campus. Even then, Mr. Anderson was interested in encouraging others to fly. He was more than congenial and was happy to take people up and let them know about flying firsthand.

We wanted Tuskegee to be a part of this new and exciting field. The government had started subsidizing civilian pilot training programs, particularly at colleges, over the nation as a whole. But black colleges were excluded.

Aviation was just beginning to come into its own as a program for college teaching and as a career. There was a growing feeling that aviation was a part of the future of America and that there would be, in time, a number of new opportunities in business, in private flying, and in other areas for trained flyers. In Alabama, white students were being trained in aviation at Alabama Polytechnic Institute at Auburn and perhaps at some of the advanced high schools. The University of Alabama may have had a flight program as well.

An aviation program was expensive. There was no way in which

Tuskegee Institute or practically any other college, black or white, could have started a program on its own. But aviation was one of those fields of promise that the federal government wanted to advance. The U.S. government has opened up most of the industrial areas of large potential, such as railroading. Most major developments had to be started with money which only the government could afford to risk.

When we learned that West Virginia State College, a black school in Institute, West Virginia, had been awarded an aviation program because of certain existing relationships with the Department of Defense, it became apparent to us at Tuskegee that we too should attempt to provide training in aviation. When we began to investigate the possibility of offering an officially endorsed and government-funded civilian pilot training program, we discovered that it operated on a contract basis. If we could supply the students and locate qualified instructors, the government would pay for everything else.

The land around Tuskegee is basically flat, and so we didn't need an airfield. We could use a cow pasture—and we did! We recruited Chief Anderson to head our program of flight instruction. G. L. Washington, who was an engineer, headed the program as a whole. Anderson's title of "Chief" was an honorary one: he had been flying longer than anybody else we knew, and he was among the best known of the black pilots; furthermore, he was completely competent and professional. We were sure of his ability and his enthusiasm for flying.

The challenge, though, was to find enough people to run the program. With Anderson's help, we searched the country to find people who could fly and were willing to come.

At this time there were black people living outside the South who did not want to come south because they had heard so many unfavorable things about segregation. Most people did not realize that Tuskegee Institute was almost completely insulated against the meaner forms of race prejudice. Although incidents could have occurred, they rarely did, because Tuskegee Institute was the biggest thing in the town of Tuskegee until the Veterans Hospital was established. Blacks there remained in charge of a sizable payroll. The preponderance of blacks and the financial base of the college together gave us the strength to undertake almost anything for which we could find the resources. We tried to stress this vast potential when skeptics considered our offer of employment.

Eventually, we assembled a staff of instructors and an allocation of aircraft, mechanics, and the other things we needed at the outset. In fact, I was somewhat surprised when black aviators proved willing to join us. Their numbers were not legion, and they were scattered around the country. They would not have been heard from unless they were brought together for one overriding purpose, such as setting up a flying school. Later, I was to find, in setting up both veterinary medicine and engineering schools at Tuskegee, that at least a few qualified black people were available. My experience with recruiting black aviation instructors in the 1930s disproves the objection often raised by those who do not wish to hire blacks: "There aren't any qualified blacks available."

The aviation school at Tuskegee was almost immediately viewed as an institution with a commercial future. It wasn't too difficult to recruit students once we had started. Flying was adventurous, glamorous, and up-to-date. Young people were naturally enthusiastic. Flying appealed to them. Many of the first aviation students were already registered at Tuskegee, and they saw flying as an unusual opportunity to try something new. On the other hand, some Tuskegee students wouldn't try it because they thought it too dangerous.

I never doubted that employment opportunities would come to blacks if they were prepared adequately. But they had to be prepared. We were concerned to make our program excellent and our students well trained. Aviation instruction involved blackboard work, but the crucial experience was the chance to fly under competent instructors. Usually, a student would be taken up, almost from the beginning of the instruction. Then, as he or she became more and more experienced, the instructor would turn over the controls. Finally, the instructor stepped out of the picture and left the student and the plane together, saying, "Now it's yours, and it's up to you to solo." That's when you really learn, by experience. No matter what someone may tell you, it's when you are at the controls by yourself that you learn what it's all about.

Our students had many adventures in the course of their civilian pilot training program. Sometimes the pilots would make a forced landing. Once the local community recovered from the shock of seeing a black person piloting a plane, the pilot was well received. The Tuskegee flyers became well known and were generally accepted. In any new situation, there will be people who resent the presence of a different type of person, but the student pilots in our program generally met with kindness and cooperation.

I found the enthusiasm of the students contagious. After being urged by "Chief" Anderson and some of the other flight instructors, I decided that I too would learn to pilot a plane. It was great. I learned to fly and got a primary pilot's license. I was able to fly solo to Atlanta and back and to one or two other places. Then I had a couple of close calls, either of which could have ended in tragedy. They made me reconsider whether I wanted to pursue flying. In each instance, I was soloing in a biplane, the kind with two sets of wings, upper and lower, on each side.

First, I was showing off when Dorothy Maynor, the singer, was visiting the campus. In those days, every biplane might have had control knobs that looked the same. But as I was to find out, the knobs might control different systems in different planes, even when they were the same "models." You couldn't assume that because a control was in a certain place, it was doing what you assumed it was doing. Instead of cutting off the heat, you might be cutting off the gas! And that's precisely what I did on this occasion. The plane was losing altitude and, in my frantic search for the proper control, I finally pulled what I thought was the heat control knob. Because it was the gas, I regained altitude at the last possible moment.

In another escapade, as I was coming in for a landing, I found myself much too close to treetops on my approach. I couldn't seem to gain altitude no matter what I tried. This time, I was sure I was feeding gas, but the plane continued dipping lower and lower. I gave it as much carburetor pressure as I could. We should have been going forward and up. Instead, we were sinking. Once again, at the last moment, on that chilly and overcast day, I realized that perhaps the gas wasn't feeding properly or was freezing before it could move through the carburetor, which controls the flow of fuel. If that was happening, the carburetor would freeze if I didn't apply heat. I grabbed the heat control and pulled it all the way out. Suddenly the plane regained altitude, and I found myself perpendicular to the ground. When I heard the wind whistling through the struts of the plane, I breathed a sigh and regained my composure.

The moisture in the atmosphere influences the way the plane functions in flight. If the day is overcast, a little heat may be needed to keep the gas flowing well. The carburetor had not been issuing the proper amount of gas because it needed heat. When I applied the heat control, the plane zoomed forward, and I landed at the field as I should have. I wasn't far from the field, and I was flying a plane with which I wasn't familiar anyway. It was a little two-seater, with a seat on the side, just like a roadster.

After these two incidents, my interest in flying waned considerably. Flying is not something to do poorly. I felt that if I could not excel at flying—which would take considerable practice as well as advanced study of meteorology and navigation—I shouldn't pursue it. It wasn't a major interest, and it wasn't something that I wanted to do halfway. It was better, I thought, for me to encourage other people to fly. I flew occasionally but gave it up altogether a few years later, when we progressed to military aviation at Tuskegee.

Our civilian pilot training program was a great success, both in training pilots and in introducing numbers of black people to aviation. Magazine and newspaper articles circulated throughout the black community about our program. In black communities in the South and all over America, word of the pilots of Tuskegee spread. The program didn't progress as rapidly as we had anticipated because of the expenditure involved in flying on a private basis. The cost of planes, the cost of parts and maintenance, the cost of training, the cost of an airfield—all of these had to be covered for aviation to be successful. But flying was a part of the wave of the future, and we wanted to keep up with developments in the field. How we were able to do so is a story that deserves telling. It is a part of the history of Tuskegee Institute that should be well understood, for in reality it is part of the story of how military aviation for blacks came into being.

Tuskegee Institute had structured itself along military lines even before it began offering instruction in civilian or military aviation. At Tuskegee and Hampton, military discipline had traditionally been regarded as an experience that would be helpful to the majority of young people enrolled in these schools. Dr. Moton had been responsible for military discipline in his earlier job at Hampton, where his title was commandant of cadets. He had earned such a distinguished reputation that when Booker Washington died, Moton was sought to succeed him. I'm sure that my experience in the Student Army Corps was useful to me in school. And I found the program at Tuskegee to be beneficial as well. The structure, the uniforms, the marching, and the experience of being a part of a military-style organization had been a positive influence on Tuskegee students since the beginning of the school. In fact, when I became president, Tuskegee students wore school uniforms.

All over the country, college military training was being officially adopted. An army colonel, Benjamin O. Davis, Sr., was assigned to Tuskegee to direct the Reserve Officer Training Corps (ROTC) program there. All of the military services were segregated, but we felt that if military training was being adopted because the nation believed such training was important, then why not for blacks as well as for whites? In addition, efforts were underway to desegregate the infantry, engineering corps, and all of the other existing branches of the service, including the navy. Military aviation was just being developed. When word reached the black community that blacks would be included in the newly created army Air Corps, there was a great hue and cry to integrate them immediately—not to bring blacks into the Air Corps on the segregated basis that characterized the U.S. armed forces. I think there was a national awareness on the part of blacks, as well as whites, that the news about the Air Corps was a part of a whole new movement toward integration, a small step but one in the right direction. Not surprisingly, there was a great sense of anticipation, agitation, pride, rancor, and disappointment—all of the ingredients in the process of change.

When I heard about the plans to include blacks in the new Air Corps, I was anxious to learn more. The argument against establishing a segregated corps and segregated training was sound, but I wanted to learn whether the rumored integration of the corps was based in fact.

My concern was genuine. If the U.S. government was at long last ready to integrate the military, well and good. With desegregation of the military, there would be no reason for starting any new program under the banner of segregation! I made a thorough investigation to discover what course the military was about to take, specifically whether the new recruits to the Air Corps would be integrated.

In Washington, I consulted the office of the secretary of war, Henry L. Stimson. I met with Robert Patterson, the assistant secretary of war. He knew and I knew—as did others—that William Hastie, a black man who worked for Stimson as assistant secretary in charge of Negro affairs, and Walter White, the head of the National Association for the Advancement of Colored People, were publicly promoting integration. I told the assistant secretary of war, "Tuskegee Institute is available if flying is going to be offered on a segregated basis. We do not want it if there's a chance of immediate integration." If integration was not a part of the initial picture of U.S. military aviation, we saw Tuskegee as an ideal place for training black flyers. We were only fifty miles from Maxwell Field, the military air base in Montgomery, and the Alabama climate facilitated year-round flying. In our opinion, aviation was another important area of technical education consistent with the direction in which Tuskegee was oriented. It would have been difficult to find a better place than Tuskegee for setting up a program such as military flying. The fact that we already had both student military training and civilian aviation at Tuskegee put us a few steps ahead of other institutions because we had experience to build on. And in its practical nature training in aviation was similar to the instructional program that was the trademark of Tuskegee Institute.

Patterson told me in unequivocal terms that military flying would not be integrated. I was told the same thing by some of the leading officers of the Air Corps. I believed that Tuskegee would by no means be needed if the Air Corps was to be integrated. But if young black men could serve their country in the Air Corps only in segregated units like those maintained by the army, then Tuskegee would make its resources available. Several years later, I was told by one of the white officers in the advanced flying program at Tuskegee that it was wise for blacks to start flying at Tuskegee rather than trying to begin on a totally integrated basis. He felt that black students at Tuskegee who had not been exposed to aviation at all would not have to overcome the burden of race in order to learn how to fly. In other words, they started in an atmosphere which was comfortable for them. If they had gone to an all-white situation—where, in the first place, they probably wouldn't have been welcome and, in the second place, they wouldn't have felt comfortable even if they had been welcome—the opportunity to learn to fly would have been complicated by too much interference or too many considerations that related to race rather than to performance.

When it was clear that military flying would be segregated, I worked to establish the program at our school. The other place being considered for a military program for blacks, we discovered, was Chicago. Tuskegee, on all counts, seemed to us the better place.

After we had learned that we could have the contract to initiate a program of military training for black pilots, the next step was the acquisition of an airfield. Until this time, we had been using our many cow pastures, but now it was time for improvement. We learned that if we could acquire the land and construct an airfield, we could obtain a contract from the government for installation of facilities and training the pilots that would cover the cost of acquiring the airfield and launching the total operation.

We had a spot in Chehaw in mind for building an airfield. Chehaw, Alabama, is on the main line of the Southern Railroad. Because of Tuskegee Institute's national reputation, Chehaw was a scheduled stop on the Crescent Limited, a train running from New York to New Orleans. For many years a little spur railroad ran from Chehaw up to the campus of our school. The spur was used mainly to bring coal when Tuskegee burned coal as a major fuel, but it also carried a passenger car. One could purchase a ticket from New York to the campus of Tuskegee Institute, changing at Chehaw. There was even a little store at the Chehaw stop that sold knick-knacks and sundries. The Tuskegee students used to laugh at the railroad because the train was so slow that you could walk to Tuskegee faster than you could travel by railroad from Chehaw.

The Tuskegee community had grown in the direction of the railroad stop, and nearby land suitable for the airfield was for sale. At the time, land in Alabama was very cheap, but we had very little money. We decided to approach the Rosenwald Fund. The initial response was not favorable. They suggested that we borrow on our endowment, which we didn't want to do: in our board's opinion, the endowment was almost sacred. Eleanor Roosevelt was on the board of the Rosenwald Fund, and through her influence, with the cooperation of President Edwin Embree, we were able to

Eleanor Roosevelt at Moton Field with Frederick D. Patterson (right), G. L. Washington (left), and student pilots. The woman on Roosevelt's right is unidentified.

persuade the trustees of the fund to meet at Tuskegee, hear our plans in detail, and give us further consideration. Mrs. Roosevelt's visit, along with that of the other trustees, proved fruitful. I can remember Lessing Rosenwald's opposing the gift to Tuskegee because he thought that the contract with the federal government was good enough to warrant our borrowing. But he was eventually won over to our point of view, and we got the grant.

The engineering firm of Alexander and Repas built our airfield on Tuskegee-owned land. It became Moton Field. Alexander, who was black, and Repas, who was white, had been schoolmates in engineering and teammates in football at the University of Iowa.

When the new aviation students came to Tuskegee, they met a number of blacks who were already proficient in aviation—the graduates of our civilian pilot training program. Charlie Foxx's name stands out among our civilian pilot training graduates. He turned out to be one of the best instructors we had in military aviation. Apart from the few white officers, some of whom taught flying, the recruits had contact only with blacks. Again, in our opinion, this made our flight training comparatively easy to institute.

Military aviation brought a lot of people to Tuskegee. A considerable number of nonflight personnel are needed for such a large and complicated undertaking. They include medical workers, engineers, a large secretarial pool, people who run dining halls, and the maintenance staff. These workers made the Tuskegee airfield a complete unit within itself. The field was also a source of much money for the local community, although there was occasionally some friction. By and large, however, the wheel of change and progress moved smoothly.

Soon after the primary school had been established, the advanced program began. Construction of the second field, the Tuskegee army airfield, was supervised by the black firm of McKissick and McKissick of Nashville, Tennessee. Built from the ground up, this field included barracks and all of the facilities for housing, feeding, and training pilots who had completed the primary program and were ready for the advanced program. A number of white flying officers came into the advanced school as seasoned personnel because they had the required training. They also knew the government requirements and regulations with which we needed to become acquainted. In fact, since there were no qualified black officers in the Air Corps, the Tuskegee army air base, as far as I know, was never headed by a black officer during the short time of its existence.

In addition to Charlie Foxx, some of the distinguished flyers trained at Tuskegee were Colonel William Campbell and Major Roberts. One of the newest buildings on the Tuskegee campus is named in honor of the late five-star General Daniel "Chappie" James, one of the Tuskegee Institute graduates who achieved brilliant careers in military aviation. General Benjamin O. Davis, Jr., was the best known of those trained in aviation at Tuskegee. Davis was born in Tuskegee, the son of an army man who raised him to go to West Point, and he did. It was said that the boy was taught to make up his bed and do everything in military fashion when he was still young. As a result, Benjamin, Jr., was a natural, so to speak. When he completed his training at the military academy, he was trained in aviation at Tuskegee, and then his career really took off. It has been an outstanding instance of what can be achieved with opportunity. Young Davis was made head of the Ninety-ninth Pursuit Squadron, the first flying organization with commissioned black flyers, all trained at Tuskegee.

A short time earlier, an article in *Time* magazine had criticized the black pilots, passing harsh and unfair judgment on them. But the Ninety-ninth Squadron distinguished itself in combat in Europe and earned commendation from the Air Corps. Although the first combat experiences were not commendable—there were some problems until the men became experienced—their record was distinguished and generated pride. After the pilots had engaged in combat and had shown what they could do—chasing the enemy all over Europe, so to speak—*Time* did an apologetic and well-deserved article, praising the pilots.

I was still piloting occasionally, and every so often, I tried to coax my wife, Kitty, to fly with me. She had finally indicated that she was willing. As we drove the route to the field, we came across a truckload of twisted metal from a plane that had been totally demolished. It was a terrible experience. The plane, with a group of officers, had flown from Chicago. A number of flyers had died in the crash. My wife said to me, "I'm not going up at all and I want you to stop trying to fly yourself. It's too much risk."

Flying, as I've said, isn't something you want to do poorly. It needs to be done well, but I didn't need to do it well. I needed to keep on with my work as president of Tuskegee Institute, doing (among other things) all I could to make aviation a meaningful experience for those in and out of uniform. Shortly after Bill Trent became director of the United Negro College Fund, I flew a plane carrying him to Tuskegee from Atlanta. Upon reflection, I concluded that for me to fly simply did not make good sense. After that trip, I decided that I would not pursue aviation as an avocation. I continued to fly with a great many of the pilots who trained me as I traveled by air to different cities, but I was the passenger, not the pilot in the cockpit.

After the war, the military flying program was discontinued. Tuskegee kept Moton Field and continued aviation training on a limited basis. At one time, we could have sold the field to the government, but we decided not to do so. We felt that aviation should be a permanent part of Tuskegee's program. As a result, although some of the other smaller fields nearby were liquidated, Moton Field continued. With a lack of adequate financing, however, the flight program became much less rewarding. Today, flying is only a small part of the operation of Moton Field. More important is the research in veterinary medicine taking place there.

Tuskegee Institute and the State of Alabama

Our new programs in veterinary medicine and engineering were brought to Tuskegee in large measure by increased state financing. In 1935, when I began studying the school's budget, Alabama was appropriating five thousand dollars a year once every two years for the Institute. Although Tuskegee had originally been chartered as a state school, both Booker Washington and Dr. Moton had always deemphasized the relationship with the state.

But in the 1940s the five thousand dollars did not seem sufficient, given the services we were providing to the state by educating people in so many different areas. I had a white trustee named Russell on the Board of Trustees. He was from Alexander City, Alabama, and operated a cotton mill, Russell Mills, in that town. Working through Russell I was able to get the state appropriation raised to ten thousand dollars per year. But when Russell wasn't able to do more, we developed a strategy: have the governor yield to the pressure to give blacks equal educational opportunity (or something that implied equality). He increased our appropriation to allow us to expand our offerings, and we increased the number of state-appointed trustees to the Tuskegee board.

One of the battles I fought at this time was with blacks who didn't want the state to name white trustees to the board. They didn't object to the one or two white southern trustees, but they felt that I was selling out Tuskegee and that control of the school would go to white southerners. But we had to do something; we were financially strapped and could not continue as we had before. Furthermore, I believe that six state appointed trustees out of twenty-four members could not sway the board. Besides, those white southerners, I felt, would be so glad to be in the company of such distinguished members of the Tuskegee board as Schieffelin and Bowers and Rosenwald that they would not play the fool.

The increase in the state appropriation—from $10,000 to $110,000—would allow us to begin new programs in veterinary medicine and in engineering. The state-appointed trustees were activated to the board on the basis of the presumption that, as board members, they would know what was happening to the state's money, although, by this time, our budget was in the millions. Actually, we gave them the same authority that we gave to the other trustees, and I can't remember a time when the Alabama trustees as a group voted differently from the others.

There were six state-appointed men on the board. At least one had to be black, and one was the state secretary of education. The others were appointed at large by the governor. I can remember when at least two black state appointees were on our board in addition to the other blacks we had there. One of the early state appointments to our board made by Governor Chauncey Sparks was a young, aspiring Alabama politician named George Wallace. He attended our meetings, but I don't think he ever opened his mouth. He made no effort to be active. I think he wanted to be regarded as a good trustee, and he did so by keeping quiet. Most of the state's trustees either were largely silent or agreed with the proposals that were presented. I regarded their conduct as completely vindicating my feeling that their addition to the board would cause no loss in autonomy.

Veterinary Medicine, 1942

Blacks who wanted to become veterinarians could attend Iowa State College (as I had), the University of Pennsylvania, Cornell University, or a few other institutions. There were only about twelve to fifteen vet schools in the whole country. Those in the South, where blacks lived, for example in Texas and Alabama, excluded blacks. Consequently both the number of available schools and the number of interested blacks were small. I felt that blacks did not really appreciate the opportunities of veterinary medicine and the fact that one could earn whatever he or she was good enough to earn. Although I had planned for a career as a veterinarian when I was a boy in Texas and when I was in college, not until I was practicing in Virginia did I have a chance to see how wide open this field was for black people. In Petersburg, I had treated livestock, most of which belonged to whites, without ever feeling any animosity. Not all whites were receptive toward black veterinarians, however. Some white veterinarians had tried to discourage me from seeking training in veterinary medicine. I disregarded them because I knew that there were other black veterinarians; I had served under two. I felt that the white vets just didn't want to see us in the field. As a student, I hadn't let such attitudes discourage me. Now, as a college president, I knew that veterinary medicine was an area that should be explored by black institutions. In keeping with Tuskegee Institute's effort to move both upward and outward in occupational opportunities, veterinary medicine should, I felt, be added to our program.

Tuskegee already had a veterinarian on its staff, and so veterinary medicine was not unknown there. But there had never been a program for professional preparation. Shortly after I became president, I described for the General Education Board several fields which I thought Tuskegee might consider developing, and veterinary medicine was one of them. The General Education Board responded, "You're asking us for money you think you need to start this school. But after beginning it, how are you going to continue it? Unless we see that you have found money that will keep the plant operating at a satisfactory level, we cannot respond to your request." Not until I had prevailed on the state of Alabama to put up the money to operate a school of veterinary medicine, a school of engineering, and graduate programs in home economics and agriculture was the GEB willing to help with additional money.

The outside help we received came not just from the increase in state appropriations but also from the Southern Regional Education Board (SREB). The South spent less money on education than did any other re-

Faculty and students constructing interior of building of School of Veterinary Medicine using Tuskegee concrete block, 1944.

gion of the United States. Duplication of various programs was costly when funds were so short. The idea of regional education was being promoted as one way of raising the level of instruction. The emphasis should instead be on providing different disciplines in different locations within a region. In the case of a highly specialized program such as vet medicine, regionalism could, and in fact did, work.

The idea of a School of Veterinary Medicine at Tuskegee was a timely one. Although nearly a quarter of a century would transpire before desegregation of public schools was under way, blacks were exerting pressure to give black college students greater educational opportunities than they had had before. Through the SREB, veterinary medicine at Tuskegee became a regional offering. Southern states—Alabama, Mississippi, North Carolina, Virginia, Louisiana, Texas, and a few others—which offered veterinary medicine to white students and not to blacks joined the board and contributed designated amounts of money to instruct black students in this

Tuskegee Institute faculty and students installing brick veneer over Tuskegee concrete block during construction of School of Veterinary Medicine, 1944.

field. Black students in these states could come to study veterinary medicine at Tuskegee.

I was loudly accused of promoting segregated education, an accusation which paralleled the criticism I received about the aviation program. Nonetheless, the regional arrangement was appropriate. The money from the SREB and from the state of Alabama helped us when we needed to begin programs, employ qualified faculty, raise salaries to a satisfactory level, and generally improve the education we offered at Tuskegee.

There was another important contributing factor in the establishment of the new vet school: Tuskegee's tradition of building with bricks and mortar made by the students and faculty themselves. At about this time, we had developed the Tuskegee concrete block, which I have already described. Our faith in the potential of this innovative and indigenous material was rewarded. The block, brick-veneered, would allow us to construct one of the strongest possible physical plants—and for a whole lot less money! I

First faculty of Tuskegee's School of Veterinary Medicine, 1945. Front row: Dr. William H. Waddell, Ambulatory Clinic and Large Animal Obstetrics; Dr. Edward B. Evans, dean; Frederick D. Patterson, President, Tuskegee Institute; Dr. Edward G. Tripp, head, Bacteriology, Hygiene, and Public Health. Back row: Dr. George W. Cooper, head, Large Animal Medicine, Surgery, and Clinics; Dr. Lloyd B. Mobiley, head, Anatomy and Histology, Small Animal Medicine, Surgery, and Clinics; Dr. Thomas G. Perry, head, Small Animal Medicine, Surgery, and Clinics.

think we built the entire veterinary medicine plant for seven hundred and fifty thousand dollars. It would have cost us at least three times that much if we had been obliged to contract for it. We used our tried and highly successful method of having faculty supervise students in the construction trades. Two years earlier we had started the Five Year Plan for students, which I have also described. The student labor together with our exploitation of the materials we found all around us on the ground gave us the push that we needed for our new school. It was a combination of limited funds applied with Tuskegee methods.

At the time when I considered how we could start a school of veterinary medicine, my idol, Dr. Evans, and I met at the Texas fair. He was attending as an official delegate of the state of Texas; I was there as a member of an official commission appointed by President Roosevelt which included Eugene Kinckle Jones of the National Urban League. Dr. Evans and I agreed at the fair that Tuskegee should have a school of veterinary medicine.

At Tuskegee we went through a period of preliminary planning for the school. When we were ready to begin, I asked Dr. Evans to visit and survey every veterinary school in the country for us. I wanted to know what they had to offer and to borrow ideas from them. The influence of our experiences at Iowa State was certainly felt at Tuskegee. We knew intimately the veterinary faculty at Iowa State, and we both sought advice there as our plans progressed. But I did not want to pattern Tuskegee slavishly after Iowa. Evans's tour of other schools would bring us the best ideas from everywhere. He made a comprehensive report, and the plans we made for the physical plant in part reflected what he had learned in his study.

Dr. Evans was employed at Prairie View when he made the survey for Tuskegee. After the survey had been completed, it was understood that he would come to Tuskegee and become a part of the beginning of the new program, as dean of the School of Veterinary Medicine. I was thrilled at the prospect of bringing him to Alabama to a position for which he was eminently qualified and which he deserved. Dr. Evans had outstanding ability and possessed the qualities needed to give good administrative leadership to the school.

We began to look for more faculty. I preferred to hire black people, although this was not an absolute requirement. It was part of the Tuskegee philosophy, inaugurated by Booker T. Washington, that black personnel should be used in as many fields as possible. This principle not only gave employment to competent blacks, who faced limited and segregated opportunities elsewhere, but also afforded role models—people who could inspire black students to achieve their potential. Comparatively few trained vets were black, but as I have said, I knew there were some. How many were in practice or could be recruited was another question. In my day, most black vets could not afford to go into private practice. Instead, they went into meat inspection with the Bureau of Animal Industry, the federal job with the Department of Agriculture that had tempted me when I was just out of college. Such a job offered no great mobility or challenge, but in segregated America, trained black veterinarians found few other opportunities.

We had money for salaries for our prospective teachers, but as modest as the money was, it was more than we were paying most of the other faculty at Tuskegee. In fact, trying to reconcile the difference between the two sets of salaries posed quite a problem. In addition, we again had to persuade prospective faculty to come to the South. We had to demonstrate that the opportunity at Tuskegee was preferable to other possibilities, even that of private practice.

Evans knew more about recruiting than I did, and credit for recruiting personnel was due largely to him. In addition to the veterinarians working with him at Prairie View, Evans learned of two doctors assigned to the army base at Fort Sam Houston in San Antonio, Texas. He made a visit there to talk with them about becoming associated with Tuskegee's new venture. Captain William H. Waddell, a graduate of the University of Pennsylvania, and Dr. L. B. Mobiley, a graduate of Kansas State University, both agreed to join us, with Mobiley as head of the Department of Anatomy and Waddell as the ambulatory clinician. Evans also knew Dr. Thomas G. Perry, who was an outstanding practitioner of small animal medicine in Wichita, Kansas. Through Evans we learned of Dr. George W. Cooper, who was a large animal practitioner and had been veterinarian for one of the largest beef herds in America. The seniority and competence of both Cooper and Perry brought early strength to the beginning teaching staff.

Dr. Charles Robinson, a Cornell-trained vet whose father was in private veterinary practice, also joined us. Young Robinson had maintained a good record at Cornell and had been recommended to us by the faculty there. There weren't many new black vets like Robinson, but we did try to find those schools in which blacks were enrolled. Kansas had more than any other state, and a representative number of our faculty had graduated from schools there. Dr. Theodore S. Williams, who succeeded Dean Evans at Tuskegee, and Dr. Walter Bowie, who ultimately succeeded Williams, were graduates of Kansas Agricultural College and Kansas State, respectively.

The school had not been in existence more than a year with Evans as our dean when Prairie View approached him to become its head. He had developed an outstanding reputation in Texas as a veterinarian and as an administrator, and a strong and large faction at Prairie View wanted him.

There had been pressure on Evans even before he came to Alabama to agree to accept the principalship of Prairie View, but he had resisted because he was strongly committed to helping to create the veterinary school we envisioned. Now, however, the situation at Prairie View seemed more compelling, and Dr. Evans reconsidered.

He decided to accept the call. Although his decision came as a shock, I couldn't blame him. The opportunity to be the head of that institution was better than the deanship at Tuskegee. Although I did everything I could to persuade him to remain, I could understand that, after so many years of service there, he felt an obligation and a love for Prairie View that he wanted to honor. He decided to return and, unfortunately, was able to remain with us only a short time after making his decision.

Evans's departure brought us to a critical juncture in the development of the program. I called the faculty of the school together, read Dr. Evans's telegram, and voiced what I felt was the challenge that we all faced at that time.

I am regarding this as Dr. Evans's final answer and am calling this meeting to discuss with you our immediate plans and program from here forward. I have regarded this as a matter of sufficient importance to attempt to think through properly the course of action which is wise; and therefore have set down in writing my thinking in order that it may be definite and as clear as possible.

The development of the School of Veterinary Medicine at Tuskegee Institute to date has resulted from thinking and planning over a period of several years. You, no doubt, have been made familiar with some of this, but allow me to call to your attention the fact that, in addition to any appropriation from the state legislature of the state of Alabama for the current operation of veterinary medicine, we have sought and received gifts of $630,000; studied every veterinary school in the country; and given careful attention over many months of planning, to create a physical setup which would represent the best features to be found in all the institutions of study consistent with the limited funds which we have. These plans likewise embody as nearly as possible the ideas of those who have been chosen to head the respective departments and divisions. Matters are now completed, with the exception of a few minor changes, which you have suggested and which will be incorporated in the finished plans as far as possible.

We believe we have, in you and other men who are to come, the best faculty that we could possibly select consistent with our plan to have this work under the total direction of Negroes. Our task at the moment is that of getting our facilities properly erected and functioning and of welding our faculty and staff into a strong teaching group devoted and efficient on behalf of a program of professional veterinary medicine. Our most immediate consideration is the nature and character of leadership that will be given to the school of veterinary medicine in view of the resignation of Dean Evans. I know of no responsibility that I regard more gravely than I do the naming of Dean Evans's successor. I have decided that when a selection is made it must be the man who, in my opinion, is best fitted through ability, character, and qualities of leadership to carry this work unselfishly to the heights which were envisioned when it was begun.

I do not feel that I have sufficient information about all the members of our faculty at the present time to make such an important choice. I have, therefore, decided that for an indefinite period I will assume the responsibility of acting dean in the School of Veterinary Medicine and I have asked Mr. G. L. Washington to serve as my administrative assistant and to give primary attention to the details and direction necessary to the erection of the physical plant of the School of Veterinary Medicine and to carry on such routine and administrative office details as will keep the work of this school properly functioning and keep me informed of any and all matters which are pressing for attention.

I shall ask you to be good enough to cooperate by carrying on the essential activities related to the functioning of the school as a whole, through committee participation and through conference with me on all matters where it is necessary.

I wish to emphasize that this action I am taking is purely in the interest of having the necessary time and opportunity to weigh carefully those factors which should be involved in the selection of a permanent dean to head the School of Veterinary Medicine. I am more than grateful to Dr. Waddell for his interim services during the absence of Dean Evans. Now that the dean's decision is final, it is my desire to decide on the deanship without favor or prejudice against anyone; the wise procedure is that which I have just outlined. I shall be glad to receive the application of anyone who feels he would like to be considered for the post of dean. I should also be glad to have the thinking of anyone who cares to give it. This invitation is extended with the hope that no person will feel that, because he is applying for the post or because he advises in regard to the same, his application or his advice must be accepted. I promise to consider seriously such applications and advice. I shall be guided, however, by the points which I have mentioned in the determination of who shall be the actual appointee. I may say just parenthetically that it is my intention not to succumb to undue pressure and that anyone who attempts to bring such pressure to bear has prejudiced his consideration.

I am happy to invite the cooperation of those who are willing to go forward under these terms and conditions. The job before us is not an easy one, but for those of us who are really and truly concerned with the development of a significant school of veterinary medicine at Tuskegee Institute, it is one which is full of challenge and the possibilities and satisfactions of a rich and useful career.

I said we had engaged those who we believe represent the outstanding men of the country who could be employed in this venture. This does not mean that we have arrived at a mature faculty and that we can as yet compare favorably with other institutions who through years of struggle, seasoning, and splendid resources have developed as the outstanding schools in the nation. One ingredient that must go into the development of any school of veterinary medicine anywhere is time. To be most effective that time must be spent in sincere and conscientious effort on the part of all concerned, with a willingness to take advantage of every possible opportunity for growth on the part of the faculty and staff. It shall be my pleasure and my constant desire to see every man surrounded with those conditions which will enable him to pursue his work with satisfaction and with credit. There are many hardships, however; there have been disappointments and there will continue to be disappointments.

Those who expect everything to be just right are doomed to disappointment. This is a pioneering job, and pioneering means hardships. It also means, however, an opportunity to become immortalized among those who have associated with this venture in its initial stages, and the opportunity to use our abilities and creative talents in molding an instrument of good that should endure long and successfully in service to mankind. Unless these are our chief goals, we are in the wrong work. It shall always be my effort to see to it that we are remunerated financially as well as possible. I am sure, however, that the best we could ever do would fall short of what a veterinarian could make in private practice and participation in certain government phases of veterinary medicine. I do not recommend this opportunity, therefore, in terms of its monetary consideration as a chief point of attraction. So far as I know this point has been made clear from the beginning. It is my hope that all of you will see in this the opportunity of extending occupational horizons available to Negro youth and that in the course of hard work and devotion necessary to effectively accomplish our purpose, you will at the same time achieve a career possessed of many satisfactions and distinctions. I hope also that no man will feel greatly disappointed if he is not chosen as Dean. The school can have only one dean who will be chief administrative and coordinative officer of the school. Neither in salary nor in responsibility will he have a job which is significantly different and certainly not more important than the other posts in the School of Veterinary Medicine.

As a matter of fact, from what I know about the administrative routine and its denial of the opportunity for intensive creative work, I would say that if he accepts the post and keeps it, he has doomed himself to mediocrity and unproductivity in the individual sense. He shall need to derive his satisfaction from the overall growth of the school of veterinary medicine. He shall have the dubious pleasure of having his pants kicked for everything that goes wrong and passing on the credit for the good that is accomplished to the respective members of the faculty. I wish, therefore, from this time forward to invite your cooperation in the difficult task which we face.

Every attempt will be made to deal with you as individuals and with the problems that confront this school in a definite and straightforward manner. If we can expect this type of policy and action on your part in return, I am sure that we shall, in years to come, look back on this period of our association together with great satisfaction.

This turn of events was stunning to the new faculty we had recruited, but with the formation of an administrative advisory committee, we were able to proceed with the myriad tasks required to get ready to implement curriculum, enroll a new and second class of students, and complete the physical plant. Of course, no matter how well planned the school, it could not function without students. We realized that this was a relatively new field for black students, and we assumed that the students we were most likely to get would come from the black land-grant institutions, particularly those in agriculture and fields related to animal and human health. We also anticipated that the credentials of some of the students who might come from these institutions could be cause for concern.

The specter of accreditation was with us from the beginning. Achieving accreditation was absolutely essential if we were to have a school whose graduates were to be recognized for their preparation. Our graduates in nursing, veterinary medicine, and teaching—all had to take standard exams and pass them before they were qualified to practice. If they weren't qualified, they wouldn't be employed and therefore would be denied the chance to receive the compensation which they expected. We discovered early that getting a favorable rating from the American Veterinary Medical Association (AVMA) meant that we would have to set far more demanding admissions and performance requirements for vet students than were associated with other programs of study at Tuskegee. Almost from the beginning, we placed demands on students, as well as on faculty, for excellence.

We sent out announcements to schools throughout the region that might supply us with students: "Tuskegee Institute is inaugurating a program in veterinary medicine and we want you to send qualified and interested students." The Institute itself offered a few small scholarships, but we especially publicized regional grants-in-aid. We informed the schools that if they offered some preveterinary subjects—in math and science—their students would be better prepared when they reached Tuskegee.

In setting admissions requirements for our program or for any program that required some background in science and math, we had to know the schools from which the students were coming to us. In its desire to be sympathetic and understanding of some students' plight, Tuskegee may have admitted students to college who were not prepared to do well in *every* program we offered. An applicant may have been at or near the top of his or her graduating class in high school. But unless we knew the specific subjects that the student had taken and the rigor of the curriculum of that school, rank in class or grade point average had little meaning.

In general, science and math were considered far more difficult than such subjects as composition, literature, and history. But we needed to establish standards of high performance in science and math for students who would be taking anatomy and physiology, those tough subjects characteristic of veterinary schools. Several land-grant schools followed our suggestions and sent us students. Our first group of veterinary enrollees began their studies in 1945. By 1950, twenty-one graduates of the four-year course held the DVM degree. They included Earl V. Brown, Alfreda Johnson, Demetrice Lyles, and Forde B. McWilliams, who entered in the first class. The fifth member of our first graduating class, Walker S. Poston, had done only the last two years of the Tuskegee program because he had a degree in veterinary medicine from Middlesex University in Waltham, Massachusetts, which was unaccredited. Prior to enrolling in Middlesex, Poston had attended the School of Veterinary Medicine in the University of the Philippines. He matriculated in September 1947 after working for two years as a full-time assistant to Dr. Perry in the small animal clinic. Several of our first graduates joined our faculty, and some stayed for a considerable time. This group included Alfreda Johnson Webb, who later moved to North Carolina, established a practice, and taught veterinary subjects at North Carolina A&T.

All of our entering veterinary students had completed high school, and even in the early years, many had completed at least two years of college. As competition for admission increased, even students with as much as a master's degree might not qualify because they were deficient in specific premedical subjects.

When I myself had entered veterinary school, my math skills were not what they should have been. Math continued to be a weakness of mine throughout my studies. If I had had better high school preparation, I might have been more successful in my studies. And if there had been an SREB when I was living in Texas, perhaps I would have been able to work fewer hours and to devote more time to my vet school work than I did. In fact, I'm sure that the situation would have been wholly different for me and for other black students who might have been interested in going to college and becoming veterinarians.

By 1948, two buildings of the new school had been completed. By 1950,

Faculty and first graduates (1949 and 1950), School of Veterinary Medicine, Tuskegee Institute, 1950.

the number had expanded to three. At that time a ceremony to dedicate the physical plant took place. With us on the important occasion was Dr. Edward A. Benbrook, head of the Department of Pathology, Division of Veterinary Medicine, Iowa State College, who was a mentor for Dr. Evans and Dr. Williams as well as myself.

The Tuskegee School of Veterinary Medicine was not immediately accredited. We were ineligible for accreditation when the school opened. When we were inspected by a team from the Council on Education of the American Veterinary Medical Association—individuals from the faculty of various veterinary medical schools—they were generally surprised and impressed with what we had been able to do in so short a time. We were informed of what had yet to be done to warrant accreditation—for example improvements in curriculum and facilities and increases in faculty. The inspections continued regularly, and each time we moved closer to full accreditation. Finally, on May 25, 1954, the AVMA's Council on Education voted full accreditation for our school. The moment, for us, had tremendous significance. As Dr. Theodore Williams remarked in the history of the school that he wrote in the 1970s, Tuskegee's achievement would have been "monumental for any institution, but for a Negro institution in the deep south, and a private school with a history of chronic anemic financial support with an all-Negro faculty, it was a fantastic accomplishment which amazed the veterinary medical educational community and the profession itself" (*Development of a Black Professional School: The School of Veterinary Medicine as an Educational Institution and as a Sociocultural System: An Historical Study, 1940–1970* [Tuskegee: Tuskegee Institute, Carver Research Foundation, 1977], p. 83). Tuskegee Institute was the first institution to start a new school of veterinary medicine in twenty-five years. And we had brought it, in ten years, to fully accredited status. Our initiative was followed by schools in Georgia, Illinois, Minnesota, Oklahoma, California, and Missouri and by Purdue University in Indiana.

As to what became of the first graduates of the school, Dr. Williams's history tells the story.

There were fifty-two graduates in the six classes beginning in 1949. Five in 1949; sixteen in 1950; twelve in 1951; five in 1952; three in 1953; and eleven in 1954. Three of this number are deceased. Of the remaining [forty-nine] all are active, twenty . . . are in private practice. One of this number has been appointed by the governor of his state to membership on the State Board of Veterinary Medical Examiners, and one has established an enviable record as an authority in the treatment and management of non-human primates. Twenty-three (23) . . . are in some phase of regulatory veterinary medicine either in the animal disease control section in this or a foreign country or in the meat inspection service of this nation. Of this number, three (3) are traveling inspectors who evaluate the status of meat inspection in foreign countries of the world to set standards for the importation of meat and meat food products from those countries into the U.S.A. One (1) of this number is Chief of Field Operations for the entire Meat and Poultry Inspection Service of Ethiopia, while one (1) other is Chief of the Program Training Branch for the Meat Inspection Service. Six (6) are in Teaching and Research as faculty members on the staffs of institutions of higher learning. All of this number have earned graduate degrees from other veterinary colleges in this country. One has earned the Doctor of Philosophy degree as well. These graduates, then, have done just about what every other graduate veterinarian might be expected to do, and in truth many have done what they do better than most.

This is educational accountability of the highest magnitude. The significance of this accomplishment is even greater if one considers that none of this group would have been admitted to any other veterinary medical institution in this country at the time they were admitted to Tuskegee Institute. While race may well have been a factor, the real reason would have been that their academic backgrounds would have been somewhat less well prepared than those of most of the other applicants. Tuskegee Institute, through its veterinary school, has demonstrated that using non-traditional educational methods, students, whose academic backgrounds may mirror weakness, can be graduated from academic programs characterized by rigorousness to lead productive lives in their chosen profession. Doing so requires a different kind of educational accountability, and may require that non-traditional methodology be an important ingredient in the process.

The eventual success of the program was due largely to the quality of the teaching faculty, to the grants-in-aid received, and certainly to the students, without whom there would have been no program. Students who were underprepared were given a one- to two-year preveterinary program, and faculty with promise were given a chance to go back to school and get the advanced degrees and special training they needed. The school has enjoyed high standing through the years. At one time, 80 percent of all black students enrolled in schools of veterinary medicine were at Tuskegee Institute.

The number of job opportunities in veterinary medicine dramatically expanded after the School of Veterinary Medicine started at Tuskegee. Black vets had a chance to work for the government, to go into research, to enter private practice, and to become faculty members in medical schools concerned with animal health and contagious animal diseases.

Vets who graduated from Tuskegee have practiced all over the world, from Alaska to Africa. There are Tuskegee grads on the faculties of schools in Africa. When Dr. Evans and I visited Ethiopia, we met several of the top animal health officials who were graduates of Tuskegee. The same is true in Nigeria, and perhaps in more places than I'm aware of right now.

Engineering, 1948

I was not a competent judge of all the needs of the times, but Tuskegee Institute had a broad-gauged faculty that was very much concerned about new occupational trends and opportunities. A good example was R. R. Taylor, a graduate of MIT, who, as I've said, envisioned and supervised the building of the magnificent architecture on the Tuskegee campus: structures such as Tompkins Hall, Rockefeller Hall, and the chapel—in which, during a 1942 visit following his retirement, Taylor was stricken and died while worshiping. Taylor's blending of art and science has been recognized in the campus's designation as a National Historic Site. During his time with us, he was aware of what were considered to be the next steps in professional opportunity in his field.

An equally good exemplar of the forward-looking character of our faculty was G. L. Washington, another MIT engineer with both bachelor's and master's degrees from that institution. Washington's impact made itself felt in a multitude of places in the Tuskegee landscape. The Five Year Plan, the concrete block program, and our academic and vocational programs—in commercial dietetics, aviation, veterinary medicine, and finally engineering—were nurtured by G. L., who had an outstanding gift for organization. I myself am an idea person. My forte is coming up with potentially workable solutions. I'm not as good, however, at putting the solutions to work. Washington, on the other hand, not only was a creative individual but also excelled precisely where I was weak, in working out the details. The trends that were developing in the country as a whole showed the Taylors, the Washingtons, and people with comparable vision that it was important to develop an engineering program. Tuskegee had a role to play if we could find the money we needed to underwrite the large cost involved.

It was pretty evident that if Tuskegee was going to maintain its leadership, then technical education, and specifically engineering, would be one in which it would need to advance. For us, developing the engineering program simply meant taking our School of Mechanical Industries to a more advanced level. We already had the building trades—plumbing, electricity, masonry, carpentry, and others—as well as a Department of Architecture. The next step seemed to be mechanical engineering. The distinguishing feature of our proposed engineering program was that we were taking a step in the direction of creating additional black engineers to serve the world.

These developments came at a time when I had applied to the General Education Board for funds to start several new programs: engineering, vet medicine, and graduate programs in education, home economics, and agriculture. As I have noted, the GEB was unwilling to help us until we could offer assurance that we could sustain programs financially after they were begun. Governor Sparks's increase in the annual appropriation to Tuskegee Institute from $10,000 to $110,000 for these programs represented a promise of continuing support which the General Education Board had hardly dreamed possible. The GEB subsequently gave us money which, among other things, allowed us to construct Moton Hall, the engineering building, at the main campus gate.

Our timing was good. Alabama was responsive, in part, because—all over the South—the pressure was on white universities to admit black students or at least on the state to provide blacks with "comparable" courses of instruction at black institutions. We felt that in such a climate, Tuskegee should be offering engineering to blacks who couldn't study this field elsewhere in the state. Engineering was thus another area in which Tuskegee should take leadership. In this respect we were more advanced than Alabama A&M in Huntsville.

Engineering was one of those several programs the state of Alabama would continuously underwrite because it was available to Alabama's white students and was not available to her black students. Several states had been sued for failing to provide this "equal" opportunity, and it was just a matter of time before each state would have to confront the necessity of providing for blacks within the state or of offering grants for out-of-state study in programs which were already available for blacks in various fields.

To find our engineering faculty, we had to look outside. Tuskegee had graduated students who had later gone to Iowa State and other places and had attained engineering degrees. But very few of those, if any, had returned to Tuskegee Institute, and none were teaching engineering. Those who taught had courses in some less advanced form of technical education. So we looked for prospective faculty at some black schools—Prairie View in Texas, Howard University in Washington, D.C., and A&T College in Greensboro, North Carolina—that had engineering programs. In fact, before he came to Tuskegee, G. L. Washington was Dean of Mechanic Arts at A&T, an area of responsibility which included engineering, architecture, and technology. There were others like him, we thought, and we wanted to find people equally well qualified to help us start our program. We recruited additional faculty in part by word of mouth and in part by contacting other institutions. The word got around that Tuskegee would be offering engineering. As a result, some qualified people approached us about positions.

One of the first people to be placed on our engineering faculty was Dr. William C. Curtis, a black man. Tuskegee had always emphasized the importance of having only black instructors, but the scarcity of talent in the engineering field made us look to the country as a whole for people, regardless of race. With our students, it was again necessary to verify that they had already completed the basic work in mathematics, physics, and other technical subjects. I don't remember the numbers exactly, but I do know we had a hard time getting a large number of interested and qualified people, whether they were to be students or faculty. Nonetheless, the fact remains that when you announce a new program, you find people who are ready and willing to participate. They may not always be qualified, but at least they find, in the opportunity of advancing, a challenge in registering and in becoming a part of that new thing. So far as I remember, engineering was one of them.

The first class of graduates in mechanical engineering was not large, four or five individuals or so, and it had taken four years to bring them to that point. We soon went into programs in electrical and civil engineering, the latter being one of the common fields where engineers could find work.

Our engineering school was another success and is today one of the substantially advanced programs at Tuskegee University.

The program's initial successes were due, in the first place, to the broadening of the field of opportunity. In addition, the quality of the instruction was adequate to the task. Graduates had little, if any, difficulty in finding employment. They didn't have to be employed in the South but could go to any part of the country. Technological advance in the United States depended upon the absorption of people who were prepared in engineering and other technical fields.

4 Tuskegee Years, III

Most of the South, black and white alike, was poor. Under President Franklin Delano Roosevelt, the South saw an opportunity to overcome some of its limitations. To the extent that Roosevelt's measures brought wealth, the white South greeted him positively. To the extent that there was some implication that leadership might be given to the non-white South, he was resented. When the Commission on Cotton Tenancy came south and held hearings, for example, it was the first time blacks had been invited to participate. This was a new day, but black participation was accepted. On the other hand, one governor of Alabama told me that if fair employment practices had been enforced in Alabama's cotton mills, he would openly have advocated rebellion or race riots.

The president of Tuskegee always had the ear of the governors of Alabama, no matter which governor it was. This was so, not necessarily out of any strong feeling of friendship, but because it was politically expedient for the governor to lend an ear. Until the time that I became president, both of my predecessors at Tuskegee, without holding public office, were able to influence—to an important degree—the climate of race relations as far as national appointments were concerned because they had the ear of the president of the United States. Dr. Moton had known several presidents and had visited the White House with some regularity. Both Washington and Moton had softened the harshness of prejudice and race relations in part by using their influence. Both men had national standing, not only with blacks, but also with the capitalists, who liked the Tuskegee model. This fact impressed the Alabama governors because many of them did not exert such national influence.

The first Alabama governor with whom I had contact was Governor Bibb Graves, who was in office from 1935 to 1939. Graves seemed to assume that although I was new to the presidency of Tuskegee, I had some contact with the nation's chief executive that might be useful to him. The governor asked me to come to Montgomery. When I went to his office, he put some money in my hand and said, absolutely seriously, "I want you to go to Washington and say to Mr. Roosevelt that I ought to be secretary of labor." I protested that I had no influence with the president. But he said, "Oh, yes you do! You go ahead and do this." And I did. But Graves didn't become secretary of labor.

I told President Roosevelt, "Governor Graves is very much interested in being secretary of labor and I'm here to bring that message to you." Of course, I couldn't tell Roosevelt he had to do it; he had to make that decision. I don't think he told me what he was going to do, but he didn't appoint Graves. Shortly afterward Graves died.

From a distance of forty years, it may seem surprising that I, as a black man, was carrying a message to the president of the United States from the governor of Alabama. But at the time, it was not suprising to me or to Roosevelt. He understood the situation and would have been more inclined to favor Graves's appointment because I had come, bringing Graves's message.

In my opinion, Graves wasn't an arch-racist. He liked to tell me, for example, that he was in school somewhere with a black person, the implication being that they were friends. This was, for a southern governor, an unusual admission.

On another occasion, Governor and Mrs. Graves came over to Tuskegee for commencement. Our guest speaker on that occasion was C. C. Spaulding, of North Carolina Mutual Insurance Company in Durham, a black company. Graves came into the chapel and sat in the front row. The chapel was filled, and people were waiting for Spaulding's speech so that they could receive their diplomas and go on about their business.

Graves sent me a note that he had only a few moments to be with us and needed to be called on soon. So I delayed introducing Mr. Spaulding, saying instead, "We are honored to have Governor Graves visit commencement and we'd like to have him at least bring greetings." Graves got up to address the assembly. To my surprise, he talked for an hour, ranting and raving about his friendship with his black classmate. Mrs. Graves was sitting on the front row, twisting her handkerchief. If she had had the

President Franklin D. Roosevelt visits Tuskegee Institute, March 30, 1939, Doro-
thy Hall in background. Left to right in the car: President Roosevelt; Governor
Frank Dixon, Alabama; U.S. Congressman Henry B. Steagall, Alabama; U.S.
Congressman Lister Hill, Alabama.

strength, she would have twisted it completely apart. She knew he was doing the wrong thing, but there was no stopping him.

Finally, Graves finished and Spaulding made a briefer speech than I think he planned. He was very gracious about it. I was the one sitting up there being embarrassed by Governor Graves and wondering, "When is this man going to finish?" But I couldn't get up and interrupt the governor of Alabama. This was just a case of a politician's doing his duty—to himself! He wanted to declare himself a friend to black people, and he wanted to be recognized as such. And he wanted word of his remarks to reach everyone. It was one of the few embarrassing moments I had with guest speakers at Tuskegee. On this occasion, the students were very decent. If Graves had used the word "nigger" or had said something else derogatory, they probably would have scraped their feet or made some other audible reaction. But he didn't; he was too smart for that.

On the other hand, Graves's successor, Governor Frank Dixon—a relative of Thomas Dixon, who wrote *The Clansman,* on which the film *Birth of a Nation* is based—was purely racist. Yet when President Roosevelt came to visit Tuskegee Institute, answering a promise he had made to Dr. Moton, Governor Dixon—the one who had promised me race riots if he was forced to eliminate segregation in the cotton mills—was the first one to plop down next to Roosevelt.

Chauncey Sparks followed Dixon in 1943, and it was he who appointed George Wallace to Tuskegee's board. Later I had further contact with Wallace and his wife, Lurleen, both former governors of Alabama.

On many campuses, black and white, the students do not speak to adults they pass. They are not hostile, they just don't pay you any attention; they don't think it is discourteous not to say hello. A friendly, courteous climate must be built. For example, the change in climate at the UNCF headquarters in New York since I've been there is a case in point. Initially, most of the staff people—local New York people who work for the Fund or for the National Urban League, which occupies the same building—didn't speak when they encountered you in the elevator or in a doorway or at a water fountain. Now that some time has passed, people have learned to acknowledge each other, and you can't get on the elevator without somebody's greeting you. If people don't initially consider it normal to speak to strangers, they have to learn that it is. The reason for not doing so isn't always that people don't want to recognize fellow human beings. They may think the strangers don't want to be greeted by them.

But when people visited the campus of Tuskegee Institute and walked along the streets and walkways there, they could not pass a student who didn't greet them. Students would say something friendly to any adult, even a stranger. The students and faculty spoke to each other as well. This atmosphere was characteristic of most black communities at that time, and it was particularly characteristic of black institutions such as Tuskegee, where we tried to build a feeling of community. It is still true on the Tuskegee campus today.

On one occasion, a governor of Alabama tested the hospitality of Tuskegee students in a way that was somewhat amusing to me. Some southern white speakers who did not know or pretended not to know how to pronounce the word "Negro" created embarrassing situations in speaking publicly in the Institute chapel. At times, student reaction was so great that I had to rebuke the students for being rude, although I understood exactly what caused the shuffling of feet and mumbled vocal sounds. In retrospect, I have wished that I had simply stopped the speaker right in the

Horace Suddeth, president of the National Business League shakes hands with Alabama governor James E. Folsom, as Patterson and other officers of the League look on, ca. 1949.

middle of his speech to explain what was creating the antipathy. Students were highly sensitive to the term "nigger." Instead of saying "Negro," southerners all too frequently said "nigra." At times, a speaker would slide beyond "nigra." That, of course, was absolutely unforgivable. In conversation with whites, I have had people say to me, "Well, that's what you say among yourselves." I said, "Yes, but don't you say it. It's not for you to say." Black people may joke or kid among themselves or even use "nigger" to denounce another person of African ancestry. Black culture will permit them to do so. But the term is never acceptable when it is used by white people.

By and large, such instances were few and far between at Tuskegee. But I remember one of them vividly. The governor was James "Big Jim" Folsom, who was more than six feet tall. He was visiting the campus for the celebration of the issuing of the George Washington Carver commemorative stamp after Carver's death in 1943.

One of the important features of such an occasion—with distinguished guests such as the governor and Postmaster General Donovan—was the line of march to the chapel. The dignitaries had been assembled and

Folsom arrived late, but I knew we had to ask him to make brief remarks. The students were in uniform—both men and women at that time (later the uniforms for women were abolished)—and were parading past the reviewing stand. From the reviewing stand we were rushing to the chapel, which I knew would be filled to overflowing.

I felt that Folsom's attitude on the race question was good. But southerners are southerners, and sometimes, under pressure, they can be offensive. I wanted to be sure he wasn't, so I called the governor to one side before we got into the chapel. I said, "Governor, we are greatly honored to have you. People here have a good impression of you. So when you are called on to give a brief expression, I hope you will be careful not to say anything offensive, like the word 'nigger.' It is highly objectionable." Folson acted as though he had been insulted. He drew up to his full height and said, "I never use that word except when I'm politicking sometime!"

When we reached the chapel, I had so intimidated the governor that, although he did not use the word "nigger," he forgot who I was. He addressed me as "Dr. Carver" three times before he began his speech, even though Dr. Carver was dead and we were eulogizing him on that occasion. Folsom was plainly struggling to avoid anything that would be objectionable. His remarks were entirely appropriate, except for the one faux pas on my account. I was almost embarrassed at the turn of events. To me, it showed a streak of decency, considering that Folsom was a rough-and-tumble type of man. I used to sit in his outer office in Montgomery, and the stream of curse words that I would hear him use in talking to those politicians was ever-flowing, although I never heard him use the word "nigger" there.

Gordon Persons followed James Folsom to the governor's chair. I had known Persons when he was head of the Alabama Transportation Commission. A group of us had gone to Montgomery to appeal Commissioner Persons's decision to segregate blacks in railroad Pullman cars despite federal regulations prohibiting such discrimination. The battles around segregation in Pullman cars and the Pullman car porters' struggles to make the Pullman Company recognize their union, The Brotherhood of Sleeping Car Porters, constitute one of the important stories of that time.

The Pullman car was a sleeping accommodation; Pullman sleeping and dining cars were owned and staffed by the Pullman Company separately from the other cars on a passenger train. During the day, the Pullman car looked like a regular railroad coach: pairs of seats on both sides of the aisle for nearly the length of the car. In the evening, however, the car was transformed into thirty or forty beds by the Pullman car porter. Each pair of seats collapsed into one bed, and a second bed was unfolded from its storage space in the wall. Bedding and pillows were brought out, and curtains were drawn between each set of upper and lower berths. At one end of the Pullman car was the deluxe accommodation, the drawing room, which was separated from the rest of the car by a door off the aisle. This room seated three during the day and slept three at night. The increased privacy in the drawing room usually rated a higher fare than regular Pullman berths. But Pullman segregated blacks—those few blacks who tried to use the service—particularly those of us who had to use the railroad for travel. These were days before interstate highways and passenger-oriented commercial aviation.

To ride a Pullman car, you had to pay your regular railroad fare plus the Pullman fare. The Pullman car ticket was even sold at a different window from the regular (segregated) ticket window in the "colored" waiting room. Usually there were so few blacks traveling Pullman that you had to go to the white waiting room in order to purchase a ticket for a Pullman berth.

When the Pullman company was forced to sell a prominent black a Pullman ticket, he or she would be put in a drawing room rather than in the open Pullman car itself. The drawing room, which was really a much nicer accommodation, carried a premium price, but if you were black, you were given the superior accommodations at the regular Pullman price.

Both the Pullman berth and the drawing room were serviced by the porter, always a black man. Sleeping car porters shined shoes, hung or whisked off clothing, brought towels and soap, tended to emergencies during the night, and did other things for the comfort of the passengers. Pullman porters held one of the important jobs in the black world of the 1920s, 1930s, and 1940s. It wasn't a professional job, but it was semiprofessional. Porters were usually people with personality and some stature. There were, among them, men who had finished college and couldn't find work elsewhere. People called it "running on the road." Most of the travelers were white people of financial substance, so the porters got a chance to see and talk to and know them. When the sleeping car porters were in their prime, they had contact with the more affluent class of whites in a traditional master-servant relationship.

Pullman porters were not paid adequately, and they were overworked. The organizing of their union, led by A. Philip Randolph, was a long and difficult process, full of reprisals by the Pullman Company against Pullman employees who protested their treatment. But the Brotherhood was a dynamic organization with chapters and members all over the country. It wouldn't take no for an answer. The porters had to fight for something like twelve years after the union had gained recognition before the first contract was signed.

E. D. Nixon of Montgomery, Alabama, recently deceased, was a Pullman car porter with whom I rode sometimes. I was familiar with Nixon's work with the Brotherhood and had seen him in Montgomery. He and I frequently discussed the race problem; he had strong feelings about breaking up segregation in the South. Some years later Nixon was in the leadership in the civil rights movement in Montgomery as one of the leaders of the famed Montgomery bus boycott, which boosted Martin Luther King, Jr., to national prominence.

When federal regulations prohibited segregating blacks in Pullman cars, Commissioner Persons decided that if blacks and whites had to ride together, he could still segregate them by requiring that a curtain be drawn between the seats occupied by the different races. When we went to see him about his decision, I asked Persons, "What are you going to do if a white person is sitting in the same compartment with a colored person?" He said, "I'll pull a curtain around him, too!"

We all laughed. We were familiar with the omnipresent "curtains" of the railroad. In the dining cars, black passengers could eat but only after the third call for dinner and then only behind a curtain drawn around a few tables at the end of the car, separating black from white. We knew that Person's Pullman curtain idea was hopeless. It wasn't going to happen. He dropped it.

The next thing I knew, Persons was governor of Alabama. When I went to see him at the state capitol, he said, "What about this fellow Gomillion?" He was referring to Dr. Charles G. Gomillion of the Tuskegee faculty, a leading member of the Tuskegee Civic Association, which was actively pushing for the ballot in Macon County. Blacks in Macon County, like their brothers and sisters in Alabama's other counties, were being denied the right to vote by obstructionist rules and terror tactics.

I said, "Well, Governor, he's simply exercising his duties as a citizen. He's not acting officially for Tuskegee Institute."

He said, "Yes, I understand that, but you and I know there isn't any difference. We can't act as a citizen and be an employee of Tuskegee without Tuskegee's influence being a part of what he's doing. I'm not going to ask you to do anything about it. I am just pointing that out to you."

I was glad he didn't because I wasn't *going* to do anything about Gomillion. I believed in the ballot, and blacks in the South were not allowed to register and vote, as was their constitutional right.

Back in the 1920s when I was teaching at Virginia State, we were trying for the ballot. One of the professors traveled around the state, arguing unsuccessfully for the vote for blacks. But in Alabama, I began voting when I became president of Tuskegee Institute. In fact, I voted as *soon* as I became head of Tuskegee. Dr. Moton had voted, and I assume that Booker Washington did also, although I don't know that he did so. I learned in 1935 that I would be allowed to vote for the first time in my life—because I was Tuskegee's president. I'm not sure who spoke to me about it, but it might have been the business officer at the school. As I recall, he reminded me not only that I had the vote but that it was important that I use it.

On election days, I went down to the courthouse and signed in just like the whites who were voting. I thought of it as an example of the kind of citizenship that we were striving for, for all black people. And I thought it would be too bad if I, having the vote, did not demonstrate my belief in it by using it.

There was a time in Alabama when, if an ordinary black person went to the courthouse and tried to register to vote, an effort was made to exclude him from voting. There were two frequently used obstacles to black voting. One was the poll tax, which all voters had to pay. Blacks   for example, the sharecroppers and tenants—by and large had not paid it and probably could not. But even if you paid your poll tax, you had to be endorsed by two registered voters. So few blacks were registered that you couldn't get an endorsement from a black voter. On the other hand, there had to be some *reason* for a white registered voter to endorse you; usually one did so because you held some position in which you could be useful. The ordinary black man or woman couldn't find two endorsers.

Even if you could find endorsers, you still had to pass a test in the courthouse. You had to read the constitution of the state and then, if the whites were satisfied with how you read, you had to interpret some portion of it "correctly." No matter what you said, they said your answer wasn't correct. I heard of one black man who was being "tested" on the state constitution. He was asked by the white person in charge to tell what a particular section meant.

"It means," the black man replied, "you white folks don't intend for me to vote."

But Gomillion, who was dean of students, along with William Shields and some of the people from the Veterans Hospital, were fighting to get the vote for themselves and other blacks in Macon County. I gave as much encouragement as I could to Gomillion and the others when the Civic Association began. Gomillion has since made speeches in New York and elsewhere about those times in the 1950s. He has said that he never knew of any instances in which I tried to curb what he was doing. The only time I ever attempted to restrain Gomillion was when he sent some notices for the association out on Tuskegee stationery. I told him, "Don't do that. I don't object to what you are doing, but don't identify your movement officially with Tuskegee Institute, because Tuskegee Institute isn't a civil rights movement, it's an educational institution."

After blacks in Alabama got the ballot, the Tuskegee Civic Association had to fight gerrymandering. One of the first actions taken by the white citizens in an effort to exclude blacks was to gerrymander just about all the black citizens out of the Tuskegee district, where their vote would have counted. The map of the election district looked like a snake. They drew lines around the houses where blacks lived; on one side of the line were blacks and on the other side were whites. Although the gerrymandering occurred after I left Tuskegee, I followed the events there and all over the nation quite closely. Governor George Wallace had come into office and had left. His wife had succeeded him. Wallace became angry because of the efforts of the Tuskegee Civic Association to get voting rights for blacks in Macon County. So when his wife, Lurleen Wallace, took the governor's chair, the same George Wallace who had been a Tuskegee trustee had his wife sharply reduce the state appropriation to Tuskegee Institute. My successor, Dr. Luther Foster, was able to get foundations to make up the difference, and when Lurleen Wallace had left office after one term and her husband had become governor again, the appropriation was restored and increased. The whole matter was part of a racially motivated, vindictive effort to punish Tuskegee because Gomillion and other blacks in Tuskegee were pushing for the ballot.

The strongest opposition I faced on campus while I was president, other than that from individuals who had personal interests, came from alumni, who were unhappy because I would not go out and buy football athletes. The alumni aren't afraid of the president. They're already out of school, and they'll say what they think. As the president, I usually tried to accommodate them within reason. Sometimes it wasn't possible.

When I visited a city in which there was an alumni club, I frequently met with its members. At these gatherings the poor athletic performance of the institution was a matter of discussion. Usually these alumni weren't contributing any money to the school to speak of, but the performance of their alma mater's athletic teams was a source of pride. For many of them, the reputation of an outstanding team may have afforded more favorable publicity for the school than what we were doing academically. The alumni wanted bragging rights.

During my administration, Tuskegee was being defeated regularly at football. Earlier, Tuskegee had had a long string of highly successful teams

composed of players from our high school right through its college se-
niors; you didn't have to be in our college division to play on the Tuskegee
team. Some students played long enough to be good. A guy named Stevens
was known all over the South as a fellow who could run with the football.
Big Mule and his brother Little Mule also had reputations. Then there was
the Adams family, a noted clan of Tuskegee graduates who were all six-foot,
two hundred pounders. However, when Dr. Moton added the final two
years of the college curriculum, transforming us from a normal school
into a four-year college, only students in the college division were allowed
to play on the Institute teams. The alumni were unhappy because they
wanted Tuskegee football teams to win as they had in the past. I wanted
good teams too, but I wasn't willing to use our already scarce resources to
entice students to come to Tuskegee just to play ball.

We were trying to give the best education the students could afford, but
Tuskegee did not have much money. If I spent money on athletes, that
money couldn't go into education. I didn't see buying football players—
and the bragging rights they might give us   as worth the expense. "Years
from now, when our hired athletes have finished college and can't make a
living at tennis or football or basketball," I told the alumni, "they will be
very unhappy people. I want Tuskegee graduates to be able, with their
education, to start a good job and hold it. I don't think football will help."

In this day and time, when football players have so many opportunities
to play after college, I might have felt differently. I might have helped to
recruit outstanding athletes and to give them whatever help I could. Today
money is involved for those schools whose alumni become professional
athletes. But in those days, all blacks had was "bragging rights" about what
their team had done. And Tuskegee alumni wanted theirs.

I remember speaking to some of our alumni in Dallas. I told them, "I'm
trying to do the best we can with what we have. I think Tuskegee's obligation to give you the best education is my first priority." Some of the alumni
said, "It's no use fighting you, Dr. Patterson. We aren't going to get anywhere with you." And they were right as far as buying athletes was concerned.

Dr. Moton was about sixty-nine or seventy when he retired. He was a
father figure, and nobody dared to challenge him. I think the Tuskegee
community's reverence for him was passed on to me. I don't say that everybody agreed with me; some didn't. But I was never challenged in an ugly
sort of way.

I found Tuskegee pretty well organized when I got there. It had to be,
because Dr. Moton was off the campus most of the time. We were really set

up by departments and divisions, with each division head more or less in charge. Within any group there are people who want leadership. And they'll create a problem in order to demonstrate their power. Even among students, you will always find some who are on the stump telling everyone else what to do.

I have a low flash point on some issues but not with students. I felt that they were there to learn. I felt that problems with students were a challenge. If the students wanted an unreasonable thing, we had to say so and let them know that we were not going to go along. But on the other hand, if there was merit in their complaint, if they had noticed something that the school ought to be doing, we had to see if we couldn't start doing it.

Plenty of faculty members disagreed with me, but I didn't have many open breaks with people. One professor made a point of being unpleasant in every faculty meeting. But that was his nature, and I think he wasn't really well. He used to make me very angry at faculty meetings, being supercritical; most of the time he was critical of the administration and me.

Faculty members enjoyed what he said, but some of them looked at him skeptically. My feeling was that the worst thing I could have done was to show anger. So I took low. I said, "That's your point of view. You have a right to express it. This proves we have a democracy. You can say that if that's the way you feel about things. But I don't have to do what you want me to do just because you are unhappy."

I let him say anything he wanted to say in the faculty meetings because it seems to me that one of the most important responsibilities of an administrator is to administer to dissent, to manage dissent. Let people get off their chests whatever they want before they become violent. It's only when they can't say what they want or feel that they become violent. But if you give people a chance to talk to each other and talk out the problems, the solutions come with less rancor. Management of dissent means providing a mechanism through which dissent can be expressed.

To manage dissent, you had to be willing to listen and analyze what people were saying. Very few people on a campus, if they are intelligent people, want to invent a problem. If they bring up something, it's usually something they're genuinely concerned about. Their concerns need to be channeled into committees where issues are presented and solutions discussed. You manage dissent. You don't let it sit like a raisin in the sun.

This supercritical professor was an Iowa State graduate like me. One of the things we fell out about was my decision to release a Tuskegee faculty member who was also an Iowa graduate and a classmate of mine, the daughter of a cook at Iowa. She had come to Tuskegee and had taught for a while. For some reason or other—I don't think the problem had to do with her intellect—she didn't turn out to be satisfactory, and I decided to let her go.

He came to me to appeal my decision. He argued that, since he and I were fraternity brothers, I should give his request special consideration. Of course, I could never be persuaded by a fraternity affiliation not to do my duty. You don't favor people or fail to favor people because of a fraternity affiliation, not if you take your presidential responsibilities seriously. I was greatly offended that he had thought otherwise.

I never made a move to retaliate against him; he was a good teacher. When he left Tuskegee, it was of his own accord, not because I did anything about the nasty things he said. He went to Prairie View. The last I heard, he had passed on to the great beyond.

Under the system, there was no tenure for teachers at Tuskegee. What the president said was law. You were reappointed every year, and you received a letter from the president inviting you to return for the next academic year. That letter was called your "ask back," but it didn't sound like that when some of them said it. Under ordinary circumstances, I would not dismiss a person unless those who worked closely with that individual suggested that the teacher in question was a liability to us. Many people, if they were not happy, left of their own accord.

People usually knew whether or not they were going to be invited to come back. They had to be mindful that their behavior—whether it reflected incompetence or some social problem—could determine whether or not they would be asked back.

I did not wait until the last minute and then spring surprises on people. As a rule, instead of writing a letter, I invited them to my office, thanked them for the year's work, and right then and there invited them to remain with us for the coming year.

No one I asked to leave ever protested. Then, too, teachers who were asked to leave didn't have any recourse. We didn't have all of the hearings and appeal procedures common in colleges today. In my day, the president had almost too much authority. If he said he didn't want you back, you weren't coming back.

The part of my job as president that I was least competent to do was preparing the budget. I therefore always tried to have a skillful financial officer at my elbow. I had only two during my entire reign. One of them I fired; the other was promoted to vice-president and later succeeded me as president.

The one I fired had been a schoolmate of mine in Texas. He was competent, but we fell out because he didn't share with me information that I should have had. The information reached me too late to be useful. We had a significant deficit in our operations at the infantile paralysis unit at the hospital. By the time he told me, we had already spent ten thousand dollars more than we had.

I couldn't do anything to correct the expenditure after the fact. If I had known, I could have taken steps to see that we didn't create the deficit. This incident was characteristic of his way of doing things; he didn't let me know in time what was going on. He was ready to give me the blame, but he wasn't ready to give me the opportunity to do something.

As president, I always put my responsibility to the institution first, and I did not allow friendship to get in the way. I needed friends, and if they were the kind who would help, fine. But if their interest did not coincide with their obligation to the institution, I couldn't afford their friendship. I thought my treasurer was someone I could trust. I had known his family; his father was a distinguished financial officer at Prairie View, and so I thought I had a good man.

My second treasurer, Luther Foster, was also the son of a college business officer. Foster was a barefoot boy on the campus of Virginia State when I took my first teaching job there. His father later moved from the business office at Virginia State to the presidency. Foster, after taking his degree at Virginia State, received a master's degree from Hampton and then a master's degree from Harvard. Then he worked at Howard University. I felt that I knew Foster when he became my vice-president. He had grown up in the field of college business affairs. After he was hired by Tuskegee, he went to the University of Chicago and was awarded his doctorate in educational administration.

Dr. Carver was both a scientist and a moving spirit at the Institute. There were many occasions when we tried to accord him the recognition we felt he deserved.

On June 2, 1937, when the George Washington Carver bust was unveiled at Tuskegee, Dr. Carver wore the same suit he had worn when he graduated from Iowa State forty years before. A number of distinguished visitors were present, and we all felt, of course, that this bust was an appropriate way to recognize Carver's life of unselfish research and brilliant service. His service addressed the needs of the region, and particularly the locale, in which Tuskegee had been founded. At the unveiling for the first time I heard Carver described as a chemurgist (one who, through scientific processes, converts simple natural phenomena—whether clay, plant or animal—to a more useful purpose). Dr. Carver was described as the world's leading chemurgist, a man who saw the potential of sweet potatoes and peanuts, plants and clay. From the latter he extracted color and produced durable paint for houses. He was a genius at converting the things about him so that they could meet people's needs. His achievement was borne out by the many honors he received. Today his work would probably be called chemical engineering.

Carver made the nation and world aware of the real value of the peanut, a plant brought to this country by Africans and grown abundantly in the South. It was well known that the Tom Houston Peanut Company, which was just forty miles away in Columbus, Georgia, turned about everything Dr. Carver did with the peanut and some of what he did with the sweet potato into a commercial enterprise. Carver was a consultant to the company, which never paid him a penny! He probably wouldn't have accepted anything. Many people have heard the stories of how Carver would not collect his Tuskegee check or, if he collected it, would not cash it. Sometimes we had to go to him and take his checks to the bank before they expired. Money making and commercial considerations were not his life. He lived for his work.

Dr. Carver was not race conscious. He had been born a slave, kidnapped as a child, and ransomed for a horse. Yet on questions of race, he offered no comment. He never spoke of it, at least not with me. There was one exception: the occasion when he turned over his life savings to me for the establishment of the George Washington Carver Research Foundation. The money was in government bonds. Carver said that buying the bonds was an act of patriotism in which all citizens could indulge, not just white citizens. He felt that his purchase of bonds had great significance for him as a Negro. It was a gesture symbolic of his Americanism. I don't know whether or not I agreed with him. I'm not prepared to say. But he had strong feelings about it. Another tribute to Carver's scientific and creative genius, the George Washington Carver Museum, grew out of displays Carver used to mount in the old Milbank Agricultural Building. A room in Milbank, where he taught, had been set aside for the display of Carver's preserved vegetables and fruits; paints and boards that he had painted with clay dyes; paintings of fruits and flowers; and other samples of his handiwork. Carver was a talented artist and weaver; he knitted and crocheted. The building that eventually housed an expanded display of his work, the museum, was originally the campus laundry. It was a handsome building located in the center of the campus. Such an important spot, thought Carver, should not be used for so mundane a purpose. He must have whispered to some of the trustees that this would be a lovely place for his museum. And it was. Initially, I kind of resented the move to create the museum. Why? Because I had not thought of it myself, I suppose. Nonetheless it came into existence and increased the awareness of the public—both students and visitors to our campus, of which there were always plenty—of the importance of the things Carver was saying and doing.

Unfortunately, just four years after Dr. Carver died, the Carver Museum was destroyed by fire. We never learned the cause. Students had constructed the building years earlier. Probably the electrical wiring eventually shorted in some way. The museum had become one of the richest expressions of the Tuskegee Institute and its purposes. The fire consumed things that were absolutely irreplaceable. It was a great tragedy, and I was devastated. As I stood and watched the greedy flames destroy Dr. Carver's work, I could not keep from weeping. Right away we began planning for the reconstruction of the museum. Today it still illustrates the genius of Carver.

There were several black businesses in Tuskegee and many more throughout the South. As president of Tuskegee, I became president of the National Negro Business League, as Washington and Moton had been. The league had originally been established in Boston by Booker Washington at about the time I was born. (We later dropped "Negro" from its name.) Our local chapters all over the country didn't have much money, but as apostles of Booker Washington, we did realize the importance of cooperation and the effort to expand opportunity in the fields of business for black people.

Segregation gave the black community a lot of structure. For example, it was very unusual for a white undertaker to accept black bodies. As a result, funeral homes became important black businesses. The same is true of barber shops, beauty parlors, dry cleaners, pool halls, restaurants, caterers, dressmakers, and the like. And some of these businesses, if they were good, served all people, not just blacks. (In the field of education, when schools and faculties were segregated, our teaching graduates returned to their own communities or to other places with substantial black populations and found work there.)

When I was living in Tuskegee, I patronized the local merchants. Tuskegee had a dry cleaner on the edge of the campus, and our family laundry was done in the school laundry, where the students did their clothes. I went to the local barber shop. One barber, named Lassiter, was married to the daughter of the man who was a carpentry or electrical instructor in the Mechanical Industries Division at Tuskegee.

I wore prefabricated clothes. Rarely did I have a tailor-made suit. The average size would fit me. At Iowa State, I had worn some kind of suit or jacket and sweater and pants but no tie. At Virginia State, I began wearing a suit and tie every day, and I've been wearing a suit and tie every day since that time. The casual dress you see teachers wearing today would have been strictly out of the question when I was teaching.

I was commended on my dress. Some people look better in clothes off the rack than do others. I was told that I looked fairly good. A woman who came to visit Tuskegee, a judge from Chicago, told me, "You look good in your clothes." I never shopped for clothes in New York, although I went there fairly often. New York was always too high and highfalutin for me. Besides, in New York, I was looking for money, not spending it. I could buy what I wanted and could afford close to home. The town of Tuskegee had some clothing stores, although I don't remember buying a suit there. Perhaps I bought only underwear, shirts, ties or things like that. One day I went into a department store in Birmingham to look at some shirts. The salesman said, "This is what all the white boys are wearing." My reaction was, "If this is what the white boys are wearing, I don't want any part of it."

At that time you could purchase a suit from companies that regularly sent salesmen around to the various college campuses. One company, I remember, was in Cincinnati. The salesman had a whole sample book from which you could choose fabrics. He had pictures of different styles, two-button or three-button, single-breasted or double-breasted, with cuffs and without. You could select what you wanted. He would take your measurements and write up your order. The suit was sent to you by mail, and the price was comparable to what you would pay in the department store. Prejudice being what it was, I preferred to buy by mail rather than to deal with the average store, although I could have shopped off the rack.

I have always been aware of the teachings of religion. While I have not been a devout follower of the Word, I have tried to take to honor my duty to my fellow man and to the community. Even when I was a youngster living in Austin, we attended the African Methodist Episcopal (AME) church. My family is largely AME. My sister Lucille was quite a strong member of her church in Washington. My sister Bessie became the leader of a choir in a Baptist church—Shiloh Baptist—in Washington after she left Hampton. She did that for the rest of her life, but she did not change her own affiliation.

I taught Sunday school at Tuskegee, but I wasn't very good. I inherited a lot of information, but I'm not a good Bible student. I just read some chapters and followed lesson outlines. We had an interdenominational church service, although we followed the Episcopal manual as far as the order of worship was concerned.

I like good preaching, but much of it is repetitive and some of it is almost intimidation. I don't get much out of it. Then, too, twenty-five years of feeling obligated to attend our campus religious services has weighed upon me. Unless you are going to do more than go to church on Sunday, unless you become a part of the operational structure, you're not considered a good church member. Rather than doing something that I don't feel up to, I'd rather listen to the world news on Sunday mornings than go to church.

I never really took a vacation while I was at Tuskegee. Although I traveled in connection with my work, I didn't spend several weeks or months away, vacationing with my family. After commencement, we had summer school. The year when my wife was pregnant with our son, Fred, she stayed home with me and spent a good bit of the summer at Capahosic as well. At other times, when summer came, she would go off to Maine or some other northern place by herself. She was still very much interested in her music and would go to study under some outstanding teacher for a month or six weeks.

Despite segregation, there were always provisions of some kind for blacks at many resort areas. For example, in Atlantic City, there were hotels for blacks, although the boardwalks and seashore were cordoned off. Blacks have never been completely without facilities, but I didn't take time to enjoy them.

Over the course of the school year, I was away from the campus from a fourth to a third of the time, attending meetings and going to see people. When I took a trip, I tried to group appointments if I could. For example, if I were going to New York or a large city and knew how much time would be involved, I'd ask myself, "Is there anyone else I can see in connection with the welfare of Tuskegee Institute?"

Traveling was such a normal part of my routine that I don't think it disturbed my wife. I think it caused my son more concern, since I wasn't able to spend time there with him. Fred attended the local Catholic elementary school a little bit. Dr. Richardson's wife, who was a teacher in our elementary school, thought that the Catholic school was not the place for him, however, and she brought him to the Children's House, where she worked.

My son was sometimes teased and badgered by other students because he was the president's son. Once, I recall, he came to me after such an incident and said, "They're doing to me what they'd like to do to you!" He didn't really expect me to be out on the campus with him because he had his own program to follow. But we were together at home and at mealtimes and in the evenings.

Ten-year reunion, Class of 1940, Tuskegee Institute.

Our home continued to function as the campus hospitality center. In it we welcomed the numerous visitors who wanted to see what was happening at Tuskegee or who had been invited to share with us something of what they were doing. Dr. Du Bois made several more trips there. He had been critical of Tuskegee and of me at one time. But after hearing me speak at Prairie View once, he accepted Booker Washington's program and agreed that vocational and technical education was important for blacks. At one time, Du Bois wanted everybody to have a bachelor of arts education and be educated as he had been. Booker Washington has been criticized for not believing in higher education, but Washington *did* believe in higher education. Certainly he employed some of the best educated people he could find. He wasn't against Du Bois. Washington simply said that Du Bois's program was too limited to promote the progress of black people.

In his change of heart Du Bois didn't abandon what he was doing—he felt that it was still important—but he felt that education of greater importance for the masses of blacks had to do with vocational education. He retracted some of what he had said about Tuskegee and, in some reasonably complimentary way, indicated that I was doing all I could to better the opportunities for black youth.

Once, when Du Bois visited our home, an amusing incident took place. He was accompanied by an associate, a sculptor from Atlanta University, Elizabeth Prophet. We were having dinner, and when dessert was served, Du Bois and the young woman disagreed as to what they were eating. She said, "The ice cream is delicious." He said, "It's not ice cream, it's sherbet." "It's ice cream." "It's sherbet." The exchange continued for several minutes before we understood what was happening. I was supposed to be watching my weight and was to eat sherbet instead of ice cream. Our cook had prepared both. When we were served, Du Bois was given sherbet, and his companion, ice cream.

In my mind, the exchange was symbolic of the educational alternatives offered in the Washington-Du Bois debate. They were both right! Both ice cream and sherbet. Both liberal arts and a technical eduation—in large quantity—were needed for black students who were denied so many opportunities in America. We needed to improve the education that was being offered to these young men and women. There was no dodging the fact, and there was no dodging the fact that improving education meant spending more money.

Finding the funds to keep these students in college and helping them advance has been the dominant theme in my life. I began life financing my own school expenses—picking cotton, driving a delivery truck, or waiting on tables—and moved, at Tuskegee, to the problems of financing an institution that served students who, like myself, had no outside financial resources on which they could rely.

Tuskegee was definitely a training ground for people interested in grappling with the questions of finance. We literally never had enough money. Tuskegee was running a deficit. And consequently I would hear from the trustees. On the whole, I think that the trustees were pleased with my work. Ten years after my installation as president, they presented me with a purse, a check for a thousand dollars. They thought I had done a good job that ought to be recongized. They made the presentation at a service in the Institute chapel, with students and faculty attending. This was a high point in my life. Before the gathering adjourned, I announced that the money would go to establish a student loan fund. Then the students really applauded. They were excited not about my getting a thousand dollars but about my plan to use it for students. Despite the general success of my administration, however, I could not ignore the need for new solutions to our fiscal problems. My search led to the creation of the United Negro College Fund in 1943.

5 The United Negro College Fund

In 1943 we had the first meeting to consider the feasibility of a combined appeal program, which became the United Negro College Fund. Our first national campaign was in 1944. Until then, practically all of the money for the black colleges had been raised largely by the president himself. I came to the presidency of Tuskegee at a time when the methods that Dr. Moton had used successfully to raise money were becoming passé.

In most small private colleges, the president based one of his primary appeals on the fact that the college had a deficit caused by enrolling so many financially poor students who wanted an education. The school just couldn't turn them down. The tuition at Tuskegee then was about fifty dollars a year. As a result, we had to raise just about all the money needed to run the institution from sources other than tuition. So we would go out and make the appeal to erase the deficit.

Tuskegee was fortunate, as was Hampton, in having some endowment, but ours was approximately $10 million, which produced only about $500,000 a year, at 5 percent, to operate the institution. Our budget was about $3 million. We had to find the difference between that and the modest tuition paid by the students and the yearly grant of five thousand dollars from the state of Alabama.

Tuskegee's fifty thousand dollar deficit became very important for two reasons. First, it meant unpaid bills. And if it was fifty thousand this year and nothing improved, it was going to be another fifty thousand the next year or perhaps even seventy-five thousand. Second, a college which is coping with deficit financing is not a college that can do new things to keep up with the times. Therefore, it stagnates. The stagnation can be worse than the deficit itself.

Either we had to reduce substantially the number of courses we were offering or we had to find new sources of funds. My analysis was that the things we were doing were sufficiently important and that we should be doing even more. Under the circumstances, I opted to see how Tuskegee could raise more money. I decided that since all private black colleges faced similar, if not identical, financial hardships, and since Tuskegee Institute, as a single institution, was having relatively little success, why not suggest to other private black colleges that we pool our resources—tell a better story and appeal to a broad base of donors as a financial constituency?

I wrote a letter to a number of private colleges. The immediate impetus for writing the letter was that I had to prepare a little paper for presentation to a group known as the Atheneum Club on the campus of Tuskegee Institute. The club was composed of faculty members and doctors at the Veterans Hospital next door to the campus. Each member was expected to present a paper which reflected something of the speaker's interests, particularly his professional interests. At the time, I had no intention of doing anything more than talking about an interest which was very close to my heart, namely the fact that Tuskegee needed money, as did, perhaps, a lot of other private black colleges.

At the time I wrote the letter, it was purely an inquiry, so I could report to the club on the general condition of the colleges, of which the members were probably unaware. I received a prompt response from most of the college presidents. They said, "We are having an even worse time than Tuskegee Institute in raising funds, and we are in serious financial trouble."

When I received such quick replies, I wondered whether the respondents thought that perhaps I had some money to give out. When Booker Washington headed Tuskegee, certain wealthy philanthropists, and the Rosenwald Fund in particular, gave him money to help Tuskegee and to distribute among other schools. This arrangement became well known, and people remembered it long after such funds had ceased to be available. I had to write an additional letter to the private black colleges explaining that I was merely trying to find out whether they were as poor as Tuskegee was. This, I am sure, was disappointing news.

My initial survey revealed that Tuskegee was better off than most of the black private schools to which I had written. Tuskegee had a comparatively long history of reasonably well organized fund raising. We had a specific office dedicated to this purpose, and two field agents who lived in the North and who, on a regular schedule, presented Tuskegee's case to people who they knew to be interested. We were raising about forty thousand dollars a year at that time, but it cost more than twenty thousand to raise it.

In my earlier efforts to find money for Tuskegee, I had already been made aware that two or three changes were taking place in the philanthropic marketplace. As I've said before, many of the wealthy people who had given to Tuskegee had lost their wealth in the depression. Others had died, and their children did not necessarily inherit the philanthropic interests of their parents. Furthermore, the Roosevelt administration was blamed, as I have said, for the changing tax situation. Despite the fact that most blacks were denied the vote, many potential contributors believed that blacks were responsible for Roosevelt's election and said they would not give for that reason.

Still another part of the picture which the record should show is that as little as we presidents—going out individually—were raising, we were competing with each other for the same philanthropic dollar, because not many people were interested in this group of institutions.

I can recall bumping into some of the presidents of other black colleges in the offices of the General Education Board. Our meeting wasn't intentional; it was just happenstance. They were going for their interests, and I was going for mine. There was no secret about who was donating what: reports were usually available indicating the gifts a particular foundation had made to various colleges.

The GEB and the Julius Rosenwald Fund of Chicago had strong minority interests in their philanthropy. While they gave to whites, they frequently gave to blacks. We, as presidents of black colleges, felt that the extent of their interest and the level of giving left much to be desired. For although the two foundations were among the major contributors to black colleges, they made greater gifts to white colleges, whose needs were comparatively less staggering than ours. As Benjamin Mays, former president of Morehouse College, has said, they always seemed to assume that blacks don't *need* as much money as whites. The Rosenwald Fund initially concentrated on helping primary and secondary schools, whereas the GEB seemed to be more interested in helping the black colleges. Very few other foundations at that time were equally interested in black higher education.

All of these factors combined to create a bleak financial future if our survival depended on traditional sources. Such at least was my conclusion in a paper that I presented to the Atheneum Club. And that was the end of my probe, or so I thought at the time.

During this period, I had been asked by the *Pittsburgh Courier* to write a weekly column entitled "The Southern Viewpoint." I had written about first one current concern and then another. I soon found that writing a column every week wasn't an easy task. Once, when I couldn't think of anything else to say, I decided I would bring to the readers' attention my findings about the colleges and suggest that a combined appeal might be a useful approach to the problem the colleges were facing.

My experience with two other national organizations made me think that the combined appeal might work. Basil O'Connor, the chairman of the Tuskegee Board of Trustees, was a former law partner of President Roosevelt, who suffered from infantile paralysis. O'Connor headed the National Foundation for Infantile Paralysis, sponsor of the March of Dimes, and he, like myself, was on the board of the American National Red Cross. Both of these organizations were trying to broaden the base of contributors to their causes rather than confining their appeal to the wealthy alone. Their aim was to encourage people, at whatever level of giving, to contribute. Thus, for example, the March of Dimes campaign sought not dollars but dimes, and the March of Dimes made its appeal with a drop box everywhere dimes could be found: in movie theater refreshment stands, in drugstores and dry cleaners, in diners and cafeterias, always sitting right on the counter near the cash register where the customers' loose change could be deposited by anyone who wanted to help fight polio.

The coming together of the private black colleges out of concern for our needs; the fact that we were not going to get the amount of money we had been receiving from our former sources; and the innovative fund-raising practices of other organizations—all of these factors contributed to the formation of the United Negro College Fund.

We should try to present the needs of black youth in the private black colleges, not as a matter of only local or restricted concern, but as something Americans of goodwill would take to heart. People could, we hoped, be united in an organizational relationship similar to that of the American National Red Cross or the National Foundation for Infantile Paralysis. We could then jointly solicit gifts from donors large and small all over the country.

In forming the Fund, we did not simply attempt to exploit the credentials of the member colleges. These credentials weren't that strong to start with. Basically, we wanted to reach people who didn't know the colleges but who did believe in education and who would be concerned about meeting the financial needs of black youth.

At this time, in 1943–44, education was rigidly segregated in the South where most black youths lived. Black colleges—nearly all of which were located in the South—needed help so that they could offer better education where it was needed most. The very heart of the Fund's rationale was the commitment of the colleges to serving as many black youth as possible. To do so, the colleges had to be strengthened.

The alumni were giving relatively little to Tuskegee Institute. Even the trustees weren't giving much. But many people knew the reputations of Tuskegee, Hampton, Fisk, Atlanta, Howard, and others, and many more people knew that there were hundreds of thousands of young people who needed to be educated. That need was the basis on which the UNCF got its start.

I knew very little, if anything, about organized fund raising, except that it had to be done and that what we actually needed was professional fund-raising counsel. We needed someone more knowledgeable than ourselves to tell us whether or not, in their opinion, this was a good idea, how much it would cost, and how much we could expect to raise.

In the Hampton-Tuskegee campaign in 1923, when approximately $4 million dollars had been raised for each of the two institutions, a New York fund-raising firm, John Price Jones, had been used. After several colleges had responded to my letter, I invited them to send representatives, preferably their presidents, to a meeting at which a member of John Price Jones would also be present. Seventeen or eighteen colleges attended the first meeting. Apart from Buel Gallagher, the president of Talladega College, who came with a paper stating why it wouldn't succeed, and the president of Fisk University, Thomas Elsa Jones, who also thought that the idea was not viable, the presidents were quite willing to try any plan that stood a better chance of succeeding than what they were doing.

Although Talladega did not join at the time, Fisk University did, and President Jones turned out to be a most valuable participant. Later, after Dr. Gallagher had resigned, Talladega joined the Fund, when Dean Cater was acting president.

From the beginning, we met with little resistance, only the usual type of criticism, mainly the objection that the plan had never been tried before. That assertion, however, was not absolutely true. I believe that some women's colleges had formed a joint campaign previously. The big question was: will people respond? The presidents thought, "I can make a case for my institution with my trustees, with my alumni, and with cultivated friends; but can I go to the general public and make an appeal? And what will be the cost?" With little or no money, black colleges individually were not able to pay for a national campaign, and there was little reason to believe that a national campaign would succeed for a single black school.

The John Price Jones representative thought that the idea was a good

United Negro College Fund Member College presidents, 1940s.

one and would work. Then we had to decide how much we should ask for. We knew there was no point in asking for what we needed. The amount we needed was far in excess of the response we anticipated. But if we had a hundred thousand dollars, how much money could we raise? Or suppose we were trying to raise a million dollars. How much would we have to pay in expenses to do so? The discussion of the million dollar goal made it appear that a hundred thousand dollar budget was sufficient for starters.

In 1943 we put together a planning committee of presidents from some of the stronger colleges. These were not exclusively prestigious institutions but were institutions that had sizable budgets, had experienced fairly substantial success in fund raising, and had presidents who were well known to the foundations.

President Tom Jones had been at Fisk for several years, was very well known to foundations, and was considered quite successful. Miss Florence Read headed Spelman College, which had come into being with the support and blessing of the Rockefeller family. She had influence. So did Rufus Clement, who headed Atlanta University, a group of colleges (including

Spelman, Morehouse College, Clark College, and Gammon Theological Seminary) that were operating in a cooperating relationship. Albert Dent was president of Dillard University, which had formed from the merger of two schools, New Orleans University and Straight College. The merger had been brought about largely by the Rosenwald Fund, with which Dent had a very good relationship. I was included because I recommended the plan and because everybody mistakenly considered Tuskegee Institute comparatively rich.

The first question put before us was: where do we get the hundred thousand dollars? We thought of our two foundation friends, the Rosenwald Fund and the General Education Board. In deciding to make the approach, the presidents—twenty-seven had decided to join by then, I believe—decided that we should show our sincerity by raising half of the amount from ourselves, dividing the costs among the colleges on a pro rata basis. Some of the colleges that had to raise as little as three hundred dollars were obliged to borrow that amount in order to participate. I think Tuskegee had one of the largest shares—ten thousand dollars, as I recall an amount more or less in keeping with our comparative financial position. Hampton Institute, having the most money, committed funds accordingly.

One of the immediate results was the positive response that came from the officers of the two foundations, which provided twenty-five thousand each. In this way we collected the hundred thousand dollars needed for the first campaign.

The distribution of the money to be raised was a matter of great concern to all the presidents. We had to decide upon a formula that reflected the relative strengths and therefore the financial obligations of each of the participating schools. For example, what was the size of the operating budget? How many students was the institution serving? Although we knew that sometimes a college might take more students than it could accommodate, we thought the size of the student body would reflect, to some degree, the size of the institution's obligations. What was the base of its financial support? In other words, did it have an endowment, and if it did not, was it church-related? If the latter, what was the annual commitment made by the church to the institution?

As we discussed these factors and worked out details of a distribution formula, we also decided that since the stronger colleges were better able to raise money on their own than the weaker ones, a part of the formula should favor the weaker institutions: 40 percent of all the money raised would be divided equally, regardless of the size of the college.

Everybody did not get the same amount. The colleges that had to bor-

Organizing meeting of United Negro College Fund, Waldorf-Astoria Hotel, New York City, May 13, 1944.

row three hundred dollars to participate would not receive the same allotment as the college able to put up ten thousand dollars. The ability to put up the money reflected, to some degree, the operating expenditures and therefore the size of the obligation of the institution.

The formula that we devised, slightly modified for capital campaigns, has operated successfully throughout the United Negro College Fund's existence. Although several efforts were made to change it, the revised formulas always brought us back to where we started. We decided that the real challenge was to increase the amount of money raised and not to quibble over the formula itself.

One of the things that gave us such an early and successful start was the complete endorsement of John D. Rockefeller, Jr., who came to the Fund's opening session at the Waldorf Astoria. His participation and active public endorsement were major contributions. Rockefeller had never before associated himself with any national appeal. Ours was an appeal, however, to which he was perfectly willing not only to lend his name and to give financial support but to write letters. He made it plain that we should call on him for assistance. Black education had long been an interest of the Rockefeller philanthropists. I think it was easy for him to sense that, as time went on and as costs became even larger, the existing philanthropies would not be adequate to sustain the colleges.

In addition Rockefeller wanted to encourage us to raise the money we needed. He knew that his name and his standing in the field of philanthropy would be a great asset. I have always said that the Fund actually picked up where Rockefeller and other foundations' efforts left off, or where they stabilized, and finally diminished, in terms of broad-based support to black colleges. The foundations continued to respond to appeals from individual colleges but mainly for special programs and capital needs for a restricted number of institutions.

The next question was how soon we could get started and where we would be located. Since New York was considered then, as it is now, the financial capital of the world, we decided to locate our new organization there. The big problems then were to find space and to figure out the minimum size of the staff we needed. The location of the office was also a prime consideration, since there were areas of New York City where the volunteers we hoped to recruit would not go.

The first executive director was William J. Trent, Jr. Trent's father, William J. Trent, Sr., was the president of Livingstone College in Salisbury, North Carolina. Livingstone did not join with the first group of colleges, but Trent was well known to some of our members. He was a graduate of the high school at Morehouse College and Livingstone. He had also received an M.B.A. from the Wharton School at the University of Pennsylvania. At the time we contacted him, he was working in Washington, D.C., in the Department of the Interior under Harold Ickes.

Trent was better known to some of the presidents in the Atlanta area than to me. They suggested him, saying that he was ideally suited for the position, provided he could be persuaded to accept it. Early in 1944, Albert Dent and I had a conference with Trent over dinner in Washington, and we found him positive in his attitude, but he pointed out that he was classified 1-A and was expecting to be drafted into the army. He was afraid, under those circumstances, to accept our offer unless he could be deferred.

It then became my responsibility to try to secure the deferment for Trent. I went to the District of Columbia draft board and was told, "We think you have a good case, but we can't do anything about it. You'll have to see the regional man, who is here in the District but in a different office." I went to him—Colonel Carlson, a very cordial man. I told him what we were trying to do. Obviously, I wanted my credentials to impress him. He said, "Oh yes, Tuskegee Institute. That's the school Booker Washington founded, isn't it?" Washington, of course, had died in 1915.

I said, "Yes, it is." He said, "Booker Washington gave the commencement address when I graduated from the University of Iowa. I don't remember what he said, but he told some good stories." After that, Colonel Carlson didn't discuss Bill Trent or the idea further; he just signed the paper.

I went back and told Trent, "Bill, Booker Washington just got you deferred from the draft." In that way the UNCF found its first executive director.

We rented space on Fifty-seventh Street and got organized. We then decided how much of the work would be done in New York and in what principal cities we should try to conduct our campaign. When we invited John Price Jones to send a representative to the first meetings of the college presidents, they sent Paul Franklin, who was assigned the responsibility of directing our first campaign. The only other person who came on board very early was Betty Stebman, who had been working with Paul Franklin at John Price Jones. First she was assigned to us as a member of the firm's staff. Later she became a full-time secretary with the Fund. A women's program was organized by one of our important volunteers, Catherine Hughes Waddell, daughter of Supreme Court Justice Charles Evans Hughes. Betty became the director of the Women's Division.

Because we didn't have enough money (nor at the time did we even fully appreciate how much money was necessary), we decided that each college president would give at least a month of his time to fund raising for our new organization at no cost to the Fund except for transportation and living expenses in the assigned cities.

Although we were asking for a million dollars, we didn't know what we could raise. That first year we raised $760,000, which was more money than we had had any right to hope for. The success of that initial campaign fully justified our continuing and our expanding. I remember that when Benjamin Mays, one of the college presidents, first joined the group, he said, "Of course, you have in mind our doing this for two or three years, and then going back to what we were doing, don't you?" Well, we didn't go back. We've never gone back because the joint appeal was so much more successful. Mays, of course, remained one of our most conscientious presidents.

Whereas Tuskegee was previously spending twenty thousand dollars to raise forty thousand dollars, after our first UNCF campaign, it spent nothing and received far more. The campaign immediately showed a successful return in terms of financial outlay.

Leadership is the key to any campaign. If the top one or two or three people in the community identify themselves with it, their endorsement will make an important difference in its success. One of the amazing things about this country is the commitment to philanthropy; compared with many European countries, the United States is way ahead. Philanthropy in the United States is an established concept. The direction taken depends largely on the person in charge, the good opinion of prominent individuals, and the extent to which those people are willing to identify actively with a cause or causes.

Another aspect of American philanthropy is that it is such an ingrained part of the American way of life. Many young people in the field of business, and perhaps in other areas, win recognition by associating themselves with causes of significance. For example, if some of the older and prestigious people invited an up-and-coming person by saying, "We want you to help raise money for this cause," he or she responded for a couple of reasons, first, because they asked, but also because a good cause will receive favorable publicity that will make the up-and-coming person known as progressive and public-spirited.

Walter Hoving was the first national campaign chairman of the United Negro College Fund. Hoving was among the top business executives in New York, head of Lord & Taylor, which at that time had the city's most racially advanced hiring policy and brought blacks onto the staff as salespeople. I'm not sure whether we learned about this policy after we approached Hoving or before, but the policy he instituted at that prominent store indicated to us the type of man he was.

We had Mr. Rockefeller inform Hoving of our intention to approach him. One of the reasons he accepted our request to chair the campaign was that it was the colleges' idea. It was not an idea that somebody else had thought up and had given us as blacks. Naturally, if Hoving accepted the chairmanship, he wanted the campaign to succeed. He probably conferred with John D. Rockefeller, Jr., and if Rockefeller asked him to take it, Hoving knew that Rockefeller would lend important support to the campaign.

While I was still president of Tuskegee Institute, I was also the first president of the Fund, so I had to be in New York frequently. I remember that Hoving scheduled visits to the Fund as a part of his regular routine. The entire staff knew that he was going to come in and sit down and talk about the campaign and what he could do to advance it. At that time, Hoving was young and handsome and one of the best-dressed men in New York. All the ladies swooned whenever they knew that Walter Hoving was coming. He was a very popular and most effective chairman.

In launching the campaign, we went to our friends for leadership from people who, in one way or another, locally or nationally, had shown that they believed in helping blacks. We reached out to people who had leadership standing and who, when they were called by people like Hoving and Rockefeller, would endorse the cause and help develop leadership throughout the United States.

In other words, in any kind of national undertaking, people want to know who leads it. "With whom will I be associated?" Rockefeller's participation was a stamp of approval to which most people would respond. If he wrote somebody a letter, it brought a lot of friends, because they wanted his goodwill. The issue wasn't always goodwill for the cause; it was the goodwill of Rockefeller and his recognition of selected individuals as people of leadership. He complimented them by calling on them. Our cause benefited from this mechanism in that first campaign.

Some years after the UNCF began, when I was doing postdoctoral study at Stanford University, the Fund decided to start a campaign in San Francisco. One of the persons who was extremely helpful and went out of his way for us was Dan Koshland. He was a businessman, but he was never too busy to see me and never too busy to call somebody. (Koshland was a joy to work with. The only thing I ever held against him was that he set our sights too low; he prompted people to give less than I think they might otherwise.)

One day, near the end of the campaign, I thanked him for his efforts and he said to me, "Don't thank me too much. This is the way I meet all the best people. Those are people I want to know and those are the people I want to know me. Those are the people I want to know that I'm identified with a good cause." Our approach, initiated with Mr. Rockefeller's influence, has been 100 percent effective for the UNCF.

After the Fund had existed for one or two years, Paul Franklin observed that we had enough publicity for a $12 million campaign and yet we were asking for only a million and a half. I was always trying to raise the goal, but because Mr. Rockefeller was conservative and wanted to be certain that fund raising reached the stated goal, we didn't increase it. I learned early in the game that many people give according to the size of your goal: if you're asking for peanuts, you get peanuts. My feeling was that even if we did not reach our objective, many people would have given larger sums toward a larger goal, had we established one. But I was persuaded that to name an amount that seemed too far ahead of reality perhaps was not wise, and I bowed to that opinion.

On the other hand, we felt we had to keep our sights high, because the amount of money we were raising was in no sense adequate to our needs, and even though we said we wanted to raise 10 percent of the annual budgets, we never did. And I think we don't do it now. We were always struggling, as we are today, for an improved procedure, in an effort to get more money.

One of the things we used to say was that we never raised as much money as people were willing to give us. We raised only as much as our procedure would permit us to get. Whereas we are now moving toward a $40 million goal, $50 or $100 million are out there. It's a question of how to gear up to raise that amount without having costs so high that they are frowned on by the agencies that accredit fund-raising programs.

The *Chicago Defender* and the *Pittsburgh Courier* were two of the leading black newspapers. We had the support of both, but my column was appearing in the *Courier,* and it was the first paper publicly to support us. The black press generally carried the picture of Rockefeller at the first meeting of the UNCF at the Waldorf and gave it great coverage. Much of the white press did so also.

After my article suggesting a united fund appeared in the *Courier,* Ira Lewis, the editor, called me and said, "I think you have a good idea here, and if you're willing to do something about it, we'll put the *Courier* behind it." His offer encouraged me. Mrs. Robert Vann, the widow of the former owner of the *Courier,* was also most helpful. The paper backed the Fund, and they gave to it. They probably thought, in the early years, that most of the money would come from blacks. We never believed that it would; we wanted it to as much as possible, but the cost of fund raising necessary to tap only black sources, in terms of the organizational structure required to raise the requisite amount of money in small amounts, would have been phenomenal. This was not a question of color; it was a question of ability to give. In almost any general campaign, most of the money comes from a small group; then the base is broadened so that everybody feels a sense of participation in line with individual means and interest.

One idea which was relatively unpopular with the college presidents to begin with—they naturally wanted to safeguard contacts associated with their own institutions—was that they had to share their leadership. Whenever any city was chosen for a campaign, it was chosen because it was already identified in some way either with philanthropy or with southern colleges. Tuskegee had had a field agent named Robinson in Rochester, New York; as a result many Rochester people knew about Tuskegee Institute. This prior experience was a good door opener for the UNCF appeal. I became familiar with fund raising in quite a few cities where we conducted campaigns. The presidents of the member colleges would spend the required thirty days in their designated cities, forwarding to our office regular reports on the status of the fund raising in those places.

The Fund conducted a campaign in Pittsburgh, where the *Courier* was located. I chose Pittsburgh as the city in which I would campaign, for I felt that with the backing of the *Courier* and some of the leadership there, our message might bring a favorable response. I also knew that the Mellon family of Pittsburgh had contributed to Tuskegee Institute.

In the early years, Washington, D.C., was never a strong city for UNCF fund raising. Still, it was the nation's capital, the home of Howard University, which was in the Fund in the early days, and a magnet for UNCF graduates, and so it seemed to have excellent prospects.

In Atlanta, Georgia, of course, there was a whole cluster of colleges; nevertheless, in terms of the white community, it took us a long time to raise significant money there. There was an excellent response from the black community, thanks to such people as Benjamin Mays, president of Morehouse College, and others who were good arm twisters and who made the colleges do their share. Furthermore, the black public school personnel were among the strongest contributors in Atlanta. The reason may have been that many of them were graduates of Atlanta University and other local colleges and therefore understood the importance of our message. All of these things are based on personal contact—personal inflence in one form or another.

In New Orleans, both Dillard University and Xavier University were members of the Fund. It took a long time to bring the Catholics in the city along, but we finally did so. They are now among the strongest of our fund raisers.

In Nashville, Tennessee, we had Fisk University, and we thought we had a toehold in the university-type community. But Nashville has never been a strong community for the Fund and isn't now. It seemed logical, however, since Tom Jones was the head of Fisk and one of the members of the Planning Committee, to select Nashville as a city in which to campaign.

Boston, of course, had a long history of philanthropy on behalf of Tuskegee, Hampton, a number of the Atlanta colleges, and probably Fisk. At one time, Boston was considered the leader in American philanthropy. Of course, a lot of wealth was there too.

Bishop College was not located in Dallas in the days of our early campaigns, but Houston and Dallas were both noted for their wealth, and we had campaigns there. I started the campaign in Houston because Tuskegee trustee Jesse Jones was there. He was on the board of Tuskegee and he headed the Department of Commerce, so I felt that I could get leadership in Houston. And the black community was surprisingly generous in Houston. It made gifts larger than many we had gotten from individuals elsewhere.

I think Chicago was picked simply because it was one of the biggest metropolitan communities and because of people like Laird Bell, who had a history of participation in philanthropic causes. After an invitation from Mr. Rockefeller, he agreed to serve us in the campaign. Also, the Rosenwald Fund was located in Chicago. I think President Dent was designated to work there because of his standing with the Rosenwald Fund.

Detroit was rather interesting as a campaign city. I am not absolutely sure how we first chose Detroit, but one of the most effective people in those early years was Catherine Waddell. Her brother-in-law, William Gossett, was legal counsel and vice-president of the Ford Motor Company. In addition, we knew that Detroit was a community of great wealth.

When the UNCF started and John D. Rockefeller, Jr., took leadership interest in our efforts, he needed someone who could follow up for him, report back to him, and target his efforts. Lindsley Kimball was the person whom Mr. Rockefeller appointed to represent the Rockefeller Foundation in working with the UNCF. Kimball continued as a consultant for as long as Rockefeller lived. Kimball had been identified with the United Service Organization (USO), which looked after soldiers in World War II. Rockefeller had become acquainted with Kimball during the war and had been so impressed that he persuaded Kimball to give up his USO presidency and join Rockefeller's private staff.

On the basis of his experience heading the USO, Kimball was invited to appraise the UNCF and to suggest improvements. In studying the UNCF's efforts, Kimball had to keep in mind that prior to the organization of the Fund, the colleges were, in a sense, in competition with each other: they felt that every dollar *they* got was a dollar that might have gone to some other college. They kept things close to their chests, so to speak, and did not tell others what they were doing. They did not want to share the names of those who had donated to them in the past, although the same donors were probably giving to several different colleges. Each college assumed that to give too much information about itself would reduce giving to it alone.

Except in a few cases—such as Hampton and Tuskegee—until the founding of the UNCF, fund raising was a single college's effort on its own behalf, although schools that were church related might have joined with the churches. But when it came to approaching sources of wealth or people of wealth, the colleges had felt in competition with each other.

One of the amusing things that Kimball said about us after studying our efforts was that he thought we had made a good beginning, but some of the precautions which we had taken to protect ourselves reflected our mutual suspicion of each other. This comment shocked us all. We realized that we were dominated by noticeable selfishness.

It's still true today that a president feels a strong sense of loyalty to his or her own institution. In fact presidents are paid to feel it. But we gradually recognize that such loyalty did not necessarily bring the best results financially and that the more ways in which we could see our common purpose and cause as being bigger than those of any one institution, the better the job we could do of educating the public, which may not have known us as individual schools but which *did* realize the importance of the job that we, collectively, were doing.

We anticipated from the very beginning that we would make annual appeals for operating funds. We never raised enough money, but after having staged the annual drive for a number of years, we decided that we should have a capital campaign as well. Our idea was to seek a large sum of money that would be distributed at one time to improve the physical plants of the member colleges. We also felt that a larger goal, associated with a capital campaign, would help us in our annual appeal. Even though this would be a temporary goal with respect to capital funds, if people responded by giving a larger sum, perhaps they wouldn't subsequently revert to the smaller annual contributions that they had been making.

We had found in a few instances that we were not able to attract the big money people because we were not asking for enough money. We knew we weren't, but our dilemma was trying to harmonize that fact with the requirement that we had to carry along the leadership. I tried two or three times to get Mr. Rockefeller to agree to a larger goal, but he would not. He knew we needed it, but he wanted a campaign goal that he felt sure would succeed. Leadership does not like campaigns that fail.

The amount of money raised for a given cause does not necessarily reflect the importance of the cause. It reflects the willingness of people to give to it. Our ability to increase giving depended on our ability to educate the people of influence, who would approve the goal. They would not approve what they felt was not achievable. Fund raising was a constant struggle. We were continually trying to broaden the base, going into new communities where we hadn't been before. As the story was told and our literature saw wider and wider circulation, more and more people from whom we could get money were brought into the orbit of UNCF influence.

At one time, corporations felt that they could not give away stockholders' money. There was a big case in New Jersey in the early 1940s in which the courts decided that corporations *could* give away stockholders' money. More than that, the decision recognized that it was in the best interest of corporations to be identified with the general welfare of the community. Therefore, a corporation's philanthropy came to be regarded as an investment and not simply as a goodwill offering for a good cause. This was a timely ruling for the UNCF. We tried to sell the concept of giving as investment: America would benefit if it educated one-tenth of its population so that this segment could enter the ranks of the professional people whom the country needed. Primarily, of course, they would give needed services to their own communities, but they would also serve the nation as a whole. The possibilities of increased contributions by corporations was, to my mind, an incentive to press for this new source of funds. But we needed, as always, the support of our leadership.

John D. Rockefeller, Jr., invited a few people—about seven, I think—to be on an advisory board for the UNCF's annual appeal. I remember going to a meeting of that group, which included Winthrop Aldrich, and suggesting that we should have a capital campaign for $25 million.

As I told the group, I believed that this should be done as a means of raising the sights of potential donors. The Fund had constantly been made aware that we were not attracting the attention of the top people in the country whose influence as well as gifts could make a difference. We needed a capital campaign not only because the colleges had a serious need for expansion, renovation, or improvement of their physical plants, but also because a larger goal might capture the imagination of people such as Richard Mellon, Alfred P. Sloan, Harvey Firestone, Robert Wilson of Standard Oil of Indiana, or Bob Woodruff of Coca-Cola in Atlanta.

Lindsley Kimball argued against the twenty-five million dollar goal I proposed. He thought that the others wouldn't buy such a large figure; he therefore said what he took to be their opinion. But Aldrich said, "I don't see what's wrong with it." Kimball immediately changed his position. When he found that the other advisers didn't think a $25 million goal was such a bad idea, he helped us to put the whole thing together. He was tremendously helpful.

The UNCF thus launched its first capital campaign in 1950 with a goal of $25 million. Mr. Rockefeller made a lead, or initial gift, of $5 million. This reflected his philosophy that, in order for corporations or people of great wealth to take our campaign seriously, we had to have a lead gift that would allow us to say, "This gift is 20 percent of our goal." He may not have thought in percentages, but he knew that his gift would have a significant impact. He expressed his interest not only by approving the campaign and inviting others to give but by saying, "I'm giving $5 million and therefore we want you to come in as generously as possible."

As a part of this capital campaign, the decision was made that our potentially large contributors should themselves be educated about the colleges. Robert Woodruff lived in Atlanta and knew about the black colleges. Most of the other advisory board members had never seen a black college, yet we were asking for their endorsement of a $25 million appeal, and so we planned a visit for them.

In order not to take much time away from the board members' regular commitments, and since several of them owned planes, we decided to fly them to Atlanta, then to travel by train to Tuskegee, where they spent the night on the campus before flying back home. The Tuskegee students called the visit "Millionaire Day."

We wanted the visitors to appreciate the atmosphere and spirit of the colleges, but we also wanted them to see the physical plants. They flew into Atlanta from different points; the Firestones had a plane, as did the Chase Manhattan Bank. With a plane leaving from Pittsburgh, we could accommodate everybody who was going. John D. Rockefeller III was there. Devereux Josephs, head of New York Life Insurance Company, came. Richard Mellon and Thomas Morgan attended. Of course, Kimball was there, and Woodruff served as a kind of southern host for the group, since he lived in Atlanta and was also a trustee of Tuskegee Institute.

We arranged an intensive tour for them to see the highlights of the several colleges in Atlanta, moving our guests from one activity to another, so they could see what was going on and what the institution represented. The group traveled from Atlanta to Tuskegee on the West Point Railroad. We had the whole train—a couple of cars and an engine—and had the entire railroad tied up. All these important people were going to Tuskegee and would spend the night on the campus!

We gave them an intensive tour of Tuskegee, with a concert by the Tuskegee Choir, a visit to the School of Veterinary Medicine—with its new set of buildings and activities—and the Infantile Paralysis Hospital, and other activities.

The trip really paid off. It made the visiting dignitaries permanent friends of the cause of black higher education. They saw what Tuskegee and the Atlanta group of colleges stood for, and they accepted what they saw as more or less typical of all UNCF colleges. They now had a new understanding. As a result they were able not only to give with pride but to sponsor intelligently. They could, from their own firsthand exposure, endorse this program of service to black youth in speaking to their friends.

Once the Supreme Court decision on school desegregation had been rendered in 1954, many people assumed that the black colleges were now temporary and only needed a little help to sustain them until they went out of business.

We had to change that point of view and let the public know we couldn't very well go out of business. The services the colleges had rendered over the years were so great that to eliminate them would be harmful to black youth. Furthermore, the schools did not want to fade away. They wanted to join the mainstream of academic life and to increase their resources so that eventually they would open doors to all qualified people. We felt that for at least the next twenty-five years, their services would benefit principally black youth. And they still do, even in these thirty-some years after the Supreme Court issued its decision.

I certainly think that the Supreme Court rendered a good ruling, although the court's admonition to move "with all deliberate speed" tended to have the opposite effect of what had been anticipated. The phrase "with all deliberate speed" gave those who saw political benefits to opposing integration a chance to develop that opposition and to organize it. Therefore, I think the decision was more placatory than it had to be. On the other hand, I think an overnight change would have been impossible, and I doubt seriously that it would have been desirable for either whites or blacks.

Some communities were faced with school integration all of a sudden, and the ruling aroused hate and opposition instead of leading to a timetable of acceptance. I think the Supreme Court meant to say, "You cannot do this overnight. But with deliberate speed, we hope you will plan the change so that it can be effected with the least amount of trauma."

The people who represented the negative atittude, that is, the vocal minority, not only did their best to frustrate integration but also intimidated white people of goodwill who might have gone along with the justice of the ruling but who at the time could not come out and speak their minds. Some of them did, but many more whites would have accepted the decision and gone along with it had favorable pronouncements been made. When the cry of nullification and interposition began, as it did in the state of Virginia, a real stumbling block had been erected.

I think that there has never been a time—certainly not in my lifetime—when blacks believed that segregation would be permanent. The struggle just before the Supreme Court's decision had been focused on equality of opportunity and not on integration per se. It was a step-by-step process. But there was always the feeling that the very pressure to maintain segregation would be self-destructive. The only question was when it would break down the inequities of the system.

The forerunners of integration were cases for equal opportunity, that is, cases that highlighted the necessity of providing "equality" in southern schools first at the graduate and professional level and later at the undergraduate level. First the states were challenged to provide fellowships or scholarships for black students to go out of state when they were denied educational opportunities available to white students within the state. The next challenge concerned the inadequacy of fellowships for study. In sequence came the Herman Sweatt case in Texas and the Lloyd Gaines case in Missouri; then the University of Maryland had to open its door. These rulings preceded the U.S. Supreme Court's finding that segregation per se was unconstitutional.

Immediately after the Supreme Court's decision, many people thought, "All right, we helped you black colleges out, but now this Court decision takes care of everything. All you have to do is close the black colleges and the black youth can attend the white colleges." We knew that this outcome would not be immediate for two reasons: many of the black youngsters were not prepared to meet the competition, nor did they have the money. The places in which blacks would normally have had the most geographical accessibility to white institutions were, initially, those that were the most hostile to them. Nonetheless, while the prospect of integration was shocking to the white South—more so than to the rest of the nation—I think much of the white leadership in the South decided that if it became the law of the land, compliance would be obligatory.

While we were waiting for integretion to happen, the immediate need was for greatly improved educational opportunity under the existing segregated system. I can remember attending a conference at Howard University in the late 1940s in which the effort was targeted in that direction, although most people believed that the tide was turning.

As we told the story of what the UNCF schools were doing—describing the problems that had to be faced in order to provide opportunities at an acceptable level—people of goodwill and intelligence were not deterred in contributing to the Fund. Some were, but by the same token, some wanted to see black people remain segregated anyway. We never asked them whether they gave because they wanted us segregated or whether they accepted our philosophy.

One of the problems we confronted when we first started was that if the Fund called on somebody who was already giving to two or three of our colleges, we might be told, "Someone from one of your member colleges was just here yesterday, and now you're asking me for money in behalf of that same college through the College Fund. Which do you want us to do?"

Frederick D. Patterson narrating United Negro College Fund presentation during the third capital campaign, late 1970s.

We needed a policy that regulated joint solicitations made for the UNCF and solicitations made by individual colleges on their own behalf. The joint solicitation policy had certain implications for each of the member colleges. Even today it is frequently necessary to explain to new presidents who come into the Fund full of enthusiasm and dedication to their own institutions that they have a responsibility not to destroy or lessen the impact of our joint appeal.

We had to say to the colleges: "If UNCF is going to raise money for current expense, your individual college may not do so during the UNCF annual campaign period. If you do, you'll only confuse the donor. If you go to the donor ahead of the College Fund, he may give you five dollars or five thousand dollars, whereas he would give the College Fund a hundred thousand dollars. The only reason for you to have membership in the College Fund is that you believe you can do better as a member than you can by yourself. You're not bound. You come to us. You ask for membership. You get it. You can leave anytime you feel that membership in the Fund is not as valuable to you as your efforts outside the Fund." (We've had one or two who left.) "But if you stay in the Fund, you have certain obligations which you must respect. If you have a church affiliation, we don't interfere. But if you're going to ask the general public for money, especially when the group's annual appeal is under way, you are in violation of the Fund's solicitation policy."

In the early years, we had to call on some of the college presidents we knew were violating the policy and ask them to cease. Calling on Mrs. Bethune was hard. She was a person of great stature, but we didn't go to anyone about infractions of the solicitation policy unless we knew they were violating the policy. And we got results. We knew our members wanted to be in the Fund, so we didn't go to them demanding anything. We did remind them that if the violations continued, they might lose their membership, but we never went further.

We do not interfere with colleges' going to foundations, because foundations do not, as a rule, give to general support or to operating funds; they give for specific purposes. We knew we couldn't stop that, nor did we want to. We wanted the colleges to have as much money as they could get without confusing the donors.

The UNCF has been endorsed by every U.S. president since its founding. The endorsement of the president of the United States indicates that a cause is of general importance to the nation. And we are seeking such a declaration. We know that the president has little time to devote to the organization, but we also know that the president's endorsement tends to make governmental departments receptive to special appeals. More important, on the national scene, a presidential endorsement is significant because chief executives do not lend themselves to many causes. The American National Red Cross, a campaign for youth, and one or two other really significant endeavors are virtually the only causes to which presi-

Christopher Edley, executive director, United Negro College Fund, and Dr. Patterson at the fortieth anniversary celebration, UNCF headquarters, New York City, 1983.

dents, while in office, will lend their names. Although presidents may come into office with certain relationships that they continue to favor, generally speaking, chief executives will not endorse a program which is not in the interest of the general welfare.

Mr. Kennedy went further than most presidents do. He actually contacted the Ford Foundation to ask for a substantial gift to our second capital campaign and had a kick-off meeting, so to speak, at the White House. Kennedy came to the UNCF for our endorsement when he was running for president, spoke for us, and dedicated the proceeds from his book *Profiles in Courage* to the Fund. He was already friendly before he took office as president; therefore, we anticipated and were delighted to have his endorsement of the second UNCF capital campaign.

There was one man who, from political motives, had earlier pledged about $300,000 to the UNCF. He wanted President Kennedy to know who he was, and after the assassination, we never heard from him.

In another instance, we had been unsuccessful in eliciting support from the Ford Foundation, yet when Kennedy spoke on our behalf, the foundation was offended. Henry Heald had been on the Phelps Stokes Fund board with me when he was president of New York University, so I had had some limited contact with him before he went to the Ford Foundation. President Kennedy subsequently tried to persuade Ford to contribute to our campaign. When I went to see Heald, I didn't expect him to reproach me as he did.

He said, "You didn't have to hit us over the head with the president of the United States." I said, "We didn't go to Kennedy to get him to speak to you. Kennedy came to you on his own initiative. We went to him because we felt this was a cause of national interest and that no one could express that fact to the nation more clearly than the president." Not long after my visit, the Ford Foundation gave $15 million to the black colleges, part to the UNCF and part to individual colleges in the Fund!

I grew up in Texas, and when I was fund raising for the Fund there, I capitalized on the fact as much as I could. I picked Houston as a campaign city partly because I had known it as a child. It is only forty-five miles from Prairie View State College, with which I had a lifelong affiliation. But in addition Jesse Jones, who, as I've said, had been secretary of commerce and head of the Reconstruction Finance Corporation, had his headquarters in Houston, and he was regarded as "Mr. Houston." Jones had brought to the Lone Star State everything that the government had, or at least every-thing of value that he could move to Houston.

Before the Fund was formed, I had gone to see Jones at the Reconstruc-tion Finance Corporation to invite him to come on the Board of Trustees at Tuskegee Institute. He said, "I'll come on the board, but I'm not going to attend any meetings." Ordinarily, one would say, "If you're not interested enough to attend meetings, thanks but no thanks." In this case, however, I felt that he had the stature and influence that we needed, whether or not he attended meetings. So I asked him to come on the Tuskegee board anyway. He was already a member when I decided to visit Houston for the UNCF campaign. I approached him again. True to form, he said, "I won't head a campaign, but I'll help you."

Blacks in Houston already knew about the UNCF schools because we had several colleges in Texas. But some of the whites had never even heard of the black schools. They responded, however, to an invitation from Jesse Jones, and we gradually educated them.

Jesse Jones had top standing with all the millionaires in Houston, and there were more than a few of them. Jones would write them little notes. I'd go out with the note to solicit, and the recipient would write a check for a thousand dollars. I'd take the check back, and Jones would write another note to someone else. Finally, after I had made several such trips, he leaned back in his chair and laughed. "Well, this is going to cost me plenty, but I'm having lots of fun." He knew that the same people were going to come back to him with their projects. This case illustrates the person-to-person relationship in fund raising.

I found among the black leadership in Houston a surprising sense of commitment and spirit of generosity. People were willing to give five hundred or a thousand dollars, even back in those days. And the churches were outstanding in their support as well.

Mrs. Mary McLeod Bethune was a very staunch supporter of the Fund. It is hard to describe her role. When she first joined the Fund, her school, Bethune-Cookman, did not have accreditation and therefore was not qualified for membership. But she brought it in anyway! It was subsequently accredited.

Mrs. Bethune had a dynamic personality, drive, and a willingness to see herself as epitomizing the capabilities of the black woman. She never settled for less because of race; she knew what she wanted, and she went after it. She managed to reach anybody she sought out. She was not inundated with money, but she certainly got excellent support.

Mrs. Bethune was a great person on a platform. Whenever we needed someone to inspire an audience and she had the time, she was available. She was very effective that way. I remember one night she came to Tuskegee Institute for our opening meeting of the year's UNCF drive. We always tried to do things right on time at Tuskegee. The chapel had a little anteroom where we always assembled five minutes early, and on the stroke of seven we walked in.

The short time in the anteroom was given to small talk of one sort or another. Mrs. Bethune spoke of two of her friends who were also in public life; one was a woman named Nanny Burroughs who ran a home for girls in Washington, D.C. The other was Charlotte Hawkins Brown, who headed Palmer Memorial Institute, a private secondary school in Sedalia, North Carolina. Mrs. Bethune said to one or two people in the anteroom, "You know Nanny Burroughs and Charlotte Hawkins say to me, 'Mary, you're just a fool. You don't do nothing but get up before an audience and talk about yourself.' And I said, 'Yes, I talk about myself, and people come to hear me talk about myself!'"

Her words were true. She told her story, how she founded her school at a time when she had holes in the soles of her shoes, how she walked great distances to see people and begged and wouldn't take no for an answer. That was her story, and it was inspiring, believe me. She's one of the most inspiring people I have ever heard. She was a good politician. She and Dr. Moton had the same kind of following, but she was really more dynamic. I don't think she ever regarded herself as capable of being only a college president. She assumed that she was a person of national stature, and that's the way she carried herself. Mrs. Bethune was a very good friend of Mrs. Roosevelt. They frequently visited one another.

I have had a little commercial venture of my own that has been very meaningful for me and my family. As I was leaving Alabama to settle in New York, I became involved in the outdoor advertising business. After starting almost accidentally in Tuskegee, I eventually found myself with some forty-two boards in eighteen different cities. The sign business had started with my purchase of a piece of property in Alabama. I felt (as I always have) that blacks ought to engage in business more often, and so I bought a little building near Tuskegee Institute on the Montgomery Highway. It housed a grocery store when I bought it with borrowed money. Since that time, it has been a dog-and-cat hospital, a funeral home, and almost anything else you could put in a small building.

When I left Tuskegee to move to New York, the building was rented to one of the wealthiest blacks in Alabama, A. G. Gaston. Gaston had fifteen funeral homes and wanted to use this building for another. He thought that as president of Tuskegee, I could help him get the contract from the Veterans Hospital, which had some two thousand or more veterans. I wasn't aware of his interest in this particular funeral business, but soon after the business opened, I moved to New York, and Gaston knew I couldn't help him. I had hardly reached New York when he canceled his lease. He canceled it properly (there was a cancellation provision with which he complied), but he left me with an empty building and less income than I had anticipated.

When I took the Phelps Stokes job, it was in what is known as the Architects Building in New York City, one block from Grand Central Station. That building housed displays of trades such as roofing and plumbing. I was trying to decide what I was going to do with my building in Tuskegee, when these displays gave me the idea of selling advertising space on an outside wall.

With Tuskegee Institute and the Veterans Hospital constituting one of the largest concentrations of black money around, why not use the building for displays for businesses in Montgomery, forty miles west, and Columbus, Georgia, forty miles east?

As soon as I had a chance to return to Alabama, I went to some of the establishments with which Tuskegee had done business. They said, "You are forty miles away. A display forty miles away, if it isn't kept up, is bad advertising. But we like your idea of putting billboards on the outside of this property."

Outdoor advertising had not yet grown into the business that it is today. Many people who have driven the highways of this country in this period remember landscape that was not cluttered with signs, only an occasional series of eye-catching signs advertising Burma Shave or various approaching roadside pecan and taffy stands. Perhaps there was an occasional ad for Standard Oil or Texaco but advertising was not the competitive business that it is today. I thought I would try the display idea to see whether I could find a way to make the building pay for itself.

I was able to rent the display space on the building locally, and I put nine signs out along the highway. With the income, I recovered all the money I had lost in the contract when the funeral director canceled. This turn of events made me think, "If this thing is this good in Tuskegee, the market in Atlanta and everywhere else ought to be even better." Since I had formerly been president of the National Business League, I knew most of the savings-and-loan people or bankers, and they all accommodated me by taking advertising.

At the start I paid rent to the persons who let me build a sign on their property. Then I'd get a contract from someone who wanted to rent the space, and I would arrange to borrow the money to put up the sign. When the signboard had been erected, I'd hire a local sign painter to paint the sign. The only real maintenance the business required was telephone calls and an occasional visit. My enterprise grew, and it's one of the easiest businesses I have ever known.

Earlier I had had a lot of traveling to do. Many of my contacts when I rented signs were incidental to my visits to Atlanta or Dallas or Memphis or wherever. Some outdoor advertising signs are still owned in the way I've just described; others are owned by major corporations, such as Foster and Kleiser. Most of my customers were black, although I had one or two whites. The big money, however, is in the major companies. A big ad overhanging a super highway may net as much as ten thousand dollars a month.

I committed at least two blunders during my years at Tuskegee. They still stand out in my mind. One which I'll always regret is that the Rosenwald Fund when it went out of existence held a final meeting which I didn't attend. The Fund had been very helpful to Tuskegee and to me. For some reason, I just did not think that my presence was important. Symbolically it was important, however, as I realized only afterward.

As a result of my absence, I made a terrible enemy of the president of the Rosenwald Fund, Edwin Embree. He didn't say anything, but he acted offended. After all, Embree's leadership had brought the Rosenwald Fund trustees to Tuskegee when we wanted the Fund to lend us the money to buy and build Moton Field. When we started the UNCF, he was in the position to give us twenty-five thousand dollars to match our grant from the General Education Board. There was no doubt that the Rosenwald Fund had made an impact not only on Tuskegee but on southern education in general. It was foolish of me to have been insensitive to the importance of being present on that occasion.

There was another important ceremony that I should have attended and I didn't. That was John Hope's funeral in Atlanta. My wife went; he had been a good friend of Dr. Moton's—much better than I knew. Moreover, Hope's role in furthering higher education for blacks deserved any kind of recognition that could have been given. And as president of Tuskegee, my attendance would have been symbolically important.

Back in the 1940s, I was a postgraduate student at Stanford University. Although I had been president of Tuskegee Institute for ten years, my training had all been more or less scientific, in veterinary medicine and bacteriology. I had had some teaching experience in Virginia, but it added little in the way of training as a professional educator. I thought that the chance to go to Stanford and study under W. H. Cowley, former president of Hamilton College and professor of higher education at Stanford, would be a good experience. It turned out to be just that. While I was there, I was asked whether I was willing to be considered for the presidency of Hampton Institute. Hampton had been in some state of change, and I promptly turned the offer down. I was also approached regarding a job at a different kind of institution, the Phelps Stokes Fund.

Channing Tobias, with whom I had served on the Board of Trustees of the Phelps Stokes Fund, approached me after he had been director at Phelps Stokes for some time. He wanted me to be his successor. He had spent his career in the YMCA and had gone to the Phelps Stokes Fund after he retired. Tobias and I had a pleasant association. Once when I met him by chance while I was traveling, I shared my thoughts about starting the UNCF, and Tobias subsequently became one of the incorporators of the UNCF. In the late 1940s when he first mentioned the idea of my going to the Phelps Stokes Fund I gave it little consideration.

But my experience at Stanford, studying some of the features of college administration, led me to realize I had already stayed at Tuskegee as president as long as or longer than the average college president in the country as a whole. Five to seven years was considered a normal tenure for college presidents, and I had been at Tuskegee far longer. Frequently, black college presidents died in office, or they stayed on as long as they could, retired, and lived with a modest retirement allowance. They did not behave as they do now, retiring at a younger age and finding opportunities in government or even business. I was moving toward my eighteenth year as president. Having assumed the presidency at the age of thirty-four, I still had about twelve or maybe fifteen years of work to do before reaching retirement. The longer I stayed at Tuskegee, though, the less appealing the jobs that would be offered me, and some jobs would not be offered because I would be too old. I decided that a change would be a good idea.

There were relatively few openings for a black person like me at that time. Since I had high regard for the work of the Phelps Stokes Fund, I decided, in 1953, after some degree of persuasion, that I would accept the offer to head it. Many thought it unusual for me to consider leaving Tuskegee's presidency, particularly since the position was regarded as one of the top jobs in the country available to black leadership. Some people found it inconceivable that I would leave Tuskegee unless I had gotten into some difficulty there. In fact, some of my former colleagues who were no longer at Tuskegee even made a trip to Alabama to find out what I had done that would make it necessary for me to leave!

Being president of Tuskegee was the greatest experience of my life. Although I had loved veterinary medicine and had enjoyed practicing and teaching, I realized in 1935 that the presidency of Tuskegee Institute was a larger opportunity—particularly in an educational institution with Tuskegee's reputation—for service to humanity. I can't imagine that anyone the least bit competent would have turned down the job.

When I first went to Alabama, I had no idea that I would do anything but run the little veterinary hospital and teach agricultural students. I didn't even have the School of Veterinary Medicine in mind. These developments emerged from the job as I tried to discover the future potential of Tuskegee Institute. In 1953, however, the time seemed right for a change.

When I announced that I was leaving Tuskegee Institute, the trustees asked me to recommend a successor. I had worked with Luther Foster and felt that he was better prepared than I to administer some of the programs I had started. I was an idea person and a hard driver, and people followed my leadership, but he was better at organizing than I.

One of the people who wanted to succeed me as president was a person who was considered vindictive. Faculty members came to me saying, "He's no good for the job. He wants to cow people. Either you do it the way he wants to do it, or you're an enemy for life." Someone on whom I relied heavily was the head of the Carver Foundation. He came with the same message: "You have built a strong morale here. If this other person takes the presidency it's going to destroy the morale, because people do not believe that he's able; they do not have confidence in him." I felt the same way. The person of whom he was speaking practically begged me for the position. We had worked together closely, and it was hard for me to say no, but I felt that my loyalty should be first to the institution. I had the confidence of Basil O'Connor, the chairman of the Board of Trustees, when I recommended Luther Foster. In spite of the fact that others were vying for the position, O'Connor listened to me.

Foster did a good job, especially with the trustees. For example, when I was heading Tuskegee, trustee meetings lasted for about two hours: I made a report, and the business manager reported on finances. The rest of the time the trustees were there, we put on special programs for them. Both Booker Washington and Dr. Moton were such powerful people in their own right that they didn't have to ask the trustees to do much work. Booker Washington and Dr. Moton did things themselves; they had relationships even with presidents of the United States. I did not have those relationships; nonetheless, the legacy of the administrations of Washington and Moton sometimes left me feeling that I had too much power. The trustees left too much to me and did not, by the same token, discharge as much responsibility as they could. I was not gifted enough to involve them more effectively.

On the other hand, Dr. Foster was able to give the trustees a more effective role. He made them better organized as a group; he had them do things; he arranged for effective committee work. He involved them more in doing work most of which I had done myself. Yet the only time the trustees were ever unhappy with me was when we overspent the budget and ran short of money.

The role of the college trustee has evolved. I think that now the role is more highly defined. There's an old expression: "Give, Get, or Git." Trustees are expected to give money or get money. There is a committee structure for the board—buildings and grounds, student selection, and so forth. Then there are faculty-board committees, so that faculty people meet with trustees about certain specific things. These provisions didn't exist when I was president. Now everybody concerned about institutional affairs, even students, meets with trustees. We were moving in this direction when I left Tuskegee. The student strike helped us to realize that we had to do so promptly.

Foster, however, brought this realization to fruition and even made the top administration of the college better organized than I did. These were his areas of strength.

In effect, I was able to pick my successor, as Dr. Moton had. Except for

Booker Washington, Luther Foster held the position longer than anyone else. He was president for twenty-seven years.

My wife was the last Moton to leave Tuskegee. She had three sisters and two brothers, all of whom had been born at Hampton, except for Jennie, the baby of the family. Allen was an adventurous type who died after we moved to New York. Bob (Robert Moton, Jr.) was the gentlemanly type and did well in business. He graduated from Tuskegee, then worked in the school's business office. He subsequently earned his master's degree in business at Columbia University and went into the investment field, becoming a pretty good salesperson in Atlanta. He died recently. Kitty's sister, Charlotte, went to college at Sargeant, majoring in physical education; then she taught dance at Hampton and worked for Tuskegee, where she supervised our commercial dietetics interns for a short period of time. Later she was appointed by President Lyndon Johnson to be deputy assistant secretary of state for public relations. She kept this position until illness forced her to resign. By the time we left Alabama, Jennie was married and teaching in Indianapolis. She has a daughter who has finished at the university and is now teaching. Robert III has two boys.

My son, Fred, was twelve years old at the time we moved to New York. He had an early interest in foreign languages and studied Finnish and German extensively in the United States and in Europe, where he was a translator and taught English. He completed his B.A. in cultural and intellectual history and philosophy at Empire State College of the State University of New York. Fred is presently a college instructor in criminology and specializes in criminal case research and analysis.

Fred's cousins, the other descendants of the children of William and Mamie Patterson, are several, as attested by the large numbers at our family reunions at Capahosic. I have already mentioned Lucille's son, Almore, who attended Tuskegee and met his wife, Marie, there. They lived in Washington, D.C. Almore become finance officer at Howard University and retired as an official of the District of Columbia. Almore's sister, Araminta, also lived in the Washington area, as did his other sister, Thelma Dale Perkins, who became an officer of the Ciba-Geigy Company.

My brother, James, has three children, James, Wilhelmina (named for Bessie), and Lorenzo. My brother, John, also had a son named James, who lives in Winston-Salem, North Carolina, and a daughter, Patricia Brown, of Richmond, Virginia.

I was sad to leave Tuskegee—the school, the people, and the town—

even though I was enthusiastic about my new position as head of the Phelps Stokes Fund. At my parting address to the Tuskegee faculty, some of whom I had known since my arrival on the campus in 1928, I cannot say whether the tears I shed were from joy or sorrow.

6 The Phelps Stokes Fund

The Phelps Stokes Fund was started in 1911 with a gift from Caroline Phelps Stokes. Under its first director, Thomas Jesse Jones, a Welsh sociologist, it focused on African education, black American and Native American education, and housing in New York. Jones had been involved in a 1917 study of the education of black children in the South which was partly financed by the federal government and involved several researchers in addition to Jones. The study was outstanding because, for the first time, it showed that the colleges and universities for black youth were hardly good high schools. They were poorly financed and were therefore inadequately operated. The implication was that any group or individuals interested in the education of black youth would have to know that these schools were not worthy of being called institutions of higher education. This criticism, of course, started a revolutionary process that involved rethinking the structure and the quality of these institutions. Although nothing happened overnight, the changes that did take place were, in part, direct reactions to the critical comments of the 1917 study of the Phelps Stokes Fund.

I knew about that study when I went to Tuskegee in the fall of 1928. And while I was at Tuskegee, it was not infrequent that Thomas Jesse Jones, as director of Phelps Stokes, made trips into the South, almost always including Tuskegee Institute on his itinerary, because of the leadership that Booker Washington had given. Washington had improved not only education at the advanced level but also primary and secondary education.

Washington's successor, Dr. Moton, had the same interests and was a member of the Phelps Stokes board. In fact, one of the restricted funds of the Phelps Stokes Fund bore Dr. Moton's name.

I had heard of Phelps Stokes throughout my tenure in Alabama. But as many as ten years elapsed after Dr. Moton's retirement in 1935 before I was invited to succeed him on the Phelps Stokes board. Mr first assignment on the board broadened my horizons by taking me to Africa.

In 1945, Mrs. Patterson and I went abroad. The extended tour was jointly funded by the Tuskegee trustee board—for the honeymoon that had been cut short ten years earlier—and by the Phelps Stokes Fund, which wanted me to visit Liberia and to evaluate an educational program there. The Fund was concerned about the Booker Washington Institute, a school that Olivia Phelps Stokes had established in Kakata, a small village in the Liberian countryside. The PSF believed that the time had come when the Liberian government should exercise greater control of the school and commit greater resources to its operation. The Booker Washington Institute, designed by Tuskegee's R. R. Taylor, was an attempt to create an institute like Tuskegee in Africa. My purpose was to examine in particular the structure of the board of trustees at the Institute, a group dominated by individuals put there by the PSF.

The European phase of the trip was pleasant and purposeful. My wife had traveled quite a bit with her family before we were married and had made several trips abroad. She is very knowledgeable about art, and we went to museums and galleries, which meant more to her than they did to me. Still, I enjoyed seeing *The Last Supper* in Milan, and the statues and cathedrals of Italy and France, particularly the Reims Cathedral, where French kings were coronated.

The working part of the European tour involved trips to the Scandinavian countries, which, I had heard, did a lot for underprivileged people. I wanted to see what they were doing. I guess I was, in part, trying to retrace some of the early paths of Booker Washington, who had been concerned to learn how poor Welshmen and other financially unfortunate people were being treated. I didn't go to Wales, but I kept Washington in mind in the countries that I did visit. What slums did they have? What happened to young unmarried women who had children? I was curious about the extent to which government exercised responsibility for the disadvantaged. On my visit, I found that the poor were well housed, looked well, and seemed to be reasonably well cared for. In Sweden and Denmark I conferred with government officials. In these countries in particular I saw for myself what could be done. I didn't see any slums of the sort that you see in the United States. All people deserve to have decent homes in which to live. And I suppose the low-cash-cost homes in Macon County that I encouraged reflect my belief in this regard. We must continue to search for ways to make decent housing and health care universally available.

England and France stood in some contrast to the Scandinavian countries. I saw more of the capitalist attitude in these places. I received the impression that people suffered more as a result of poverty in England than in Scandinavia.

The second part of my trip was in Africa. Although the University of Liberia, the largest school, was chiefly liberal arts oriented, at the Booker Washington Institute I found some elements of agricultural and trades education. The school did not begin to fill the educational needs, but at least the verbal commitment was there. I found that the amount of money which the PSF was putting into the school was far from adequate. As a result of my report to the PSF, it was decided that both the control and more of the financing should come from the government of Liberia.

Liberia was created by black Americans who later became known as Americo-Liberians. Because of the PSF's interest, I was asked several times to appraise the educational opportunities there. In fact, my involvement was more or less continuous; I visited Liberia three or four times a year for many years.

When I became head of the PSF in 1953, my first African assignment came, however, not from the Fund but from the World Bank/International Bank Commission to Nigeria. In fact, the invitation was addressed to me as if I were still president of Tuskegee Institute. The Commission had been charged with evaluating the resources of Nigeria. My role was to study the educational programs and the organizational structure of advanced education.

It wasn't difficult at all for me to use the knowledge I had gained at Tuskegee because Tuskegee's philosophy had encompassed "education for life." Tuskegee was not considered a highly sophisticated college or university. Until that time it had been principally a trade and agricultural school. It was very much concerned with bettering primitive conditions in the South, particularly those involving sharecropping low-income black people.

The South had largely a plantation economy, and very few blacks were wealthy enough to own plantations. Some of the changes which we were trying to bring about through education in the South thus seemed to have an important bearing on the situation in Africa at the end of the colonials' regime.

The African people were exploited and received very little life-related education. The top jobs in government civil service were all given to Europeans from the colonizing country. Educated Africans—for the most part graduates of Oxford, Cambridge, and other institutions of higher learning—could aspire only to civil service jobs of minor rank.

I saw the need to revise this type of education, which led to white-collar jobs without the necessary undergirding substance. Far too little was being done, even by the white colonialists, to alter the basic socioeconomic structure. The Commission study was concerned with the transfer of control from the colonial powers to the indigenous people and with assessing the raw human resources of Nigeria: How well are the people equipped to do anything about their condition? What kinds of education would be needed so that the scientists of the future would be African—to change the picture from a society of relief to one of productive involvement in modifying raw materials?

Nigeria was under the administration of the governor, and the governor was an Englishman. As a matter of fact, throughout the whole of Nigeria, the officials were whites from the colonizing country, and they were running everything. It is true that colonialists were beginning to develop assistantships of one sort or another, but mainly whites were in control. We found far too few Africans prepared to undertake the new roles that independence required. American education was not as well known as British, and some of the educated Africans looked with disdain on American training. I think African leadership was just beginning to realize how unprepared the educated Africans were to take over. For the most part, African leaders were looking for guidance.

It was a thrilling experience for me as a black person to be in Africa. As a matter of fact, my prejudice against white people surfaced visibly. I resented the colonials so much that I wanted to do everything I could to help blacks prepare themselves for the eventual assumption of control and power. I did not like to see white Americans coming over and running things. I'm afraid I was unwise in some of my attitudes toward white American leadership. I thought that black Americans should exercise a more prominent role. Of course, they have increasingly done so, but even now much of the American leadership in Africa through the Peace Corps and other programs, such as Operation Crossroads Africa, is white. Nevertheless, overall I was really delighted to find that even under the colonial regimes, the colonials could not avoid training Africans in some technical fields to do things like run the trains as conductors and engineers. In this respect, Africans were doing more than blacks were doing in the United States because they had more opportunities.

It was important to look at Africans not as they were but as they could be if they came into responsible leadership. That perspective was thrilling. Of course, the quality of the African mind was one of the things I learned to appreciate more. Blacks have been downplayed everywhere in the world. Some of the Africans I met were brilliant. The problem lay in the quality of their exposure, not in the quality of their minds. Africans have a great past and are people of great promise.

On one excursion in Africa, I went with a group to visit Dr. Albert Schweitzer in the little African village of Lamborene in Gabon. Schweitzer was already recognized as a great man, but the trip was not as exciting as I had expected. As we traveled to his camp, we were met by some of his white assistants, women. They came in their white coats and boots, and we were rowed up the river in a great long canoe that had been cut out of a log—the primitive form of transportation. But while we were being rowed, an African came along in a boat with an outboard motor and passed us! I thought, "Schweitzer's trying to hold back progress in Africa. He's not trying to promote it."

We had a chance to meet Schweitzer and to tour his facilities, including the compound where the sick stayed. As a veterinarian and bacteriologist, I was genuinely disturbed to see flies swarming all over the mouths and faces of people who were sick. Sanitation was inadequate, and the camp was really not what I had expected. We stayed overnight and I remember hearing a sound all night which, though at first I thought was human, turned out to be a singing bird. Its cry was distinctive and, combined with my observations during the day, made the visit memorable, if less than enlightening.

My work with Phelps Stokes involved me with a number of agencies, among them the African Science Board of the National Academy of Sciencs, which organized a field trip to Nigeria and Ghana for scientists from America and from the two African countries. Ours were not extensive visits, and our observations were limited. Nonetheless the African potential was always clear. The developments taking place in the urban areas contrasted greatly with the primitive conditions of the rural areas: only an elite class was being trained, and the number of people involved in educational programs was tiny, considering the magnitude of the problems which the training was designed to address.

In Nigeria, for example, the question was whether training a few doctors at the highest level was more important than training many more medical assistants. Though assistants would be much less sophisticated, they could be placed all around the country to manage small health stations. The country could never have found enough fully trained doctors to do this job. The same was true of nursing: we found the health needs greatly exceeded the trained people available.

Our study groups had to address reality; there was always a shortage of money. When I served on these various commissions, the colonial governments were beginning to put more money into the different countries. By so doing, they could gradually move out and leave the African people in charge. But the amounts of money they spent for this purpose were totally inadequate, given the size of the job to be done. I guess the problem is not too difficult to understand in the United States.

At the end of the colonial era, Nigeria, for example, was obliged to decide not only how many of which health care officials to train but also where the training should be given. Most of it, of course, had been given outside the African countries, but not everybody could be sent to schools outside of Africa.

Another set of questions emerged concerning the role of the United States in meeting the training needs of the African countries: what people could be brought to the United States for instruction, and in what areas should they be taught? There were a few government-underwritten projects in which black American colleges participated. Tuskegee Institute—having been so long identified with the Phelps Stokes Fund, Liberia, and the Booker Washington Institute at Kakata—was naturally one of the schools frequently asked to help in African educational development. Tuskegee sent commissions to Africa to undertake training projects, mainly in the fields of primary education, social work, and agriculture. Tuskegee as well as Prairie View and West Virginia State College sent faculty to spend time in Liberia working on these programs. I was decorated Knight Commander of the Liberian Republic by the commissioner of education, but I think the award was made in appreciation of the work which the Phelps Stokes Fund had done over the years. In addition, I had worked in the United States to win recognition for visiting Liberian president William Tubman, and I was partly responsible for the honorary degrees he received from a number of black U.S. colleges, particularly Tuskegee.

In Liberia I had had pleasant relations with President Tubman and officers of government administration as well as with school officials at the University of Liberia, the Booker Washington Institute, and Cuttington College. It distressed me greatly to learn that many persons, official and otherwise, had been killed in the takeover by the present Liberian administration. They included the minister of agriculture, James Phillips, a graduate of Tuskegee University and a personal acquaintance of mine. He was the son of Anna Cooper, a former dean of the University of Liberia, in whose home I had lived during many official visits to Liberia.

Over the years I came to feel greatly disappointed with my work in Liberia. The Liberian people, whom I intended to help, would not follow up when I wasn't there. They would come to meetings and do a lot of big talk, but when I left, they went about their business, doing something else.

The Liberian government had very little money and was not looking for places to spend it; it was looking for places to get money. The white U.S. volunteer groups were well funded and tended to denigrate the work of the Phelps Stokes Fund. Since they had money to spend, the president listened to them and not to us. We were not treated discourteously, but we were more or less ignored.

My African travels also took me to Ethiopia, where I learned that, when the Italian military had overthrown the government of Haile Selassie, many of the ablest people had been killed. Human destruction of indigenous talent was a deliberate technique of conquest. Despite this holocaust, I met many outstanding Ethiopians struggling to rebuild their country.

The fiftieth anniversary of the Phelps Stokes Fund, in 1961, was celebrated with a trip by the trustees to West Africa, where much of Phelps Stokes's interest had been directed for many years. The trip was made possible by Lansdell Christy, a Phelps Stokes trustee, whose corporation had iron ore mining interests in Liberia. A highlight of this trip was an audience with President Kwame Nkrumah of Ghana, who greeted our group and expressed gratitude to Phelps Stokes for the financial help given him during his student years at Lincoln University in Pennsylvania. Nkrumah said that many Africans engaged in professional careers had been educated in the United States and that many more needed and wanted the same opportunity. Therefore, he suggested, the newly independent countries should make grants to Phelps Stokes to assist the program of aid to African students studying in the United States. Unfortunately, this objective has not been realized.

I also recall on this trip an amusing incident. When the group of trustees visited the office of Ghana's minister of education, a female trustee asked about polygamy in Ghana. The minister, taken aback by the question, advised her that polygamy was not a part of his portfolio!

Fourab Bay College is one of the oldest institutions of higher learning in West Africa. A trip to Sierra Leone, where Fourab Bay College is located, gave me another memorable experience. We participated in a conference with government and education officials who were seeking further assistance from Phelps Stokes.

The visit of the Phelps Stokes trustees to Nigeria reached its culmination when we sat in on a cabinet meeting and had an audience with the prime minister in Lagos. He and leading officials from other regions of Nigeria were assassinated during the civil war that followed soon after our visit.

One of the best programs developed by the Phelps Stokes Fund in response to the situation in West Africa was the Aggrey fellowship program. This award was designed to help African students go to graduate school in the United States. The program was named for James E. K. Aggrey of Ghana. He was vice-principal of Achimoto College, a distinguished secondary school in Ghana. Aggrey had lived a good part of his life in the United States and had early been inspired by the concept of education for life. Because of his work at Achimoto, where many of his ideas on practical education were adopted, Aggrey became a kind of patron saint of African education.

Aggrey had received a British education of high quality. His subsequent experience in the United States profoundly influenced his ideas on education. He married a black American woman, and his son, Rudolph, recently retired from a distinguished career as a U.S. ambassador. The Aggreys lived for much of their lives at Livingstone College in Salisbury, North Carolina, where Aggrey was a highly valued member of the faculty. He later returned to Africa and worked to bring his ideas to fruition there. His life typifies the educational values which we were trying to foster through Phelps Stokes's efforts in the grant program for African graduate students, and so we named the program for him.

Since the purpose of the Aggrey fellowship program was to assist African universities in upgrading their faculties by sending teachers to earn advanced degrees, the selection of Aggrey fellows required us to consult with African educators. In my travel in Africa to confer on awards, I met with officials at the University of Liberia at Monrovia; the University of Ibadan in Nigeria; Makerere College in Kampala, Uganda; and Haile Selassie University in Addis Ababa, Ethiopia. The first fellows were named in Accra on December 12, 1957. These students received grants from the Phelps Stokes Fund, which had itself received a grant from the Hazen Foundation for the purpose. Later, the Danforth Foundation joined in support as well.

Aggrey fellows, many of them accompanied by their families, were provided with full transportation costs from their country to the United States, full university tuition, and a maintenance allowance. Normally, a student received a grant of at least one thousand dollars for one year. It was not unusual for a fellow to be reappointed for an additional year or two to complete studies for an advanced degree. Awards were concentrated on students studying in the humanities and social sciences, areas frequently neglected in other African graduate assistance programs.

The first Aggrey fellow to complete his studies was Isaac Boateng, from

Ghana. He finished his training at Teachers College, Columbia University, and also studied at the Educational Testing Service at Princeton, New Jersey. Boateng returned to Ghana in July 1963 and began work at the West African Examinations Council headquarters in Lagos, Nigeria. Other Aggrey fellows from Ghana included Obed Y. Asamoah, a student of international law at Columbia who was selected by the Carnegie Endowment for International Peace to conduct a seminar on international relations at the Hague; Godfrey Gyekeye, who received his M. A. in African history at Harvard University; and Dr. Nicholas Anim, who received his Ph.D. at Columbia in 1964 and became head of the faculty of education at the University of Cape Coast, Nkrumah University. Anim was later a visiting professor at Columbia. Kwamina B. Dickson, also from Ghana, studied geography at both the University of California and the University of Wisconsin.

An African student of French literature, André Kumuamba, from the Congo, was named Aggrey fellow and studied at Howard University. Frederick Okatcha, a Kenyan, used his grant to study psychology, earning the Ph.D. at Yale University. And Kosonike Thomas, from Sierra Leone, studied at the University of Illinois, doing research there on prestressed concrete.

By 1965, twenty individuals from ten African nations had been awarded Aggrey fellowships, and by 1969, the last year of my tenure at the Phelps Stokes Fund, the Aggrey fellowship had become the most prestigious study grant in many African universities.

In addition to projects concerned with Africa, my time at the Phelps Stokes Fund involved me in work on programs and activities for American blacks. There were times, however, when my work in the domestic field was sharply criticized. The criticism stemmed, in part, I believe, from the way my predecessor, Channing Tobias, had conducted *his* work there. Tobias had begun his directorship at Phelps Stokes when he was already chairman of the board of the NAACP. His main time and efforts were, in fact, spent on matters connected with the NAACP rather than with the Phelps Stokes Fund. Tobias, A. Philip Randolph, and others were always in the public limelight, doing good work in the struggle for equality. I, on the other hand, was seldom in the limelight.

When I went to Phelps Stokes, Randolph bawled me out for what he said I was not doing. I had gone there to direct the educational program, and although I was interested in what Tobias had been doing, I didn't have the time for it, nor was I inclined to do just exactly what he had done. In all my years at Tuskegee, I had had to watch my conduct, lest I get Tuskegee Institute in trouble and damage its value to students. I thought it wisest to steer clear of controversy on the race issue. Dr. Moton had done so;

Booker Washington had done so; and I simply fell into the same pattern. I did take some actions, such as desegregating the elevators in Birmingham. But I did so quietly, without marches. I didn't publicize anything.

When I went to New York, in other words, I went with certain preconceptions regarding my role vis-à-vis the race problem. It wasn't that I didn't agree with Randolph and Tobias; at one time I had attended the NAACP meetings annually. I took out a life membership and contributed every year, as I still do. But I was not terribly active as some people were or thought I should be.

In one meeting, Randolph indicated that I wasn't doing all I should be doing; I wasn't active enough, he thought, in what *they* were doing. I listened to what he had to say, but I didn't do any differently. After working for forty years, you form habits. I just didn't regard Randolph's kind of activism as the reason for my joining the Phelps Stokes Fund. I joined it as an educator, and my accomplishments would reflect that emphasis. Nonetheless, I participated in the March on Washington and spoke to Randolph there to let him know I was present. I also joined the 1965 Selma-to-Montgomery March in Alabama, which was concerned with voting rights. I don't think I spoke to Martin Luther King or other civil rights leaders there. I was simply present in the crowd, mixing with the marchers.

A strange thing happened when I became head of the Phelps Stokes Fund. Because I had been a member of the Board of Trustees before I left Tuskegee, I knew that PSF programs focused on education in both the United States (mainly the South) and Africa, and so I had no great program surprises once I arrived at Phelps Stokes. One thing, however, that I had not anticipated—although the PSF annual reports were available to me—was the extent to which the monetary resources were limited. As a result I found that the things that I wanted to do at Phelps Stokes required seeking funds just as my work at Tuskegee had. Instead of becoming a donor, I remained a fund raiser.

One of the early things I did was to arrange for the Fund to assist in securing the Virginia property of Dr. Moton as a retreat for fund rasing. With the meeting space, sleeping accommodations, and small staff trained in commercial dietetics that came up from Tuskegee, we had the beginning of a conference center for fund raising. The more we thought about it, the more we thought it would work. Capahosic could serve as an interracial setting for meetings of people in a position financially to further the concerns we shared.

Rapid social change was under way in Africa, and as a result, the U.S. government was beginning, in a modest way, to assist African education financially. This budding interest, I felt, provided an opportunity for raising some money.

To understand the usefulness of the property at Capahosic on behalf of African and U.S. education, it must be recalled that in the early 1950s segregation of the races was still strong throughout the South, including Virginia. My feeling was that we needed a place in the South where people, regardless of race, creed, color, or sex, could, under the aegis of the Phelps Stokes Fund, discuss African and U.S. problems which fell within the purview of the Phelps Stokes Fund.

During the more than twenty years that Dr. Moton had lived and vacationed at Capahosic, he had conceived a desire to build a colonial home on the five acres of land he had acquired as a homesite. This beautiful home, in a beautiful setting, was completed in 1935, the year he retired from Tuskegee.

After Dr. Moton's death in 1940, his widow continued to live in the house, called Holly Knoll for the holly trees on the river bank, until she died in 1942. The members of the family, of which I am one by marriage, had the responsibility of deciding what to do with the property.

The family heirs could not afford to maintain Holly Knoll, and we did not know who might buy it if it were sold. Unless the property was preserved for some useful purpose, we would waste a resource that Dr. Moton had, over a period of twenty years, created and developed. For a while, no decision was reached. For several years, following the annual autumn meeting of the UNCF board, some of us—known as the Holly Knoll Associates—traveled by train together from Atlanta to Richmond, Virginia, and by car from there to the Moton home at Capahosic for a weekend of fishing and card playing. This trip was usually made at about the time of the World Series. The house had been closed for most of the year. As the UNCF group expanded and used the home for fellowship, the thought occurred to me that while card playing and fishing were pleasant enough, perhaps we could find a better use of the property.

At Capahosic the Phelps Stokes Fund could talk about need and about money. The insights gained might lead agencies such as the Sloan Foundation and the General Education Board to consider how they could wisely spend their funds. The Moton mansion would provide a site for such a conference.

I mentioned this idea to the Phelps Stokes Fund, and I persuaded the Moton family to sell the property for the modest sum of twenty-five thousand dollars for the house and five acres of land—a price for which the family continues to condemn me. I then went out to raise the rest of the money, from whatever sources I could, to establish a conference center through a vehicle created for that purpose, the Robert R. Moton Memorial Foundation. Soon I found that the name "Foundation" was wrong. When you say "Foundation," people think you have money to dispense, and we did not. With a change of name, we became the Robert R. Moton Memorial Institute, which functioned as an operating agency. I went for help to the usual sources: foundations. Some of the members of PSF's Board of Directors were respresentatives of foundations, such as Jackson Davis of the Rockefeller Foundation.

Alfred P. Sloan himself was alive in the early years of the Moton Institute. He admitted that he had not known anything about educational opportunity in the South, particularly as it related to black Americans, until he was informed through the Sloan Foundation's participation in a Capahosic conference. Thus, getting a conference center meant being able to educate those agencies that had the goodwill but lacked the information to help alter race relations both in Africa and in America.

For example, in response to the question of what could be done about African educational needs, Phelps Stokes in 1958 sponsored a conference entitled "Patterns of Public and Private Responsibility for African Education in the United States." Many church groups working in Africa sent African students to the United States with the false belief that, once they arrived, all of their problems would be solved. The Phelps Stokes Fund, with its long historical commitment to African students, stepped into the picture with limited resources—scholarships, student aid, and conferences—and tried its best to assist.

I can recall two other Virginia conferences for African students, one for African women and another for African men who were leaders. Some of the conferences were supported by government funds, but usually we had to find the money for a given conference, since we did not have an overall fund out of which we could set things up as we pleased.

Another conference at Holly Knoll was spawned by the actions of black college students in Greensboro, North Carolina. On February 1, 1960, five freshmen students at North Carolina A&T College took seats at a segregated lunch counter at Woolworth's. By refusing to leave until they had been served, Ezell Blair, Jr., Joseph McNeil, David Richmond, and Franklin McClain initiated the sit-in movement. Other Greensboro students, including those at Bennett College, joined in the protest. Dr. Willa Player was the president of Bennett, a UNCF college for women on whose Board of Trustees I served. When the Greensboro students began their actions, the entire black community, including the college community, was affected.

Dr. Player really showed her mettle when Bennett alone gave Dr. Martin

Luther King an assembly hall in which he could speak after being invited to Greensboro by the local NAACP. The numbers of students who sat in and were jailed grew as Woolworth's continued to resist the inevitable. Player did not try to change the attitudes or the actions of the students, although she was under some pressure to persuade the students to stop. Instead, she said, "No, they are a part of this protest, and as long as they are willing to stand up for their beliefs until the problem is properly resolved, I'm not looking for an exceptional way to get them out of something that is very difficult but very important."

Soon thereafter the sit-ins spread throughout the South. We could see that the protest was going to continue. We also knew that it was going to meet with a lot of resistance. For example, even at the beginning, demonstrating students were being burned by cigarettes put down their backs while they sat at lunch counters. Martin Luther King was telling them, "Don't fight back. Stand your ground, but don't get into physical combat. And you'll overcome."

In the matter of segregation, the businesses—chain stores and the like—were simply following the pattern which they thought the white community wanted. At the Phelps Stokes Fund we said, "We've got to go for the top and try to get some of the people who run these establishments from the central office to meet and hear these students and their demands."

Under the ordinary circumstances of these times, a place to hold an integrated meeting in the South like the one we were proposing was hard to find. Public accommodations were, of course, segregated. There was virtually no place where such a group could meet except on a black college campus. Fortunately we had the Moton Conference Center, and the gathering took place there.

We picked four or five of the students publicized as leaders in the sit-in movement and invited them to meet with us at Capahosic. We also asked some nearby representatives of the white South. And we sought representatives from S. H. Kresge, Sears Roebuck, and other businesses. Many of them did not come, but those who did sat down under the trees at Capahosic and listened to the bright youngsters, who were extremely literate and knew how to express themselves. The students were not bristling with fiery tempers; they were just normal human beings who wanted to be treated decently.

Always there are some decent people of courage, of whatever race, who will respond to a challenge. Most forms of discrimination and meanness persist long past the time when people know they are wrong. What they need is the opportunity to face up to that wrong and to the challenge to do something about it.

The students were the motivators. They said, "We've taken it long enough." The representatives of businesses really wanted some insights and came to the conference thinking, "Maybe we had better find out what's going on. If this is going to be something that's going to cause our businesses a lot of trouble, maybe we'd better get some insights as to what can be done about it." It's awfully easy to measure human problems in terms of the cash register.

For weeks thereafter, I received calls from the central offices of companies that had attended the Capahosic meeting. (I can't recall whether or not I got a call from Sears Roebuck, but the man from S. H. Kresge called and said, "Well, we've desegregated the lunch counters in such and such a place!") Business people who had attended our conference took great pride in the fact they had responded to the challenge by desegregating their facilities.

Some people resist change because all they've known is the way things have been. Usually, if the issue is black versus white and the white's on top, the masses of whites oppose change. But most of the time the decent people in the leadership go for change, although there are exceptions. For example, one of the white persons who had been so pious and such a warm friend to blacks had three elevators in his office building in Birmingham. Blacks could ride in only one of them. This elevator, supposedly reserved for blacks, was often so crowded with whites when the "white" elevators were full that the blacks could hardly get in "their" elevator.

I went to the building's owner and said, "I don't understand this. Here the whites are with blacks in the car reserved for blacks, and yet you won't let the blacks ride in the others reserved for whites. This is just frank humiliation to black people." He finally desegregated the elevators, but he did not attend any more meetings.

Another example: in the early days of the College Fund, one banker said to me, "Well, you should *expect* to be segregated." He meant: "Because you are black, the order of the day for you is segregation, something that is a part of your life, that you have to live with." I never accepted that idea. I accepted his money, but I didn't accept his pronouncements on the inevitability of segregation.

Very often other African students studying in the United States appealed to the Phelps Stokes Fund. Missionaries had told them that when they arrived they would have no trouble finding jobs and money. Of course, most students did not have such good fortune, and at best, they needed pin money; many also needed money for clothing, food, and basic necessities. We did not have a lot of money, but word got around that the Phelps Stokes Fund would make grants of $50 to $100 to $150. Usually we had to pick and choose the students to be helped because we could not respond to all the requests that we got. Even so, a good number were helped each year. If, upon investigation with the counselor at the institution where the student was enrolled, we found this was a worthy student who was making academic progress and who would find modest help meaningful, we gave it.

The Phelps Stokes trustees were debating how the rather modest monies we had should be spent. Until that time, even with the small funds which the PSF had, we had paid a fair amount of attention to making grants. But we decided that we had nowhere near enough money to meet the important needs in the grants area. Instead, our limited resources could best be spent in conducting programs in which we could provide leadership.

I did not find the trustees at Phelps Stokes as inclined as I to raise money to operate programs. Bishop Anson Phelps Stokes, one of the trustees, did not wish the Phelps Stokes Fund to search for funds. Finding the money with which to "do something" therefore continued to be a problem. The money available was insufficient for even the limited programs we wanted to run to help black students and colleges in Africa and the United States.

Meanwhile I wrote some papers on the subject of African education here in the United States. One in particular was entitled "Education for African Development." It stressed the importance of having African students come to the United States and attend American land-grant colleges where they could receive down-to-earth training in agriculture, engineering, and applied sciences, which they would then take back to their home countries. I believed that too many educated Africans had been miseducated where their countries' needs were concerned and that these students and their countries primarily needed the land-grant type of education.

Even money for the relatively small projects was often hard to come by, especially for an organization like the PSF, whose directors were black.

Other groups competed with the Phelps Stokes Fund and siphoned off much of the money because their leadership was white. We developed a little handbook for African students in the United States, and I tried to get some money from the Carnegie Corporation to publish it. Carnegie would not agree because, it said, the handbook had been badly reviewed. In fact, we did not receive the money because a white person at another foundation had reviewed the book. The person in question gave it a poor rating because he wanted the Carnegie money to publish *his* foundation's handbook for African students. I said to the Carnegie Corporation official, "I wouldn't ask a Chevrolet salesman what he thought of a Ford car."

This incident illustrated our problems. The issue of race invaded practically all relationships. And my job required me to deal skillfully with the issue. Yet in my life it has been important to make things happen. You say, "You can't do it," and I say, "We'll find a way."

I had a dilemma. Having acquired a site in Virginia for a conference, we now needed money to develop it and to operate programs there. The Moton Institute had been created to develop the conference center, but the Institute lacked the necessary funds. Once again I saw what I felt were important needs—on two continents—crying to be met.

I believe that the people who need to talk to each other must be brought together. The PSF needed to provide the opportunity and as a private organization was in a position to do so. Nobody looked over our shoulder and said that we couldn't do something.

At the Phelps Stokes Fund, I did not find very many people concerned with the kind of project that interested me. I had to hire staff to move in the direction that I identified for the Fund: designing and operating programs instead of making grants. People like Ida Wood, who's still at Phelps Stokes, and Dr. Aaron Brown—who studied ways of improving the quality of U.S. education in the high schools as a means of making black students better prepared for college work—joined the staff of the Fund at that time.

Following the Supreme Court decision in 1954, Earl McGrath completed his study on the black colleges. It was entitled *Predominantly Negro Colleges and Universities in Transition*. He gave me the opportunity to review it. I had served with McGrath in the 1940s as a member of the Truman Commission on Higher Education during the time that the United Negro College Fund was started. McGrath knew of my connection with the UNCF and thought that I would have great interest in the conclusions he had reached.

He told me, "I think you're going to be greatly surprised. After a two year study" (financed by a grant from Carnegie Corporation to Columbia University) "I've seen every black college in the country. And contrary to the proverbial wisdom—that the way to promote integration is to do away with the black colleges and just let the black students go to white colleges—my conclusion is that this would be disastrous! In the first place, many of the black students, poorly educated at the primary and secondary level and from low-income families, are not ready for higher education, and the white colleges and universities are not ready to receive them sympathetically." It seemed to McGrath that, for the time being, all of the black schools worthy of being called colleges—and some that were not—should remain in existence and be given an opportunity to improve the quality of their efforts significantly. As the colleges improved, many of them would no doubt open their doors to students without regard to race and would be regarded as normal American institutions of higher education. But advances in quality, the report concluded, would require money.

We decided then and there that the view of the black colleges' immediate future, as described in the McGrath study, was consistent with the UNCF's statement about the black colleges in the wake of the new "law of the land": they were not going out and should not go out of business; they needed, as always, money to thrive and to grow.

The Phelps Stokes Fund decided to call a conference to discuss the findings of the McGrath study and invited participants from education, industry, and religion who were concerned with opportunities for black colleges. We arranged for the Alfred P. Sloan Foundation to finance the convocation, which was attended by Dr. Willa Player, President Rufus Clement, Dr. Albert Dent, and Bill Trent, as director of the UNCF. Peter Muirhead, from the U.S. Office of Education, and representatives from U.S. Steel also attended, along with McGrath, who served as a resource person to the group. We hoped to generate some money to help the colleges address the issues that McGrath's study had raised—issues of which the schools were already aware.

As a result of the conference, the Sloan Foundation said, "Now that we have funded this meeting and we have seen the implications of the study, what steps can we take?" We suggested two ways in which the Sloan Foundation could help the colleges. First they funded precollege training for students. The students had been admitted as freshmen by ten UNCF colleges but had not yet enrolled. Programs were set up at Atlanta University and Dillard University for summer study in the social sciences, mathematics, and English to better prepare them for the freshman year.

The idea for the second proposal grew out of my involvement with the UNCF. As the McGrath study had indicated, if the black colleges were to remain in existence, their financial needs in the future would be far greater than they had been in the past.

The College Fund had started its first capital campaign, the one which included "Millionaire Day." For this campaign, we were clients of Marts & Lundy, professional fund-raising organization. Marts & Lundy invited all its clients to attend a luncheon meeting at which we heard James F. Oates, Jr., chairman of the Equitable Life Assurance Society of the United States, speak on a campaign he headed for Princeton University that had raised $80 million.

The United Negro College Fund is presented with the first transcript of Dr. Patterson's reminiscences in the Columbia University–UNCF Oral History Project, 1981. A portrait of Dr. Patterson is in the background. From left to right: Gregory Hunter, UNCF director of archives and history; Elizabeth Mason, acting director, Oral History Research Office, Columbia University; Dr. Patterson; Christopher Edley, executive director, UNCF; Dr. Martia Goodson, interviewer.

Most of the people at the luncheon were college development officers, whose work is raising money for the colleges, or were training to become college development officers. But the black colleges were almost totally without development officers. We had seen and heard of this administrative post before but largely in terms of the major colleges and universities. It was certainly not found in the black colleges. We had not thought of development officers as functionaries to be integrated into our staffs, even down to our smallest institutions. Until that point, as I've said earlier, all of the burden of fund raising, as well as public relations and even recruitment, was pretty much the responsibility of the president.

The presence of these development officers at the Marts & Lundy meeting suggested that we should help the colleges organize their fund-raising activities and organize programs to train college development officers. So we suggested that the Sloan Foundation make a grant to black colleges to undertake a study of the training required.

How do you staff a college's development office? How do you relate it to the office of the president? How do you carry out all of the things that ought to be done in order to seek the kind of support that is needed? The Sloan Foundation voted fifty thousand dollars for this training, with the understanding that each college would put up twenty-five hundred dollars a year for three years, an amount that would be matched by the foundation.

At first, Sloan officials wanted only private colleges involved in the program. But I indicated that, although I favored helping the private colleges, the fact was that more black students were in public institutions than in private ones, that if the intent was really to help young people, training development officers for the public colleges was crucial. Sloan acquiesced and, I believe, agreed that a third of the twenty or so institutions would be public ones.

Some of the people in training as development officers in this program went on to become college presidents. They included Norman C. Francis at Xavier University and Benjamin Perry at Florida A&M University. After learning how to seek and manage funds, they so impressed their administrative boards that they were selected to head their respective schools.

So the conference on the McGrath report helped higher education for blacks by illuminating the need for improvement and support.

My acquaintance with Willa Player turned out to be a real asset for the development effort, particularly at the time when I was, again, searching for funds. I had first met Willa Player when she was coordinator of instruction at Bennett College, a school for young women. At that time, I was still president of Tuskegee Institute. When Player was offered the presidency of Spelman College, Dr. David Jones, Bennett's president, who had known her for fifteen or twenty years, persuaded her not to accept the offer. Instead, he wanted her to succeed him at Bennett. In his final illness, Jones spoke to the Bennett trustees about Player, and she succeeded him, serving as president for ten years. During much of that time, I was chairman of Bennett's board. At the end of her tenth year, in the 1960s, Player received an invitation from John Gardner, U.S. secretary of education, who had been a high official at the Carnegie Corporation. He had had a chance to meet her when she was looking for financial support for Bennett and had been very much impressed by her. The Title III program—which provided support for "developing institutions"—was just being inaugurated, and Gardner wanted Dr. Player to direct the Division of College Support.

Even before Dr. Player was offered the job in Washington, she had said that, after twenty-five years at the school, she should be finding a new position. As chairman of the board, I was nevertheless shocked when she informed us of the federal appointment, and I tried to keep her from leaving. She went anyway, and of course, the rest is history.

Player left Bennett and worked in that division perhaps ten years or more until her retirement. She had performed an outstanding service as president of Bennett College, and she did the same as director of the Division of College Support. Having seen the problems of black colleges from the ground up, she was in a position to advise members of her staff, many of whom were white, as to how Title III could help developing colleges, many of which were black.

One of the ways in which we felt the Division of College Support could be effective involved expanding the training of development officers we had started under the program funded by the Sloan Foundation. With Player's help Title III support for the black colleges began with training college development officers. Later it branched out to include admissions and financial aid and various other administrative functions. Dr. Player was for several years the mainstay of the Division of College Support and did much to redirect the administration of higher education for black people. Small white colleges received help as well.

Because of our knowledge of the McGrath study and of the history of the College Fund, and with Dr. Player's influence, the Phelps Stokes Fund became one of the important contractors with Title III. Our job was to conduct training in those areas of technical assistance that would be useful to the colleges. We increased and improved their physical plants and personnel resources in quality and quantity; worked to overcome their academic isolation; and established officers concerned with overall financial development. Many of these schools had, through the UNCF, started cooperating in raising operating funds. Title III funds made it possible for these same schools—fifteen of them—to cooperate in receiving training together in other areas.

This program was called the Cooperative College Development Program (CCDP) and by 1969 had been expanded to forty colleges. This work was most important to the colleges and allowed Phelps Stokes to do what, in my mind, was a most useful service to institutions that had to improve if they were to survive.

7 The Moton Institute

It was 1970 and by this time I had spent seventeen years at the Phelps Stokes Fund and had worked four years beyond my sixty-fifth birthday. Fortunately for me, I had not been unemployed since I took my first teaching job in 1928, but I knew that I could not go on forever. I planned my retirement from the Phelps Stokes Fund. Since there was still no mechanism by which to keep the Moton Center thriving, I decided to try to create one. Originally, all of the staff of the Institute had been Phelps Stokes staff. But by the time I retired, Moton was able to acquire a staff of its own.

If we were trying to raise money for the conference site and its programs, no one would give unless giving was tax-exempt. I had therefore already set up the Moton Institute as a separate nonprofit agency.

Dr. Player indicated to me that, if Moton wanted to conduct technical assistance programs for the black colleges, much as Phelps Stokes was already doing with its CCDP, Title III could fund them. This was a very fortuante stroke of luck that came just when we at Moton needed it. When I began to work full time at the Moton Institute, we set up a program in Washington that would help the black colleges identify federal monies for which they might be eligible and apply for them. This program helped our black colleges compete with other colleges—many of them not serving black youth in numbers—which were better equipped institutionally to apply for the federal funds which the civil rights movement and the demand for equal opportunity helped to generate.

Another Moton program helped the colleges address the problems of acquiring and retaining students. This program focused on helping the schools identify both the students they wanted to enroll and the sources of financial assistance that the students needed to stay in school.

In addition, there was a continuing need to train development officers for the colleges. Once they had been trained, development officers were very much in demand. There were always job openings for people trained in this work, and I considered our program successful in preparing them.

The Moton Institute was designated an assisting agency; colleges could hire our services to do the work of training. We had a staff of up to forty people and were succeeding. Meanwhile I began to work on the College Endowment Funding Plan.

The college presidents always complained that they were able to raise for their schools only restricted funds, whereas they needed unrestricted funds. I heard this complaint again and again, and I could understand it.

If a college president wanted to create a program at his or her college and found money to operate that program at a foundation, the program might be started. But the arrangement itself created problems for the president. First, if you received, for example, a ten-year grant, the implication was that the school would spend those funds over the ten-year period. Every year the college was required to spend not only one-tenth of the money with which it started but also any earnings it received. This practice did not even encourage saving. In addition, at the end of the ten-year period, the school had increased its quality but had incurred new costs. It no longer had money with which to finance the program. Unless some way could be found to offset the cost, the operating budget would have to increase.

The colleges needed an endowment. Endowment is gift money that the school invests for the long term while spending the earnings annually. It is the only unrestricted money an institution can receive which supplies income available every year for any purpose that requires special funding. Usually schools acquire endowment money when somebody dies or when, from the goodness of their hearts, people make earmarked gifts. And small colleges, black or white, didn't receive such gifts. We spent everything we had. "Raise all the money you can. And spend more than you raise." That's the way it usually went. But the presidents now realized that what you have to spend on a current basis needs to be cushioned by funds in endowment income.

I was trying to decide: how do you get this money for operating expenses? Foundations won't give you any: the average foundation seems to feel that yours should be a life of constant struggle and that too much money would be required to supply what was really needed, especially when the rate of return on the investment was 3 to 5 percent. I knew that no one would give us enough endowment; we had to create it. Some institutions, such as Tuskegee, Hampton, and Spelman, did receive some limited gifts for endowment, but it was not practical for the smallest of the colleges to count on receiving gifts. And of course, the church-related colleges had a hard enough struggle persuading the churches to contribute to their annual operations.

It seemed to me that the only way the colleges would ever get unrestricted funds was to create a challenge grant, a sum of money given to an institution if certain conditions are met. Perhaps we could do something with money borrowed from savings-and-loan banks. Perhaps we could get the money at one price and spend it at another, or save it and get a return from it, or get it at one rate and invest it at a higher rate. The difference would be income or endowment.

Under a plan that I conceived, participating colleges would first raise a certain amount of gift money. Next, those who were successful in meeting their goals would receive a bonus from the UNCF derived from capital campaign funds. Finally, the two-part package would be supplemented with money borrowed from insurance companies in the form of twenty-five-year loans. For example, a college raising $300,000 would receive $50,000 from the UNCF. This $350,000 would be supplemented with a $400,000 loan, so that the college would have $750,000 as an investment unit.

Under this arrangement, called the College Endowment Funding Plan (CEFP), the college pays back only the interest for the first fifteen years. The principal compounds during this time. Then one-tenth of the balance with interest is paid off during the last ten years. Meanwhile, the college receives an additional thirty thousand dollars of its operating budget during each of the twenty-five years.

The ideas for this plan emerged gradually. I first started with the idea that we would get forty-year loans. But when the Moton Institute received a grant to hire professional help to study the plan, I had to revise my ideas. After studying my proposal, Arthur D. Little reported that the idea was worth trying but that a forty-year period was too long. He suggested that we look to insurance companies, because they traditionally have large sums of money which they invest for various periods of time over a long term, such as twenty-five years. We had to have long-term money. Insurance companies are in the habit of dealing with twenty-five-year loans. I remember discussing the matter with an officer of the Teachers Insurance and Annuity Association. He said, "What you're saying is all right if you can do it." I had met Robert R. Goheen at some of the social affairs that the

UNCF had sponsored to raise funds. I knew that he was a very fine person. President Goheen had just retired from Princeton University and was head of the Council on Foundations, a private organization. I remembered his contact with James F. Oates, Jr., an insurance executive who had been the guest speaker at the Marts & Lundy conference. I decided to speak to him about the CEFP, telling him how far we had gone with the study and that we would like to meet some insurance company executives. Goheen sent me to Kenneth Albecht, the public relations officer at Equitable. When I said, "Goheen sent me," Albrecht immediately arranged for several companies to meet and hear our plan.

Christopher Edely, the current president and chief executive officer of the UNCF, and I met with them and presented our proposal. After a week or two, I received a letter from Robert M. Hendrickson, senior vice-president for investments for the Equitable Life Assurance Society, stating that he thought our plan was workable and that Equitable was willing to make a twenty-five-year loan of $5 million!

Until then we had been thinking in very modest terms. It was stunning that this major insurance company would mention a figure such as $5 million. I thought, "The plan must be as good as I believed because this man is a seasoned financial executive and wouldn't talk that kind of money unless he believed it was a sound investment and a good way to carry out Equitable's public service mission."

On the strength of that commitment, I intensified my efforts. First, I went to John Gloster, whom I had known by reputation. He headed a small organization that had some funds for black business. Gloster said, "Your program does not meet our requirements, but I think if you talk to Stanley Karson, he might be interested." Karson is the director of the Center for Corporate Public Involvement of the life and health insurance industry. Our initial commitment of $5 million from Equitable impressed him.

To my pleasant surprise, Mr. Karson said, "You know, I've been trying to do something like this for the industry. This strikes me as a good idea." Thus the College Endowment Funding Plan was created at the Robert R. Moton Institute. Today it operates in cooperation with the United Negro College Fund.

I deeply appreciate the important contributions that Stanley Karson has made to the CEFP. Thanks to him, we developed successful relationships with insurance companies, whose loans have provided the critical funds to make the endowment plan work. Karson's personal efforts in identifying and making contacts with the right companies have been and continue to be indispensable. And the plan is reinforced by frequent articles and mentions in official publications of the insurance industry, such as *Response,* published by the Center for Corporate Public Involvement.

William J. Kennedy III of North Carolina Mutual Insurance Company, a black company, was a member of the Committee for Corporate Involvement. Kennedy made a motion endorsing the plan and asked the insurance industry committee to sanction the College Endowment Funding Plan officially. Other black insurance companies participating as leaders in the CEFP in addition to the North Carolina Mutual are Atlanta Life Insurance Company, Booker T. Washington Life Insurance Company of Birmingham, Alabama, and Universal Life Insurance Company of Memphis, Tennessee.

When we had amassed enough money to begin, we worked out the formula of participation. I have felt that in fund raising, the person or agency that is going to receive the money should participate in raising part of the required money. Money raised by the colleges represented an endorsement of the college and, combined with the bonus from UNCF and the money borrowed, provided generous collateral for the loan. All of the money involved is collateral, when the loan is collateralized the risk to the lender is reduced to almost nothing.

I worked on the plan for four or five years before we had enough money to make the initial investment for six colleges. During that time I met with people who were knowledgeable in the money field to discuss and criticize the plan. Our first colleges were funded under the plan in 1978 when nine insurance companies made loans totaling $2.4 million to a group of six colleges, all of which were members of the United Negro College Fund. Since that time, thirty-two life and health insurance companies have provided more than $30 million in below-market loans through the CEFP. The plan is expected to generate more than $160 million in endowment for the participating thirty-six black colleges over the life of the investments.

One of the best operations we've had under the Moton Institute—the technical assistance programs to black colleges—was broken up by a change in the government regulations under which the Title III operated. The federal government decided to discontinue allowing colleges to contract with assisting agencies such as Moton to do the things that Moton was doing. Originally, the colleges were allowed to set up budgets that would permit them to contract with the Institute for services. The budget included 15 percent in overhead for the agency, to help us cover the cost of the organizational structure needed to make the agency function. The change in regulations meant that the schools could no longer contract with Moton. Colleges could set up programs of their own and invite qualified personnel to work with them. But this arrangement handicapped Moton and meant that we had to let staff go. The colleges, too, were less well served. There were Senate hearings in Washington, and we were given a chance to defend what we were doing. But our relationships with the developing colleges continued to disintegrate.

One U.S. senator from the Far West thought that the black colleges were getting money which ought to go to schools for Hispanic-American students out his way. But instead of adding to the appropriation to provide for those students, the Senate committee stopped it. In fact, the legislators cut several programs whose importance they did not even understand. The senators insisted that the programs were not necessary.

In politics today, it doesn't matter how "important" your program is. If you do not have on your side politicians who share your perspective, your programs get short shrift. A proposal is not necessarily funded on the basis of merit.

As a result of the cutbacks in government funding, the Moton Institute had to phase out the programs it was operating. Eventually we were totally without programs offering technical assistance. Other assisting agencies had to do the same; some of them survived because they had certain political relationships. We didn't, and we never tried to play things politically. Maybe we should have done so. The changes were so severe that we were forced to develop a closer relationship with the United Negro College Fund. This will no doubt turn out to be a good thing; it is certainly desirable at the present time.

The UNCF has an office in Washington that stays abreast of government policy and analyzes the implications for black colleges. That office is proving its worth to the UNCF, I believe. But Moton didn't have the resources to do what the UNCF is doing.

The only way to continue federal funding is to be on top of the politics. You must be sure that the people who can save you will do so because it's important to them to save you.

Until very recently, the CEFP was doing very well. When the insurers had done as much as they thought the insurance industry ought to do, they stopped making the loans. We've gone through a whole series of economic changes, many of which have affected the insurance industry. As time went on, fewer funds were available. The situation resembles that which I encountered at Tuskegee Institute when the foundations told me that they were not interested in financing Tuskegee's deficits. It's the way life is. In a private foundation, one of the challenges is to create programs that reflect need and the availability of funding. If you don't get the funding, you're out in left field. If one thing doesn't materialize, you go to something else. Many programs that I thought were good did not receive funding.

Despite the current obstacles and challenges facing the Moton Institute, the College Endowment Funding Plan has been shown, I believe, to be an important device, particularly at a time when college costs are high. From the beginning there have been supporters who believed in the soundness of the idea and helped make the plan a reality. Equitable Life Assurance Society has served as the "Lead Lender" from the beginning of the College Endowment Funding Plan. Coy Eklund, president and chief executive officer, gave his personal leadership to this initiative until his retirement. John B. Carter, who succeeded Eklund, has continued Equitable's generous sponsorship of the CEFP.

Other participating insurance companies have repeatedly provided loans to the program. John H. Filer of Aetna Life & Casualty chaired the insurance industry committee that approved the plan. At Prudential, Robert Beck and John E. Person were both helpful. Person, Prudential's current chairman, has written letters to other companies urging them to participate as lenders. Beck chaired the third UNCF capital campaign.

George Keane is president of the Common Fund, a multibillion dollar organization investing money for many of the nation's colleges. Keane has, from my early contact with him about the endowment idea, helped in a number of important ways, visiting companies and serving as chairman of the Investment Committee for CEFP colleges. He has also made indispensable contacts for advice and money among individuals highly competent in the investment field. The UNCF's Investment Committee under Keane's chairmanship consists of W. Curtis Livingston in Los Angeles and W. Clair Garff in New York. The Moton Institute today continues to develop the CEFP and seeks loan funds from insurance companies and other sources.

There is now a close working relationship between the United Negro College Fund and the Robert R. Moton Institute. The Moton Institute wants to continue serving educational institutions in almost every area except fund raising. We're not interested in competing with the UNCF, which has established itself in a rather successful way as the fund-raising organization which solicits support from the nation as a whole. Moton would like to continue to cooperate with the UNCF in the Fund's commitment to help the colleges become stronger: in recruitment and retention of students, in better financial management of the monies under the control of the colleges, and in any program which would improve the quality of education being offered or would offer new avenues of employment for the young people whom the colleges are graduating.

I strongly hope that Christopher Edley and the UNCF member colleges develop an in-house revolving loan fund by using $10 million from the next capital campaign as a supplement to, and later as a replacement for, insurance loans. As the revolving fund is repaid with interest and principal from borrowing colleges, this fund would continue to grow and would become a permanent source of loan monies. The fund could be used by colleges that become eligible to participate by raising the required gift money and by getting the bonus money from UNCF.

Anything that comes from a given U.S. presidential administration is on shaky ground because the administration in question isn't going to last. And no Congress can bind a future session of Congress. Someone influential must be on your side—someone who finds it to his or her credit to work for your program's salvation. Unless you've done an awfully good job of selling your cause, the administration or the Congress will feel that it must undo what has been done just because it was done by a predecessor. These are the inevitable pitfalls and the problems. You constantly hear about "education." President Reagan favored reducing spending on education. Secretary of Education William Bennett frequently criticized the colleges and what they do with the money. Current funds and programs will probably see further reductions.

For the first time, the federal government is earmarking funds for black colleges in the federal budget. Many people don't want to see monies earmarked in this way; I'm not sure I'm happy about it. I think the black colleges ought to move into the mainstream, not away from it. It could be argued that the black colleges are so far behind that these are "catch up" funds. But catch-up funds can become awfully permanent if you aren't careful. And if they can be earmarked in a budget, they can be earmarked out. I wish we could replace them now with regular appropriations that would give us what we need.

Epilogue

My sister Bessie died in Washington while I was on a Phelps Stokes trip in Liberia. She had been conducting the Shiloh Baptist Church choir and was planning to retire. Before I left the United States on the Liberia trip, the choir had been planning her farewell banquet. She died before the event could take place. Bessie's passing was a low point in my life. I knew she wasn't well, but her death was very sudden. She was, I think, seventy-one. I had paid for her to have an operation a year or so earlier. I guess I had had some inkling that she was failing, but I did not expect to lose her.

We had always been very close; I regarded her as both my sister and my surrogate mother. I bought her a home in Washington which we shared. I constantly helped with the expenses, and whenever I want to Washington I stayed with her. Although I had lived with my married sister, Lucille, I always felt closer to Bessie. I loved Lucille, but she had her own family and her own children, and Bess didn't. I was the closest thing she had. I loved her and appreciated everything she did for me.

She cared greatly for me. She also tried to run my life, even after I was president of Tuskegee. She never stopped telling me how to behave or what to do. She set high standards for me, even during my boyhood. I think as a child I was a disappointment to her because of her standards, in music and in everything. I think she was proud of me, but I had a kind of lackadaisical attitude.

My three brothers were the first of the six children of William and

Wilhelmina Bessie Patterson and Lucille Emma Patterson Dale, sisters of Frederick D. Patterson, 1950s, in Washington, D.C.

Mamie Patterson to die. Lorenzo went first, when I was young. John died next, in South Carolina, after I had moved to New York. John worked part time for Tuskegee Institute with *Service,* traveling from hotel to hotel, trying to enlist support for the publication. He was home in South Carolina when he became ill and died.

The next to go was James, and then Lucille, who passed in 1983. Her husband died in 1984. Lucille had always been the sickly one, but she lived longer than some of the others. And although I was a sickly baby, so far I've managed to outlive all of them.

It is a red pentagon with a golden circle of eagles with wings outspread. A white star sits on the pentagon, extending beyond it to the golden circle. The center of the star is a blue circle, rimmed with gold and filled with golden stars. The reverse is inscribed with my name and the date June 23, 1987. It is the Presidential Medal of Freedom, the highest civilian honor the United States of America confers on its citizens. It was awarded to me by President Ronald Reagan at a White House luncheon. Both the date and the place have special significance beyond the medal, which I prize. I received the award on the ninety-eighth anniversary of my sister Bessie's birth, and the ceremony took place in the city where I was born and where she died. My parents had died in Washington. Bessie, their firstborn, had been entrusted with my care when she was quite young. Bessie was a powerful influence on my life. The successes that the Medal of Freedom recognizes cannot be separated from the ideas and ideals that she imparted to me. They represent a faith that has moved my life.

I believe in black youth. My work with institutions such as Tuskegee University, the Phelps Stokes Fund, the member colleges of the United Negro College Fund, and the Moton Institute always focused on those youth, and on programs to benefit them and their schools. Bessie, as a music teacher in the public schools, was like thousands of other black women and men who have worked since the end of slavery to educate black youth. They also share my faith. The devotion and guidance they have given to the cause of those young people is no different from Bessie's gift to me. She, like her counterparts across the nation and the world, may never go to the White House and receive the Presidential Medal of Freedom, but the cause she and others served produces its own medals of freedom, the youth who have benefited from their efforts and who stride out across America and the world, ready to give to the world and to learn from it.

The opportunities today for leadership are greater than ever before. In my early life, blacks could be leaders only in the ministry, law, teaching, and medicine. Although you encounter cycles of opportunity, new fields and new areas of specialization are now coming into existence. The options are greater than ever.

With society changing all the time, unexplored areas of need beckon to the ambitious individual. Dr. Carver went to Tuskegee from Iowa State

Dedication of Frederick D. Patterson Hall, School of Veterinary Medicine, Tuskegee Institute, 1982. Left to right: Dean Walter Bowie, Frederick D. Patterson II, Frederick D. Patterson, President Luther H. Foster.

College. He left some of the richest soil in America, the Iowa black soil, and went to some of the poorest soil in America, the sandy soil of Alabama. Carver saw that the people were undernourished because they were underfed. He found hitherto unsuspected sources of nourishing foods. By examining the situation at hand and employing the education he had received, he found many ways to improve the lives of the people and the nation.

Leadership is more than confrontation. It can have a number of different dimensions. And if people seeking leadership will select areas in which they want to excel, they can draw on their special skills to improve the circumstances in which all members of society live out their lives.

Appendix

Appendix

Little-Known Facts about F. D. Patterson
J. R. Otis

Increasing enrollment of students at Iowa State College in the 1920s made it difficult for students to find living quarters, even in private homes in Ames. The colored students experienced the most difficulty, and as a result of their common needs, they formed an organization called the Interstate Club and rented quarters upstairs over a ten-cent store located at 202½ East Main Street.

Here they lived together and kept house. The clubhouse had a long hall that served as a bedroom with a row of cots arranged side by side and placed along the west wall in army barracks style. The four other rooms were used as sitting room, study, dining room, and kitchen.

At times there were as many as twenty-seven students at the Club, but sometimes there were so few that the Club could hardly be maintained. The original members were James J. Fraser (Jimmy), A. C. Aldridge, John Lockett, Cornelius Bibb, C. V. Chapman, G. T. Lucas, R. B. Atwood, H. G. McGuire, John Sweatt, Ben Crutcher, C. B. Smith, L. A. Potts, J. R. Otis, and Frederick Douglass Patterson, or "Pat," as he has always been known to students.

Each club member took turns at performing household duties, but Pat seldom had to clean house or wash dishes because he was the cook, and a good one, too–so good that many of the boys gladly did his turn at dishwashing and cleaning in hopes that he would continue cooking.

Most of the colored students at Ames between 1920 and 1925 had to work to help support themselves. Some found work at the college, some worked at the Sheldon Munn Hotel half a block from the Club, and still others earned wages as janitors in stores and offices or did housecleaning in private homes. Pat worked at the Sheldon Munn Hotel until he and Aldridge formed the Ames Rug Cleaning Company.

To gather and deliver rugs, the Ames Rug Cleaning Company needed a truck. This Pat bought with fifty dollars his sister had sent for his tuition. Even then fifty dollars couldn't buy much of a car. Pat and Jimmy, an engineering student, had to work at night for about a week before they succeeded in getting the old 1920 model Overland touring car to run.

On the first night when they drove the Overland up on the block, Pat rushed upstairs and invited the boys to come down and see his "pickup" business-and-pleasure car. Reluctantly the boys stopped studying and rumbled downstairs. It was a creation in more ways than one. Lockett said, "What in heck are you doing with a lantern back there?" The others quickly went around to the rear to investigate. As the original tail light had been past salvaging, Pat had made one by painting the globe of a barn lantern red, then wiring it to the car. Now with a slow grin and a determined stride, Pat marched to the rear and after striking nearly half a box of matches, lighted the lantern and said, "Climb in." As many as could did so. The old car coughed, spat, and coughed again, then chugged on down the street. Everything was working surprisingly well until the Overland got out in West Ames. Then it refused to cover another foot of land. The boys had to push it back to town. And when they reached the Club at about two in the morning, they were ready to fight anybody who mentioned the word "Overland."

Somehow Pat managed to get enough money to pay tuition and enroll in school that quarter. That time he had to use a little more midnight oil and bring up his scholastic average, which had slipped a peg or two while he had been occupied with the rug-cleaning business. Aldridge, his partner, spent very little time on the job, though the rugs piled up. After some weeks' delay in cleaning them, Pat was called by the sheriff, who gently suggested that he deliver the rugs to their owners within twenty-four hours. Bright and early the next morning, all the fellows (including Aldridge) hurried downstairs, bought all the carpet beaters in the ten-cent store, and went across the tracks back of the Club, where they beat rugs all day long. I cannot vouch for how the rugs looked, but every one was delivered within the specified twenty-four hours, and the Ames Rug Cleaning Company ceased to exist as of that time.

Another incident involved a Chinese schoolmate's suit. The Patterson cleaners were to clean it, but in the process, Aldridge wasted peroxide on it and spotted it noticeably. Pat told the schoolmate about it and asked his permission to do a guaranteed dye job on the suit. Permission was granted, and the suit was dyed. In the process, it shrank three sizes. Just what adjustment was made is not known, but Pat and Aldridge did no more cleaning, and Pat gladly returned to Sheldon and Munn as a waiter, though he still harbored the belief that cleaning was a profitable business.

With his ideas and Otis's money, in the fall of 1923 the two formed J. R. Otis and Company, which did cleaning, pressing, and repairing. Pat solicited clothes, and Otis dropped out of school for a quarter to establish the business. For a while it flourished. But when Otis went back to school leaving a tailor in charge, receipts fell so much that he had to drop out of school again in order to protect his interest. Later Otis sold out, in the process losing all the money that he had saved, and Pat lost several weeks' pay. From this experience they both learned not to try to do two things at once.

Pat and Otis shared many experiences both as students and teachers. There was the time at Virginia State College when these teachers hoped to earn eight to ten dollars for skinning a dead mule and selling its hide. They earned just $1.80. "That's better than nothing," Pat said.

Later they joined the faculty at Tuskegee. While returning from Columbus, Georgia, one night, they ran into a rainstorm. The unpaved highway was soon filled with ruts. Otis promptly drove into one and had to get out and find a mule team to pull them out. Thereupon Pat insisted that he could see better, and he took the wheel. He drove into a swollen stream that had overflowed its banks. The motor of the car was soon flooded, and the wheels were held fast by sand and mud. The two of them, with their feet up on the dashboard, had to keep a night long vigil in the Model T Ford until the water receded. Then Pat, the heavier of the two, got out, dug the sand away from the wheels, and pushed while Otis coaxed the little Lizzie out of the stream.

Today, in private life, Pat delights in reminding Otis of the salary he didn't get from J. R. Otis and Company, and Otis delights in recalling for Pat the Ames Rug Cleaning Company and its "pickup" Overland with the red lantern tail light.

The Military and Civilian Pilot Training of Negroes at Tuskegee, 1939–45
G. L. Washington

The following account is based on George L. Washington, *History of Military and Civilian Pilot Training of Negroes at Tuskegee, Alabama, 1939–1945* (Washington, D.C.: n.p., n.d.).

August 1939

Tuskegee Institute in August 1939 applied to the Civil Aeronautic Authority for participation in the Civilan Pilot Training Program.

The federal government had allocated $4 million to inaugurate a program of civilian pilot training in universities, colleges, and high schools throughout the nation. The program was to be developed and administered by the Civil Aeronautics Authority (CAA) (at the time Robert H. Hinckley was chairman of the authority).

President John W. Davis of West Virginia State College had sent Mr. James C. Evans and Mr. Joseph W. Grider to Washington, D.C., in July to contact the proper official regarding West Virginia State's participation. Two or three other Negro colleges had done something similar.

President Patterson approved my making an application on behalf of Tuskegee Institute. Certainly Tuskegee students shouldn't be left out, nor did I want my brother-in-law (Mr. Evans) at West Virginia to get ahead of me. I obtained instructions on filing an application.

Commercial pilot Joseph W. Allen, head of the Alabama Air Service, was contacted with respect to the flying training of our students. Ground school instruction was to be given by the Institute. (I don't recall how I came to contact Mr. Allen, who was a white man.) It was my understanding that Mr. Allen had permission to fly from the Montgomery Municipal Airfield, then Gunther Field, which was later taken over by the air force in developing Maxwell Field.

Aside from one flight instructor, Mr. Allen ran a one-man operation, and I don't think he had a contract for training under the Civilian Pilot Training (CPT) program. Furthermore, I am sure he was very anxious to get one. I attributed his willingness to train Negro students to this concern. Mr. Ralph W. Swaby may have referred him to me.

Mr. Allen agreed to my incorporating him in the application to the CAA as flight contractor, with Tuskegee Institute specified as ground school contractor. I proposed to use people in the School of Mechanical Industries for ground instructors, Mr. William Curtis and Mr. Joseph Fuller. The application was completed the last of the month, was presented to Dr. Patterson for signature, and was forwarded to the CAA.

The flying bug had already bitten Tuskegee students. Within the preceding two years two Negro pilots had landed airplanes on Tuskegee property. Colonel John C. Robinson, the "Brown Eagle," who had flown in Ethiopia's air corps, was one. His arrival caused much excitement among the students and other people. While he was at Tuskegee we tried to persuade Mr. Robinson to join the staff of the School of Mechanical Industries to develop aviation mechanic training. In the spring of 1939, commercial pilot Charles A. Anderson piloted Dr. Wright (a banker from Philadelphia) and his airplane to Tuskegee Institute. Mr. Anderson spent several days at Tuskegee Institute, taking students on flights and talking to groups of them about flying and aviation in general. After he left, a flying club was organized.

During the summer of 1939, Ralph W. Swaby (a white man and an enthusiastic pilot from Columbus, Georgia) flew to Tuskegee, giving students flying lessons and pep talks on aviation.

July 1–21, 1940

The flying field! Alabama Polytechnic Institute (API) at Auburn had a field built with WPA money, and so we decided to explore the possibility of using it. Professor Cornell of Auburn's faculty (and one of our ground instructors) discussed the matter with President Duncan.

As Mr. Cornell reported to me, he called on the president and put the proposition to him. The president was unpersuaded, and things weren't going well until the president's secretary, an elderly woman, interrupted to admonish him. "We have been going to Tuskegee Institute as guests at various cultural and other affairs all these years, and now we can't let its students fly from our airfield?" Eventually the president told Cornell to put the matter to a vote among the aviation students. They unanimously agreed. (Cornell told me in reporting that it would have gone badly for the student who had disagreed, but none did.) It should be pointed out that Tuskegee's flying activities in the heavy, fast airplane would overshadow API's cub flying program. Auburn didn't offer the secondary course until the spring session of 1941.

Auburn was only twenty miles away, but since the trainees were to take aviation only, we would divide them into two groups. One would fly at

Auburn while the other did ground school work, and vice versa. CAA approved the flying field arrangement.

July 30, 1940

Tuskegee Institute began flight contractor operations which developed into comprehensive flight training activities involving the CAA's civilian pilot training, army pilot training, and the CAA war training service programs.

When Dr. Patterson signed the contract between the CAA and Tuskegee Institute on July 13 to conduct flight training, as well as ground school instruction, Tuskegee became a flight operator, though it had not been issued a certificate granting it this function. The contract made Tuskegee an advanced flying school which would certainly also be qualified to offer the elementary or private pilot's course.

Thus Tuskegee started without a certificate but with CAA authorization. The only disqualifying factor, in regard to advanced flying certification, was the lack of an airfield at which to base the advanced flying school, one owned or controlled by Tuskegee Institute and approved for advanced flying. The authorization given was predicated on the use of API's field at Auburn, which was certified for advanced flying.

Flight instruction of the first trainees in the CPT secondary course began Tuesday, July 30, at Alabama Polytechnic Institute, Auburn, Alabama.

Anderson was eager to make up for lost time. He had doubled up on ground school for a week, thereby creating an opportunity for the students to catch up on flying, since ground school ended ahead of the original schedule, but Anderson flew the students seven days a week anyway, the July 4 holiday notwithstanding.

Interest in our flying activities developed at Auburn, just as it had at Tuskegee, except that the audience was white. Of course, the Auburn aviation students, as well as other students, were keenly interested. As noted above, this course was not approved for API until the spring of the following year. But the people from the town and the rural surroundings watched with great interest.

I am sure that the students of the secondary could tell many interesting experiences, particularly about expressions of the whites, when a perfect landing was made, "Did you see that nigger land that plane!" Not a single unpleasant experience was reported by the trainees. I think they enjoyed being the center of attention before large audiences, particularly Sundays.

Tuskegee Institute must have created great goodwill among the whites. An occasion could have been found to set fire to the Waco or otherwise to damage it, regardless of watchman service, but no incidents occurred.

September 1940

Director Washington appealed for funds to leaders of various Tuskegee alumni clubs so that an airport could be constructed on Tuskegee Institute property. Small contributions were forthcoming from the Detroit and Chicago clubs. The club deserving special mention was that in Cleveland because of the hard work done by Robert P. Morgan, a graduate of the electrical division of the School of Mechanical Industries, and his wife. At one point in their drive, Mr. Morgan asked me to visit Cleveland to encourage the alumni. Mrs. Washington and I did so, and it was most encouraging to note the activity of the drive.

Charles Alfred Anderson

It was, of course, a foregone conclusion that Chief Anderson would head the flying training of the primary program. He remained chief pilot throughout the program, and later, when classes became large, two squadron heads, Charles Foxx and Milton Crenshaw, worked under him. George Allen became chief pilot in the civilian pilot training program, when army flying began.

Flying and teaching others to fly were Chief Anderson's life. He did not have the time, the bent, or the desire for paperwork and administrative details. The logical choice to be director of training was Lewis Jackson, to whom I looked for the administration of training activities at both fields.

No history of aviation at Tuskegee Institute would be complete if it did not pay the highest tribute to Charles Alfred Anderson. I would call him the "daddy of flying training" at Tuskegee, just as Dr. Patterson once called me the "daddy of aviation" there.

He began flying training or instruction on July 30, 1940. Every student, CPT students and aviation cadets alike, knew and was inspired by "Chief," as he was called. He would go out of his way to help students over troubles in beginning their flying, sometimes offering them, I am sure, a little extra flying time that wasn't logged in the books.

His home became a hangout for students who wanted to learn and hear more about flying from the very beginning. Mrs. Anderson joined him in welcoming and encouraging the young people. He was a great motivator and aviation salesman; he was a good salesman of anything he believed in. To many a student his efforts meant the difference between elimination from the course and persistence until the work had been completed successfully.

Furthermore, no one could expect greater loyalty, cooperation, and hard work from an employee than that which Anderson gave willingly and without being asked. He was given to little jokes and occasional mischief. For instance, one day my pet dog came home from the field with his tail painted red, just the stub of the tail. He and the students were responsible. But try as I might, over many weeks, no student would admit to knowing anything about the incident. In later years, after the programs were over, he acknowledged the prank.

One more example: CAA Inspector Hudson, who flight tested CPT students, flew in to test the second group of secondary course students in acrobatic flying. Of course we were told whenever the inspector was due to arrive. Chief made a setup for him. Charlie Foxx was about the best student in the class to be tested and may have been the best among the many students trained at Tuskegee. Chief had the students practice sitting around, "looking all dumb." Foxx was to look the dumbest, which he was capable of doing.

Inspector Hudson (who was considered one of the best inspectors that the CAA had) looked around for the first person to be tested and spotted Charlie Foxx. He may have thought, "Here's one I can get out of the way quickly because he looks too dumb to pass." Foxx outmaneuvered him on practically all the acrobatics. And when Inspector Hudson came down and got out of the plane, he walked over to Anderson, pointed his finger at Chief, and said, "You tricked me."

What I have said about Chief's loyalty, cooperation, and service, and assistance holds for Mrs. Anderson as well. In a very short time after Chief arrived with the Waco on July 29, 1940, Mrs. Anderson joined him. We housed them in the guest quarters of Sage Hall. Secretarial work relating to aviation was a heavy burden on the Mechanical Industries School staff. Then there was much CAA paperwork in connection with the secondary course. After a few days, Mrs. Anderson became my secretary for aviation activities. Instead of a secretary I got an assistant and hard slave driver. Many an evening she telephoned me, if she hadn't told me before leaving work, to say that she would come by and pick me up to go to the field and prepare something urgent that had to go to the War Department or to the CAA the next day. It was often something that I had let lie too long on my desk. She also contributed many valuable ideas which I used in promoting the program. And I have never seen anyone who could do a better job than Mrs. Anderson in pursuing details about anything. Mrs. Anderson joined me at the primary as my assistant but continued to perform or oversee the accomplishment of administrative work at Airport No. 1.

June 19–20, 1941

At the request of General Henry H. Arnold, chief of Air Corps, President Patterson and Director Washington inspected the training of the initial ground crew of the Ninety-ninth Pursuit Squadron being conducted at Chanute Field, Illinois.

Arrangements were made for our transportation to and from Chanute Field in military aircraft as well as to and from Montgomery in staff cars. We departed from Maxwell Field Thursday morning (9:45), June 19, and arrived at Chanute Field at 1:30 P.M. On our return the next afternoon we departed Chanute Field at 1:20 and arrived at Maxwell Field at 5:10. The aircraft used was a light bomber. We spent most of the trips in the bombadier's compartment, beneath the pilots, out in front, with clear vision ahead and to each side. The crew was most attentive, explaining the various features of the aircraft and its use in combat and identifying from the map of our course the various landmarks on the ground.

Upon landing we were welcomed by the acting commandant, Colonel R. E. O'Neil, Lieutenant Colonel A. C. Kincaid, Captain Maddux, and other staff officers. The officers were careful to see that our needs were met but refrained from such attention as might circumscribe us in our mission.

Immediately after lunch we went about our mission, assisted by officers. Soon we were joined by Sergeant Mack, an old soldier who had the personality and qualifications for his role as "father" for the group of trainees. The trainees were assembled, and Dr. Patterson and I both had the opportunity to speak to the men. We felt the group did credit to the War Department, the great majority of whom, if not all, were there as a result of the recruitment efforts of Tuskegee Institute.

We visited the quarters of the Ninety-ninth, and though we were quartered in the post's officers' quarters, we asked to have our evening meal alone with the Ninety-ninth in their mess hall. The food was wholesome and of good quality. Mealtimes created an opportunity to ask individual trainees questions and to give answers where we could. Sergeant Mack was with us. Quarters were those of the original Chanute Field.

Dr. Patterson and I decided to see a movie one evening. A staff car and chauffeur (white) came, and Dr. Patterson, Sergeant Mack, and I started for the movie in the nearby town—Rantoul, I believe. When we had parked near the theater, Sergeant Mack and Dr. Patterson were deep in conversation, so the chauffeur and I walked on ahead, bought our tickets, and were seated in the theater. Since the theater was full, we did not expect to see Dr. Patterson and Sergeant Mack until after the show. Outside we waited and waited for them, however. I was curious about what had happened. At the officers' quarters that evening, Dr. Patterson said that the ticket sellers wouldn't sell them a ticket. Things got so rough that he had to ask for the manager, who explained the policy. Dr. Patterson went to battle, saying that he was a guest of Chanute Field, invited by the chief of the Air Corps, and would see that reports were made of the discriminatory policy. The manager decided to let them in.

Considering the separate mess and barracks on the field and Dr. Patterson's experience in the adjoining town, I wondered at the time about the fate of Negro aviation cadets in other "northern" posts, or rather communities. When Dr. Patterson went to sleep, he was still cussing about the incident.

1944

On one occasion, Pilot Charles Anderson flew me to Jacksonville, Florida, in the five-seater Stinson. Our visit was expected, but we did not anticipate the reception we received. Virtually every leading Negro businessman in the city was there, including President Lewis of the Afro Insurance Company, his son, Mr. Betsch, his son-in-law, and so many others that I couldn't remember their names when I was introduced to them. I would say 100 or 150 Negroes were present.

Chief gave Mr. and Mrs. Lewis, Sr., and about a dozen or so others short flights over the city. We spent the whole day in well-organized visits to the various businesses of the city run by Negroes. Each was expecting us. We were all well entertained, and I believe the citizens took a lot of pride and pleasure in our visit. We must remember that Negroes flying airplanes were something new to Jacksonville, particularly those from Tuskegee Institute, which had been acclaimed for its aviation activities. A clipping was mailed to me by a friend. The friend failed to identify the newspaper, but I believe it was the *New York Times*.

NEGRO FLIERS WIN BATTLE
Five German Planes Downed—One of Ours Lost

ROME, June 20 (AP)—The only Negro fighter group in the United States Air Force, penetrating ahead of the Fifteenth Air Force bombers bound for Munich yesterday, battled twenty Nazi attackers and sent five of them crashing to earth, it was disclosed today.

Only one plane in the Negro fighter group was lost. The encounter occurred near Udine in northeastern Italy. The group, commanded by Col. Benjamin O. Davis Jr. of New York, was flying new Thunderbolts.

October 17, 1945

The 332nd Fighter Group comprised all the fighter squadrons activated at Tuskegee—99th, 100th, 301st, and 302nd. At first, the group did not include the 99th, but it was added shortly after the group entered combat.

On at least two occasions, in striking up a conversation with a seatmate on an airline, I learned that he was a bomber pilot overseas who praised the fighter groups trained at Tuskegee. Every time, it was said, the Tuskegee flyers accompanied the bomber personnel deeper into enemy territory than most accompanying pursuit squadrons.

Recollections of the United Negro College Fund
Albert Dent

When five of us met for the first time to organize the United Negro College Fund, we were sitting on the front porch with President Read at Spelman College, talking about the potential of the proposed united appeal.

The president of Fisk was Thomas Elsa Jones. At one point, when the discussion was particularly positive, Jones jumped up and pounded the table. "Why do we want to include all these little schools? They wouldn't know what to do with that much money if we gave it to them. Why don't the five of us just organize the College Fund?"

President Jones stayed at Fisk a number of years thereafter. He left Fisk to become president of Earlham College in Indiana, and there he took the lead in establishing a state college fund, copying all of the ideas of the United Negro College Fund, to raise money for the colleges in Indiana. Afterward there were state college funds all over. Two-thirds of the fifty states have some kind of a joint campaign for private colleges in that state.

This new committee of five went to the General Education Board of the Rockefeller Foundation. The board considered the idea a good one, and it agreed to recommend to the foundation board a grant of half of the fifty thousand dollars we needed. Next we went to the Carnegie Corporation. It didn't think well of the idea and told us flatly that it wouldn't put up twenty-five thousand dollars. So there we were, hoping to get twenty-five thousand dollars from each of the foundations to start the Fund.

After we left Carnegie, we met somewhere, in a hotel, I guess, and said, "Well, let's try the Julius Rosenwald Fund," which was a much smaller fund than either Rockefeller or Carnegie but had very, very progressive leadership under its president, Edwin Embree.

So we telephoned Mr. Embree from New York and told him we'd like to see him. He said he was leaving town the next afternoon and would be gone for some time—a month maybe. He'd be glad to talk to us if we were in Chicago the next morning. We asked ourselves how we could get to Chicago.

There were no available plane reservations, and we tried to make reservations on a train. They were hard to get because the military had first choice, but we finally got seats on a train leaving New York that afternoon, which would put us in Chicago the next morning at eight or nine o'clock.

Not all of us could go; some had made other appointments in New York for the next day. A college president never goes to New York with one thing to do—he or she lines up appointments. But Miss Read and Dr. Patterson and I could go. Dr. Patterson was staying, I think, at the Roosevelt Hotel. I don't know where Miss Read was, but she was in one of the midtown hotels. They could return to the hotel and checkout, but I was staying up at the Theresa Hotel in Harlem. I couldn't go back to the hotel, but Rufus Clement, the president of Atlanta University, was there, and he said he would check me out of the hotel and send my bags to me in New Orleans.

I boarded the train with nothing but what I was wearing. We reached Chicago and saw Mr. Embree, and he was impressed and agreed to recommend twenty-five thousand to his board. We didn't spend more than an hour with him. Afterward I caught the next train for New Orleans. We now had fifty thousand, and the schools came up with another fifty. We had a hundred thousand dollars to begin the expenses of a campaign.

The next step was to decide who was going to run the operation. Each of us had a job back home at the colleges. The College Fund would need an executive director. Bill Trent was a man we thought would be a good choice.

Several of us knew Trent. Rufus Clement, who was on the planning committee, had been dean of Livingstone College in North Carolina when Bill Trent was a student there, and so he knew him. I knew him because we'd been at school at Morehouse together. Somebody else may also have known him. Patterson and I went to Washington to talk to Bill and ask him to take the job. None of us has ever forgotten the meeting.

Dr. Patterson and I met Bill Trent for dinner at a restaurant. On the menu we saw lamb chops. We decided lamb chops would be good for dinner that night. Dr. Patterson said to the waiter, "How many lamp chops come with an order?" And he said, "Two." He said, "Well, you'd better make that three." Bill said he got suspicious then that he was in for something.

His reaction was that the proposed job with UNCF would be a stimulating thing to do, but he was subject to the draft. He had been deferred because at that time he was working for a federal agency in Washington. If he joined the UNCF, he'd be subject to the draft.

Recollections of the United Negro College Fund
Betty Stebman

I was to be the secretary and the officer manager. There was Paul Franklin, and there was me. I was hired by John Price Jones. I worked for John Price Jones in those early months and worked with Paul Franklin.

At this time I began to learn a great deal. It was my first experience in the whole business of race relations. We worked at John Price Jones until we could find our own office.

Dr. Patterson was coming up from Tuskegee to have lunch with Mr. Franklin and somebody else. I can't remember who it was. Mr. Franklin said to me, "Dr. Patterson's coming up for lunch" on, say, Friday, or whatever day it was. "I'd like to take him to White's." This was a restaurant downtown, on Nassau Street, an important, famous restaurant. I don't think it's there anymore.

Franklin said, "I'd like to take him to White's, but I don't want any embarrassment. Would you do me a favor and go over there and just check it out and make a reservation." Say that the gentleman who's coming with me is a Negro.

I said, "Oh, God, do I have to do that?" And he said, "I hate to ask you to do this, but I really don't want to take a chance of anybody's embarrassing Dr. Patterson."

I said okay, and I walked over to that restaurant, and I tell you, I was sick inside. I really thought, "What a horrible thing! Why do I have to do this?

This is ridiculous." And it was ten o'clock or so in the morning when I walked in. I walked into the restaurant, and I looked around. There were people cleaning up things and so on.

So I said to some man, "Could I see the manager, please?" The manager came forward, and I said, "I'd like to make a reservation for tomorrow at lunch." And he said, "Fine." And I said, "One of the people who are coming is a Negro." And he looked at me and said, "So what?"

And I felt marvelous, and I ran back to the office and I told Mr. Franklin what had happened. Franklin said, "Oh, that's great. I picked the right restaurant, then."

Then I started trying to find a place for us to work, to rent an office. We'd worked out how much space we needed, and we'd also worked out the location. Because we were going to have to set up an office and have a lot of volunteers—we were going to set up committees—we wanted a place that would be convenient for the people we hoped to recruit.

So I had an area. It was east of Fifth Avenue, or slightly west, between Fifth and Lexington—not north of Sixtieth Street and not south of about Forty-eighth Street or so. The offices should be in that area. But it had to be really on the East Side.

And in late 1943 and early 1944, offices were reasonably available in New York. Not until later, I guess it was 1945, did things begin to get tight. But when I was looking, there was plenty of space available.

I started by looking at signs. If I saw "Office to Rent," I would go in and say I needed *x* number of square feet and so on. The people would show me some space, and they'd say, "What's it for?" When I said it was for a group of Negro colleges that were coming together, I was told, "No, we can't. This space is not available to you."

I walked the streets day in and day out, looking for space. I found lots and lots of space, and the minute I said what it was for, it was not available. And it was the most sickening, discouraging experience, trying to find, in January 1944, a landlord in that area of town who would rent space for this purpose.

One day I was out, and I was walking on Fifty-seventh Street, really downhearted. I'd been repulsed so many times. Then I came to a sign by a little building at 38 East Fifty-seventh Street, and it was a marvelous location. I thought, "Well, here I go again."

So I walked into that building, and there was an elevator man. The hall was very small. There was no lobby at all. And I said to the elevator man, "You have an office for rent?" He said, "Yes, I'll take you up." On the top floor was the owner of the building, and his name was Mr. Briscoe. The elevator man said, "Mr. Briscoe's on the top floor, so I'll take you up there."

So he took me up to the top floor and I met the man. I said, "I'm looking for *x* number of square feet." He said, "Well, the space we have is a whole floor. You see, this is a small building. It's not quite as much as that, but I'd be glad to show it to you. What do you want it for?" And I thought, "Oh, here it comes."

And I repeated my story. "It's for a group of private Negro colleges that are coming together to form an organization to raise money." And he said, "Isn't that interesting! Is Hampton one of them?" And I said, "Yes, indeed, Hampton is one of them."

The world suddenly began to look bright for me. And we began talking about the idea. He told me that his family had connections with Hampton. He was an elderly man himself. I think he said something about his father having been on the board of Hampton, or his uncle, or something like that. Anyway, he knew about Hampton.

And he thought this was a lovely idea, and he would be delighted to show me the space. So he took me down—it was the second floor—and there was the space. It was sort of a loft right through, and you could do what you wanted with it. It was somewhat less than we had had in mind, but I could see that it would do, for the moment anyway. It would be wonderful if we could have it, and the location was perfect.

So I said to him, "Oh, this is really wonderful. I am going to check back now with the director of the campaign and also with Dr. Patterson, who's president of Tuskegee, who is the founder of this organization, and we'll get back to you. I'll ask them to come up."

So I dashed out of there and I ran to the first telephone I could find. I called Paul, and I said, "I got it, I got it, I got it! It's at 38 East Fifty-seventh Street." "Oh, a wonderful location, that's marvelous!" he said. "I'll call Dr. Patterson and get him up here right away."

Paul called down to Tuskegee, and Dr. Pat came up, and they went over and looked at the space and signed the lease. So we had our first office at 38 East Fifty-seventh Street.

We moved in and we put up some temporary partitions in the place. I think we signed a lease for only a year. I think we had to sign it for a year, but we took that chance and if it didn't work, what the heck, it wasn't going to be too bad. The rent was very reasonable.

So we moved into 38 East Fifty-seventh Street. And then we, the John Price Jones organization, provided a campaign director and a publicity director. The publicity director was Hal Hazelrig. He had to write the first brochure, and we really sweated when we wrote that one. Finally, Hal went to Washington. The nearest member of the Fund, Howard University, was there. Howard was a member originally, you know. And Hal went there so that he could familiarize himself with one of these colleges.

I remember he came back, and he said to me, "Boy! I had some experience in Washington. I got out of the Union Station, got into a cab, and asked the driver to take me to Howard University, and he looked around: 'What are you going to that nigger college for?'" You can see what the situation was like in 1943 and early 1944.

Anyway, that first brochure was called *America Is Free to Choose*. On the front cover it showed the wonderful statue of Booker T. Washington at Tuskegee.

One day we had a meeting of the Planning Committee, and the members were really discouraged, because they'd asked maybe three or four people to head the first fund-raising campaign by that time and had gotten no's. And so they began going through the list again. They reached the name Walter Hoving. Mr. Franklin said, "Walter Hoving. I've worked with him." And somebody said, "Well, who is this man, Walter Hoving? We keep seeing his name all the time."

Franklin said, "I worked with him in war bonds, and he's a really top-notch worker. He's president of Lord & Taylor and would be an excellent person." Then they began asking him questions. He said, "The reason I think that it is terribly important that we have a man like Walter Hoving is because he has absolutely no connection, never has had a connection, with the Negro colleges. What we need is somebody brand new to come onto the scene who can attract a good many people who are also brand new. That's how we have to raise the money for this campaign."

At the end of that meeting they finally decided, "Well, why don't we ask him?" They were really not keen about the idea. They preferred one of their old buddies. But we didn't want one of their old buddies. One of their old buddies wasn't going to get us anywhere.

So they said, "Okay, let's try Mr. Hoving."

At that point, John Price Jones really got going. Mr. Hoving was the man we wanted, and we finally got this group together to agree to that. And the discussion, led by Paul Franklin, who finally had his patience rewarded, came around to his man. Then we began talking about how best to reach Hoving.

Hoving was an active Republican. At the time, the governor of New York was Dewey, and Hoving had worked with Dewey. If we could get the governor to ask Hoving to help us, to be on our side, he might do it. Unfortunately, nobody knew the governor well enough to go to that point. Some of them knew him but not well enough to go to him and ask him to do this.

And so they began talking about other people. And then Franklin had a very good idea. He said, "Of course, there's another man who could be very useful in this, and that's John D. Rockefeller, Jr. Dr. Patterson, you know Mr. Rockefeller?" And Dr. Patterson said yes. Franklin said, "Well, would you be willing to ask him to help us?" Patterson said, "Yes, of course."

With that decision, the meeting was concluded. And then we sat down and tried to work out the strategy. The strategy was that Dr. Patterson would go tell Mr. Rockefeller what our problems had been because Rockefeller was clearly involved in the General Education Board, knew about this whole operation, and had given his blessing for the General Education Board to give twenty-five thousand dollars with the Rosenwald Fund to start this operation.

And the idea was to try to persuade Mr. Rockefeller to write a letter to Walter Hoving, to say, "Very shortly you will be asked to see Dr. Frederick D. Patterson, President of Tuskegee Institute, who will come to you with an invitation to serve as chairman of a new organization called the United Negro College Fund. I have been very much interested in these colleges, and my father before me. One of the colleges is named after my mother, Spelman. I think the idea merits your consideration, and would you see them when you are invited to do so?"

And Mr. Rockefeller agreed to do it. Mr. Rockefeller was to write this letter, which he did himself, and it was a two-page letter in which he really expressed his own feelings about how important he thought our idea was and said that it really needed leadership if it was to succeed. It needed leadership, and if Mr. Hoving would consider assuming that leadership, it would be a very useful job.

And so the letter was sent and when we knew—the post was much more reliable in those days—that the letter should and would have arrived, Paul Franklin phoned Mr. Hoving for an appointment.

I think Paul phoned Mr. Hoving, who had already received the letter, and said, "I'd like to make an appointment for Dr. Patterson of Tuskegee to come up from Alabama to see you." And Hoving said, "Sure, I can see him on Thursday afternoon at three o'clock" or something.

And so Dr. Patterson came up—it was Dr. Patterson, Channing Tobias, I believe, and one other person, who went to call on Mr. Hoving. And Hoving asked them a lot of questions. And then they left and we kept our fingers crossed.

Well, the next day at about four-thirty—Paul Franklin and I were the only ones in the office—Paul came out of his office and said, "I'm leaving.

Hoving hasn't called. There isn't much for me to do." And he didn't tell me where he was going.

He left, and I was busy doing whatever I was doing. The telephone rang, and it was Walter Hoving. I almost fell through the floor. He was calling Paul Franklin. And I said, "Mr. Franklin isn't here. I will try to reach him and call you back." And I hung up, and oh, my goodness, was he going to say yes or not? I've got to find Franklin! So immediately I called John Price Jones. I called the office. "Did Paul Franklin show up there? No, he's not here." And then I called his home. No, he wasn't there. And finally I called back again, and I said, "Let me talk to Mr. Jones." And Jones wasn't there. He was at another account. They finally got me in touch with Mr. Jones, and I said to him, "Hoving is trying to reach Paul and I don't know where he is, so maybe it would be a good idea if you got in touch with him."

And then, the next morning—well, I got to the office before Franklin. Franklin lived in White Plains and he came in. He came out of the elevator and I said, "Did you get Hoving?" He said, "Yes, he's going to do it."

Oh, hallelujah, we're off!

Franklin went into his office. He had been there no more than about five minutes when the elevator came up again. In walks the most handsome man I've ever seen in my life. He walked up to me, shook hands, and said, "I'm Walter Hoving. Where's the boss?"

Paul Franklin came out of his office. Paul Franklin was about six three or four, a tall, lanky man. And Hoving was about the same size. And Franklin walked out and said, "Well, hello, Walter." And Walter said, "Hello, Paul. Let's get to work." Just like that. Just like that.

It was the most fantastic thing to see. That man came to that office at nine o'clock every morning on his way to his job at Lord & Taylor. He spent an hour or more, if necessary, every morning. On Saturdays—we worked Saturdays then—on Saturdays, dressed in his country clothes, he would stop by on the way to the country and give us a half hour, an hour, whatever we needed of him.

I will say this, and if Paul were still alive and here, he would say this too, that if it hadn't been for Walter Hoving in that first year, there might never have been a second year for the United Negro College Fund. And I don't think Mr. Hoving really knew how extraordinarily important he was to this organization. He was doing the job that he could do. He guided us. He did not let us stray as we might have had there been a more liberal person.

His politics were, to me, revolting. I mean, he really was politically on the other side of the coin from most of us. But he was so much the right man to get this thing, because at that point, you know, Communism was so much associated with anybody black that you really had to be terribly,

terribly careful that you were absolutely clean and not get involved with anybody who might be too liberal.

After all, we were still fighting a war, and our ally was the Soviet Union, and it was very tricky business. And we had a conservative Republican who hated Roosevelt's guts—and boy, did he hate Roosevelt's guts! And every time he would say anything, I would get sick inside, and say, "Ugh, I cannot stand this man's position, but God, thank you for letting us have him."

We called a meeting of the advisory board, and also of all the contributors to the various colleges, who were in New York, for the first meeting of the United Negro College Fund, to tell them about the idea and about our plans. We would launch the campaign from that meeting.

So that was what we decided to do. Okay, we needed to find a place, so Hoving said, "I think the kind of place we would want would be about the size of the Perroquet Suite at the Waldorf." So he looked at me and he said, "Why don't you see if you can book the Perroquet Suite at the Waldorf for this particular date?"

So I picked up the phone and called the Waldorf. I said, "I'd like to reserve the Perroquet Suite for the March or February 14, whatever date it was." "What is it for?" "It's for the United Negro College Fund." "Just a minute, please. I'm sorry, that suite is booked for that day."

Then I had several dates. I said, "Can you do it on such-and-such a date?" "No, it's booked for that day."

So I said to Hoving, who came in the next day, "I can't get the Perroquet Suite, it's booked for all the three days that you gave me."

And he said, "Well, why don't you try and see if they have another suite? And he told me another suite or two suites that were about the same size." So again I called, and no, they didn't have any room.

Then, when he came in the next morning, I said, "You know, Mr. Hoving, they're not going to give us any room at the Waldorf, and I can tell you that I know why from my own experience in trying to do this. I've already learned. They're not going to give us this room. They're not going to have the United Negro College Fund in the Waldorf."

And Hoving said, "What do you mean, they're not going to have the United Negro College Fund in the Waldorf? Get me Lucius Boomer." Lucius Boomer was the manager of the Waldorf, a very important man around town.

So I got Lucius Boomer on the telephone, and Mr. Hoving, sitting right there in the office, said, "Lucius, John Rockefeller and I are planning a meeting for a group that we're both involved in, the United Negro College Fund, and we've tried to get a suite at—the Perroquet Suite is what we wanted—for such and such a day, and it seems that you people are all booked up. Would you see what you can do for us?"

So Boomer said, "Oh, certainly, Walter, I'll call you back." That afternoon Mr. Boomer called back and said, "I can make the Perroquet Suite available to you. We had a temporary booking on it, but they've taken another date and it's perfectly okay. You can have the Perroquet Suite on the date that you have asked for." And we all had big smiles on our faces. You know, we'd licked it.

So then we put it all together and got the invitations out and made telephone calls, and Mr. Hoving, who was so terrified that we wouldn't have enough people there, got a whole gang of Lord & Taylor floorwalker types to come to be sure that we had a big room full of people.

I got to the Waldorf to start making the arrangements for this meeting. It was a late afternoon meeting. And I got out of the elevator, got out at the Perroquet Suite, and walked up to the room, and there was a sign: "Hoving-Rockefeller Education Meeting." I went downstairs, just to be sure, and looked on the bulletin board, and there was the "Hoving-Rockefeller Education Meeting" listed.

Well, I got it all together and got the chairs together, got the men working to get it all right for the meeting, and then Mr. Hoving arrived. Before he got into the room as he was coming up, I came to him, and I said, "Look." And he looked at the sign, and he reached up and tore it down. He was mad. But then we had the meeting.

And that was the first meeting of the United Negro College Fund. It was at the Waldorf, but there was no name "United Negro College Fund." And it was the first time that they had Negroes at the Waldorf.

We had another meeting the next year at the Waldorf, and we managed to have another Hoving-Rockefeller room made available to us. We had managed to get Mrs. William Henry Hays, who was an older woman, but who had been the chairman of the Women's National Republican Committee. Mrs. Hays was quite an elegant, wonderful, fiery lady. Mr. Rockefeller and Mr. Hoving worked to convince her that she ought to take the chairmanship of the National Women's Committee for the United Negro College Fund and that we ought to have a luncheon. We would have it at the Waldorf.

I was there again to make the arrangements. I came into the Waldorf, and there on the bulletin board was "Mrs. William Henry Hays Luncheon."

I went up to where the room was, a dining room, and there was a sign, "Mrs. William Henry Hays Luncheon." Well, at this point I just figured that was a little much. So I went downstairs, and I stood there at the bulletin board, waiting for Mrs. Hays. Mrs. Hays came in and I said "Look at that sign." And she said, "Why, it's not my luncheon at all." I said, "I know it's not your luncheon. It's the United Negro College Fund's luncheon, and I wondered whether you'd come with me to the manager's office and see what we could do about that." She said "I certainly will. I certainly will."

We walked into the banquet manager's office. Mrs. Hays—she was in her seventies at that point—stood there in all her glory and said, "Young man, there's a sign down there that doesn't belong. I'm Mrs. William Henry Hays, and I'm having a luncheon, but it's not my luncheon. It's the United Negro College Fund luncheon, and I'd like you to have a sign made immediately. Change that sign on the bulletin board and also put it up on the room."

He said, "Yes, ma'am."

And by golly, he changed the sign, and for the very first time in its history the Waldorf-Astoria had the word "Negro" on the bulletin board and on a sign.

The College Endowment Funding Plan
Luther F. Foster

The College Endowment Funding Plan is a new concept proposed to address one part of the critical problem of financing higher education. The plan offers a practical way for a college or a group of colleges to increase and stabilize current income and, in the long run, to generate endowment. It is designed to serve especially the small private colleges that are often at unusual disadvantage in the financing of today's higher education. CEFP is in the tradition of the American free enterprise system, combining the volunteer philanthropic-entrepreneurial-financial strengths of the American setting to provide colleges, through self-help, with a new measure in fiscal stability, a stability that in recent years has rapidly been eroded.

CEFP is a creative combination of several long-established concepts in higher education finance, fund raising, and program development. CEFP encourages responsible college stewardship, for it challenges the colleges' constituencies to preserve and enhance the quality of their institution. Such care may help avert the loss of financially plagued but needed colleges. Because CEFP is feasible at various levels of funding, the college development officer can approach small donors and special interest groups within the alumni or other constituencies as well as persons who might contribute more substantially. CEFP gives the college a vehicle to financial salvation or at least some portion of it.

The federal government and various other governmental units benefit indirectly from the operation of CEFP. The availability of higher education experiences for Americans, regardless of their state of residence, is a keen concern of government—at federal, state, and lower levels. The public is the beneficiary when any college, working with initiative and through the private philanthropic and financial sectors, can strengthen its finances to render vital educational services. These private efforts may well be multiplied and enhanced significantly, with direct benefits accruing to government, if governmental units can work out appropriate arrangements to share in CEFP through such means as federal loan guarantees, interest subsidies, and demonstration programs. History suggests precedents for such involvement.

The College Endowment Funding Plan, a creative approach to fiscal stability in college finance, has been developed under the able guidance of Frederick D. Patterson, who has had long experience in addressing the financial concerns of institutions with modest income potential. CEFP is a practical idea which appeared at a critical time.

Tribute to F. D. Patterson
Hollis Price

I have the very pleasant and happy privilege of recording a word about one of our numbers who has served as our friend, counselor, and leader for many years.

It is comparatively easy to speak about Dr. Patterson. He is a straightforward, direct, and ingenuous person. If he says something, it is not hard to understand what he means or where he stands. In other words, he uses the Engligh language to communicate and not to mesmerize or obfuscate. This is a rarer and more significant quality in human beings than many of us often recognize. Dr. Patterson is an individual in whom other individuals can and do have faith and confidence.

Dr. Patterson has been graced with an innovative and creative mind. He has the unusual ability to grasp new and viable interrelationships of ideas and programs and to break new paths for others to follow. It has been observed that little minds talk about people, slightly bigger minds about events, and great minds about ideas. If there is any truth in this observation, then we would all have to agree that Pat is endowed with a great mind.

The causes of any problem or institutional arrangement are multifaceted and complex. As a rule, however, a few basic and determinative factors at work in any given situation are more fundamental than others. Some of us have the knack of seeing what is basic; others of us are so bogged down in the minutiae and inconsequential details that we never understand the nature of the problem with which we are dealing. Incidentally, for some reason which I cannot fathom, those of us who fall into the latter category are generally the most argumentative. Pat has the unusual capacity to bypass all the side issues and ancillary factors and to lay bare for all to see the real nature of the problem or institution with which we may be grappling.

Thus far I have described the characteristics of F. D. Patterson as I perceive them. I have not mentioned anything that he has done. I have done so deliberately because the man's character is the matrix of his activities. We must first know something of who he is before we can accurately evaluate what he has done.

Dr. Patterson taught at Virginia State College, and he served as head of the Department of Agriculture and as president of Tuskegee Institute from 1935 to 1953. From 1953 to 1970 he served as president of the Phelps Stokes Fund. He holds the A.B., M.A., D.V.M., and Ph. D. degrees in addition to many honorary degrees.

It was my privilege to work under his direction during part of his tenure as president of Tuskegee. He treated me with great kindness and consideration during that period. For this I remain personally grateful to him.

He assumed the presidency of Tuskegee, following in the footsteps of a great leader of the day, Robert R. Moton. It is instructive of Pat's values to reflect on his attitudes as he assumed the presidency of Tuskegee at thirty-three years of age. He was respectful, attentive, and warm in his relationship with the outgoing administration, but he was also then, and he is now, his own man. He listened, but he made his own decisions.

Pat was the founder and first president of the United Negro College Fund. In this connection, it is important to note that had his concerns been limited to the needs of Tuskegee Institute, then there would have been no overriding reason for him to have conceived of and promoted the idea of the College Fund. His work to establish the Fund showed that his concerns and interest transcend any single human institution, and there is evidence that his interests are coextensive with human need wherever it is found.

The United Negro College Fund has helped many private colleges and has no doubt been responsible for the survival of some. All over this country and abroad, thousands of graduates of these colleges are making their contributions to society. Many of them might never have received a college education without the foresight and dedication of Patterson.

When we think of UNCF, we are thinking of an institution which means different things to different people. I sometimes think that the UNCF is regarded today as a fund-raising organization which serves the colleges but with which the colleges have only tangential affiliation and ties.

I was privileged to work with the Fund during its formative years, and I know that Pat has never shared this narrow concept of UNCF. I earlier described Pat's ability to cut through the unimportant elements to the essential characteristics of a problem. This ability is clearly exemplified in his approach to the problems of the UNCF. He has cherished the UNCF and its member colleges, but he has not worshiped them as a shibboleth. Whenever a problem has arisen in the UNCF, he has always kept the students and their needs foremost in his mind. Sometimes he has expressed this priority in words but not often. Always, however, he has acted with this principle in mind. It is axiomatic that the development of the student is the only raison d'être for the UNCF or its member colleges. Pat understands this and has acted accordingly.

No listing of Pat's activities should omit mention of his effective work as president of the Phelps Stokes Fund or the establishment of the Moton Foundation and the Holly Knoll Conference Center. Either one of these activities would have been a life's work for the average person.

Pat now bears the weight of many years. It is accompanied by breadth of wisdom and understanding of the human condition, a priceless jewel that is rare in a human being of any age. We rejoice that he remains strong in mind, body, and spirit.

Print and Oral Historical Sources

To prepare to interview Dr. Patterson was to prepare to study the history of the descendants of the ancient Africans in the twentieth century. It was, I felt, a big job. Patterson's interests were so diverse (yet singular), his working life so long, and his intellect and curiosity so deep that preparing to probe his life was for me, at first, a bit intimidating.

I am an oral historian who likes to go into interviews knowing something about everything concerning the topic and the interviewee. My goal is to go into the interview "knowing" the answers to the questions I am going to ask. With Dr. Patterson, I fell far short of that goal. There were too many questions to ask, too many answers to try to anticipate. Besides, I had trouble understanding the differences between the various institutions—Tuskegee Institute, the United Negro College Fund, the Phelps Stokes Fund, and the Robert R. Moton Memorial Institute most especially—with which he had been associated. Like most of us, I knew, of course, of the United Negro College Fund, but with his other enterprises I was less familiar.

My first interviews with Dr. Patterson were in connection with an oral history of the UNCF. Patterson was one of several interviewees in a project conducted by the Oral History Research Office at Columbia University. It recorded the founding and early history of the UNCF through interviews with those who were participants as member college officials, UNCF administrative staff, and volunteers. Patterson, as the head elder and founder of the Fund, was my first interviewee.

I had prepared by combing multiple boxes and files in the United Negro

College Fund Archives. Paula Williams at the UNCF Archives has helped me there with archival records of the administrative history of the United College Fund as well as with materials about individual colleges and persons connected with the history of the UNCF, particularly its founding. Earlier, Greg Hunter offered the same services. These archivists' knowledge of the UNCF saved me lots of time in preparing for the dozen and a half interviews I was to conduct for the oral history of the United Negro College Fund now housed at Columbia University. The interviewees included Albert Dent, Harry V. Richardson, Walter Hoving, Benjamin Mays, Lindsley Kimball, Hollis Price, Betty Stebman, William J. Trent, Jr., George L-P Weaver, Edward Weeks and Stephen Wright, Naomi Williams, James Colston, Vernon Jordan, Thelma Berlack Boozer, Norvelle Beatty, James Smothers, Albert Manley, Turner Battle, and Christopher Edley. By the time I had spoken to each of them and several spouses, I had learned a great deal. It was perhaps the best background.

I read two dissertations that provided helpful background on the College Fund: Lea Esther Williams, "The United Negro College Fund: Its Growth and Development" (Teachers College, Columbia University, 1977), and Richard Timmins, "A Study of the Three National Efforts in Fund Raising for Colleges and Universities" (Columbia University, Teachers College, 1962).

Book sources on the UNCF that I consulted at this time were: Charles S. Johnson's *Negro College Graduate* (Chapel Hill: University of North Carolina Press, 1938) and Benjamin E. Mays's autobiography, *Born to Rebel* (New York: Scribner's, 1971).

I consulted histories of the individual UNCF colleges where they were available, either from the UNCF archives records or from the individual colleges.

When Dr. Patterson decided to keep the oral history format for his autobiography, expanding on the recordings done for the UNCF oral history project at Columbia University, I did more research in the written records concerning Patterson and his endeavors in preparation for additional interviews.

The bibliographic sources used in preparing these reminiscences consist, for the most part, of materials I used to prepare for interviews. Patterson did not write a lot, and so I read what I could about Tuskegee Institute and Tuskegee, Alabama. I had read the autobiographies of his predecessors at Tuskegee, Booker T. Washington's *Up From Slavery* and Robert Russa Moton's *Finding a Way Out*. A volume of essays on Moton which Dr. Patterson edited with William Hardin Hughes in 1956 was very useful in understanding the continuation of the Booker Washington model at Tuskegee

Institute. It is entitled *Robert Russa Moton of Hampton and Tuskegee* (Chapel Hill: University of North Carolina Press, 1956). Dr. Patterson also published a column in the *Pittsburgh Courier* for several years during the 1940s.

When we started the autobiography project, Dr. Patterson himself suggested some things for me to read. I recall Charles S. Johnson, Edwin R. Embree, and W. W. Alexander, *Collapse of Cotton Tenancy* (Chapel Hill: University of North Carolina Press, 1935); Thomas Monroe Campbell, *Moveable School Comes to the Negro Farmer* (Tuskegee: Tuskegee Institute Press, 1936), on Department of Agriculture–Tuskegee Institute extension work; Theodore S. Williams, *Development of a Black Professional School: The School of Veterinary Medicine as an Educational Institution and as a Sociocultural System: An Historical Study, 1940–1970* (Tuskegee: Tuskegee Institute, Carver Research Foundation, 1977); and George L. Washington, *The History of Military and Civilian Pilot Training of Negroes at Tuskegee Alabama, 1939–1945* (Washington, D.C.: n.p., n.d.).

I also found J. L. Whiting, *Shop and Class at Tuskegee* (Boston: Chapman and Grimes, 1941), interesting. I had read James Jones's *Bad Blood* (New York: Free Press, 1981), on the U.S. Public Health Service syphilis "experiments" in Tuskegee, Alabama. It and Rackham Holt, *George Washington Carver: An American Biography* (Garden City: Doubleday, 1943), were useful in giving perspectives on the times in which Patterson and his Tuskegee predecessors lived.

The *New York Times* regularly ran articles about Tuskegee Institute and about Dr. Patterson during his presidency as it had about Dr. Moton. For example, see the several articles concerning Moton's impending retirement (October 28, 1934, and January 30, 1935), Patterson's election to the presidency of Tuskegee Institute, (April 28 and May 13, 1935), and Patterson's departure for the Phelps Stokes Fund (March 12, 1952).

Tuskegee Institute publications of the Patterson era (1928–35) were also useful. Three in particular stand out in my mind: *Negro Yearbook,* produced annually by Monroe Work and then by his assistant, Jessie Parkhurst Guzman; *Low Cash Cost Housing,* Tuskegee Institute, Rural Life Information Services, Bulletin Number 2 (1950), describing the production of the Tuskegee Concrete Block; and *Service,* a serial publication of Tuskegee's commercial dietetics program. George L. Washington edited and contributed to this "national journal dedicated to the men and women who spend their lives administering to the physical comfort of those whose pursuits of business or pleasure require the use of facilities maintained for the commercial lodging, transportation and feeding of guests."

The annual reports of the Tuskegee president offer a running narrative on the changes at the school and highlight the achievements of which, as president, Patterson was proud. Minutes of trustee meetings, college catalogues, clippings files, proceedings of the annual All-Institute Conference, and other material on Patterson's presidency are found in the Tuskegee University archives. Dr. Daniel Williams was my guide to all of this.

Patterson's work at the Phelps Stokes Fund was a bit harder to document from archival sources. *Phelps Stokes Fund and Its Work, July 1, 1963–June 30, 1965* was informative. The Fund history contained in *A Self-Study of the Phelps Stokes Fund* (November 1979), although it was written after Patterson's tenure, contained useful comparative information on the history of the Fund. The Phelps Stokes Fund papers housed at the Schomburg Center for Research in Black Culture, including the two documents mentioned above, contained material on the development of the Robert R. Moton Institute. Edward Berman's doctoral dissertation, "Education in Africa and America: A History of the Phelps Stokes Fund, 1911–1945" (Columbia University, 1969), chronicles the Fund's history.

The Moton Institute's main thrust, in Dr. Patterson's mind, was the College Endowment Funding Plan, which is described in Frederick Patterson's *College Endowment Funding Plan* (Washington, D.C.: American Council on Education, 1976).

During the time that we worked together, Dr. Patterson and I read and discussed several autobiograhies. Although this book is not patterned on any of them, we did discuss aspects of Joe Louis's *My Story* (New York: Harcourt Brace Jovanovich, 1976), Winnie Mandela's *Part of My Soul Went with Him* (New York: W. W. Norton, 1985), and Mark Mathabane's *Kaffir Boy* (New York: Macmillan, 1986). Both Patterson and I were impressed with Kenneth Manning's *Black Apollo of Science: the Life of Ernest Everett Just* (New York: Oxford University Press, 1983), particularly with regard to his discussion of the role of philanthropic foundations in the support and lack of support for black colleges and black scientists. Ironically, Just was the first Spingarn Medal winner in 1915; Patterson was awarded the Spingarn Medal posthumously in 1988.

Dr. Patterson's papers and memorabilia will be housed at the Library of Congress, making many materials available for the first time. They present challenges for a study of a giant of our times whose life began with the twentieth century and whose impact will be felt in the next.

Index